ACADEMIC FREEDOM
AND CATHOLIC
HIGHER EDUCATION

ACADEMIC FREEDOM AND CATHOLIC HIGHER EDUCATION

James John Annarelli

Foreword by Charles E. Curran

CONTRIBUTIONS TO THE STUDY OF EDUCATION,
NUMBER 21

GREENWOOD PRESS
NEW YORK · WESTPORT, CONNECTICUT · LONDON

Library of Congress Cataloging-in-Publication Data

Annarelli, James John.
  Academic freedom and Catholic higher education.

  (Contributions to the study of education,
  ISSN 0196–707X; no. 21)
  Bibliography: p.
  Includes index.
  1. Catholic universities and colleges—United States.
  2. Academic freedom—United States.   I. Title.
II. Series.
LC487.A56   1987   378'.121   86–27152
ISBN 0–313–25425–7 (lib. bdg. : alk. paper)

Library of Congress Catalog Card Number: 86–27152
ISBN: 0–313–25425–7
ISSN: 0196–707X

First published in 1987

Greenwood Press, Inc.
88 Post Road West, Westport, Connecticut 06881

Printed in the United States of America

The paper used in this book complies with the
Permanent Paper Standard issued by the National
Information Standards Organization (Z39.48–1984).

10 9 8 7 6 5 4 3 2 1

For Anna
With Love

Contents

Foreword

Educational institutions play a vital role in the life and culture of the United States. Academicians should rightly analyze and criticize the issues facing American higher education. Such studies are not only of great importance from a theoretical perspective, but they also can have lasting and permanent practical effects. At the same time, churches play an important function not only for their own members but also in the society at large. The Roman Catholic Church is the largest church or denomination in the United States and thus by its size it exercises a considerable influence.

Over the years, there have been many issues involving the church, on the one hand, and other institutions of political, social, and cultural life, on the other hand. Think for example of the role of the churches in public policy on such issues as peace, race, the economy, and abortion. Professor Annarelli in this volume is addressing a very significant issue for the Catholic Church and for American higher education—academic freedom and Roman Catholic institutions of higher learning.

The purpose of this foreword is not to repeat the reasoning so clearly presented by Professor Annarelli but to develop the historical background for understanding better some of the tensions involved in the present dispute about academic freedom in Catholic higher education in the United States. This issue has become even more timely in the light of recent developments within the Roman Catholic Church itself.

In general, the history of the Catholic Church in the United States can best be seen in the light of the basic question—is it possible to be both Roman Catholic and American at the same time? From the very beginning of the Catholic Church in the United States and throughout its history, there have been those who from the viewpoint of Roman Catholicism have feared that the Catholic Church was becoming too

American. On the other hand, non-Catholic Americans have been fearful that the Catholic Church was so Roman that it could never be truly American.

The question was first posed for the immigrant church in the nineteenth century in pastoral terms—how best to deal with the immigrants who were flooding into this country? Should the Roman Catholic Church urge and help its members to accept American culture and ways and thereby enter into the mainstream of American life? Or should the church urge the immigrants to hold on to their own customs, language, and traditions and thereby hold on to their Catholic faith? Were the American ethos and culture seen as a threat or a help to the Catholic faith of the immigrants? Americanizers, who advocated a rapid assimilation of the immigrants into American life and culture, ultimately won and such a policy was followed by the Catholic Church at large in the United States.

However, in the nineteenth and twentieth centuries fear and suspicion continued to exist on both sides. In 1899 Pope Leo XIII condemned the heresy of Americanism. Rome expressed the fear that the Catholic Church in the United States was becoming too American. That condemnation, together with a later condemnation of modernism at the beginning of the twentieth century, created a climate that stifled creative scholarship in all areas in the Catholic Church in the United States. At the same time, many other Americans remained suspicious of this immigrant Catholicism which owed allegiance to a foreign ruler. In the nineteenth century there were three different waves of bigotry against Catholics and other foreigners, ending with the attack of the American Protective Association at the end of the nineteenth century. In addition to the anti-Catholic bigotry and discrimination, many Americans were skeptical that Roman Catholics could totally accept the American political system and ethos.

From the nineteenth century until recent times the primary reason for the suspicion of American Roman Catholics by their fellow Americans was the Catholic Church's unwillingness to accept the principle of religious freedom and the separation of church and state. At best the official Catholic teaching could tolerate the American system of religious freedom but never wholeheartedly endorse it. The change finally came at the Second Vatican Council in 1965 with the promulgation of the decree on religious liberty. Roman Catholicism now could unreservedly accept the United States' political structures with their emphasis on freedom in general and religious freedom in particular.

From a practical perspective, the 1960s marked the beginning of a new era. The election of John F. Kennedy as President of the United States in 1960 laid to rest the generally accepted political axiom that a Catholic could never become President. Thus in the 1960s there was the growing recognition on the part of both Rome and non-Roman Americans that Roman Catholicism and the American political ethos were compatible.

However, before the 1960s had ended, a new reality entered the picture with the emergence of what has been called "the Catholic left" with its strong opposition to United States policies, especially in the area of peace and war. The Catholic left maintained that Catholicism had become too American and in an unquestioning manner accepted all too easily American policies and programs. The Gospel and the Church must protest against the glaring moral deficiencies in both United States foreign and domestic policies. The recent pastoral letters of the United States Roman Catholic bishops on peace and war show that the Roman Catholic Church in the United States can accept the basic structure of United States political life but still be critical of particular policies and positions.

The relationship of Roman Catholicism to American educational institutions is a more specific example of the general issue of being both Catholic and American. Roman Catholicism in the United States built and supported its own educational system from grammar school through college and university. The particular question under discussion in this book is the relationship between Catholic colleges and universities and the accepted American understanding of such institutions. Institutional autonomy and academic freedom are the distinguishing charcteristics of American colleges and universities. No outside authority of any kind has the competence to make judgments affecting the academy. The hiring, tenuring, promotion, and dismissal of faculty is done only by academic colleagues and peers.

Can Catholic colleges and universities accept the autonomy of higher education and the academic freedom that are necessary for them to be truly American institutions of higher learning? Before 1960 there was almost unanimous agreement both on the part of American Roman Catholics and on the part of specialists in higher education that Catholic institutions could not accept the autonomy and academic freedom characteristic of American colleges and universities.

However, the decade of the 1960s marked a dramatic change especially in the Catholic self-understanding of its institutions of higher learning. The first impetus began with a few articles in the 1960s and reached its apex with what became known as the "Land O'Lakes Statement" signed by twenty-six leaders in higher education in the United States and Canada, including the presidents of the most prestigious Catholic institutions. According to this statement, "To perform its teaching and research functions effectively, the Catholic University must have a true autonomy and freedom in the face of authority of whatever kind, lay or clerical, external to the academic community itself." This acceptance of academic freedom involved a quick and dramatic change, and since that time the leaders of Catholic higher education have become even more firm in their support for academic freedom.

A number of factors influenced the change, which coincided with a growing Catholic acceptance of political and religious freedom. From a theological perspective, Vatican II not only accepted religious freedom but also called for a dialogue with the modern world and recognized the rightful autonomy of secular institutions. From a cultural perspective, Catholics were no longer an immigrant church but now became part of the mainstream of United States life and culture. In 1955 John Tracy Ellis first pointed out the failure of Roman Catholicism to contribute to the intellectual life in the United States. In the light of these criticisms, questions about Catholic higher education were raised. At the same time, changes were occurring in the 1950s and the 1960s in Catholic colleges and universities themselves. Lay people were assuming more significant roles on the Catholic campus. Catholic institutions began to strive for academic excellence and to establish more graduate programs. Professors trained in secular universities came into Catholic institutions. Especially in theology and religion there was a move toward a greater professionalization. The Catholic college and university came to see the need for and acceptance of academic freedom and institutional autonomy. The availability of government funding was also a consideration which became even more significant as the 1960s gave way to the 1970s.

Thus, the leaders of Catholic higher education in the United States strongly supported the need for institutional autonomy and academic freedom. Catholic colleges and universities best serve the church by being good institutions of higher learning and not by being a catechetical arm of the pastoral mission of the church. The most touchy aspect of the question concerns the academic freedom of theology, but the commitment to academic freedom in the theological enterprise was seemingly firmly established in a number of somewhat celebrated cases involving Catholic higher education in the late 1960s.

However, recently there have been strong threats to the academic freedom of Catholic institutions from legislation introduced and/or proposed by the Catholic Church. In 1979 the Vatican Congregation for Catholic Education issued new norms for ecclesiastical faculties, that is, those institutions and schools which give Vatican accredited degrees. In the United States there are very few such faculties or institutions, with the department of theology at the Catholic University of America in Washington, D.C., being the best known example. According to these norms, Catholic theologians in these faculties teach in the name of the church and need a canonical mission from church authorities. The church authorities existing outside the academy thus have the power to give and to withdraw this mission or license to teach.

The 1983 Code of Canon Law proposed for the entire Roman Catholic Church in canon 812 maintains: "It is necessary that those who teach theological disciplines in any institute of higher studies have a mandate from a competent ecclesiastical authority." This canon provides that a church authority, external to the academy, can and should make decisions directly involving the hiring, promoting, and dismissal of faculty in theological disciplines. At the present time it seems that this canon has not been applied in the United States, but it is definitely on the books. In addition, in April 1985 the Vatican Congregation for Catholic Education sent out for consultation proposed norms for all Catholic colleges and universities throughout the world. These norms include and build upon the regulations of canon 812, calling for competent ecclesiastical authority to give a mandate to all who teach theological disciplines in Catholic institutions of higher study. The leaders of Catholic higher education in the United States have strenuously objected to these proposed norms. At the present time it is uncertain what will ultimately occur, but there is no doubt that existing Roman Catholic law and proposed norms threaten the academic freedom and autonomy of Catholic colleges and universities in the United States.

Within this context, Professor Annarelli's book is even more important and timely. The shape and even the future of Catholic higher education in the United States is now at stake. The particular issue is of great importance to all those interested both in higher education and in the Roman Catholic Church.

Annarelli's defense of academic freedom in Catholic institutions is scholarly, clear, and complete. Some readers like myself might differ slightly from him, but all should agree that this is a significant and timely volume which makes a valuable contribution to the understanding of both Catholic institutions of higher learning and the demands of academic freedom. All those interested in Catholic higher education should read this clear and scholarly defense of academic freedom for Catholic higher education.

Charles E. Curran

Acknowledgments

I would be remiss were I not to thank publicly those who aided me in various ways during the course of this project. I owe a large debt of thanks to Dean Thomas W. Ogletree, Ph.D., and Professor Edward LeRoy Long, Ph.D., of Drew University, and Professor Charles E. Curran, S.T.D., of the Catholic University of America for their helpful suggestions and encouragement. I also wish to thank Gerard A. Hefner for his proof-reading assistance, Maria Ptakowski and Patricia Schuettich of St. John's University Library, through whose efforts I was able to secure long-term loans of library materials, Jack Rose for allowing me unlimited access to his office equipment, and Mary Sive, John Donohue, and the staff at Greenwood Press for their guidance and assistance.

I note with loving appreciation the continuing personal support and encouragement given to me by my parents. Finally, I offer my loving, heartfelt thanks to my wife Anna, who has been the source of great inspiration, encouragement, and assistance. Not only did she do every-thing in her power to provide me with a distraction-free work environ-ment, but she also assumed the task of typing the manuscript.

Introduction

In the United States, academic freedom for the teaching scholar is defined as "the freedom of professionally qualified persons to inquire, discover, publish, and teach the truth as they see it in the field of their competence,"[1] while the academic freedom of the student is identified as the "freedom to express and to defend his views or his beliefs, the freedom to question and to differ, without authoritative repression and without scholastic penalization."[2] This book will address the problem of finding a model of academic freedom that is applicable to the American Roman Catholic college or university as a religiously-committed institution, yet is consonant with its nature as an American university devoted to the free pursuit of truth and the dissemination of knowledge.

Scholarly debate concerning the role of academic freedom in the Roman Catholic college or university continues. The claim has been made by many secular educational theorists that the notion of academic freedom defines the true university.[3] It has been argued that to the extent that academic freedom is qualified or limited on the Catholic campus, the words "Catholic university" constitute a contradiction in terms.[4]

In contradistinction to this position, some Catholic scholars—among them S. Thomas Greenburg and Germain Grisez—maintain that academic freedom in its secular formulation must be qualified insofar as the Catholic university has a special relation to (and, thus, responsibility to) the *Magisterium*, or teaching office of the Church.[5] This qualification of the secular notion of academic freedom becomes most important in the area of theology.[6]

There are, however, other Catholic theologians such as Charles Curran and Frederick Walter Gunti who have championed the cause of academic freedom in the Catholic context.[7] They argue that with a "correct" understanding of scholarly competence, the secular notion of academic freedom can and must be applied to the Catholic college or university, even within the sensitive area of theology.

It is the thesis of this work that current Catholic models of academic freedom are inadequate guides for the American Roman Catholic college or university as an American college or university, while the American secular model—although not without defect—is, when correctly interpreted, applicable to the Catholic institution and necessary to its proper functioning.

Problems inherent in the more restrictive Catholic models of academic freedom include the limitation of institutional autonomy, unacceptable notions of scholarly and juridical competence, a static view of theology, and a limited and highly ecclesiastical/pastoral view of the role of university theologians. Similarly, less restrictive Catholic models have not fully resolved the problem of the nature of scholarly theological competence and continue to betray an implicit ecclesiasticism in their conceptions of university theology and the role of the university theologian.

The methodological approach of this book will consist of an examination of, and critical reflection upon, the Catholic models of academic freedom as these have developed in the American Roman Catholic context since the Second Vatican Council (1962–65). A critical analysis of the American secular model of academic freedom and a discussion of its applicability to the Catholic context will also be included. Through the critical examination of current models of academic freedom, criteria for the interpretation of academic freedom in the American Roman Catholic university will be generated. It is hoped that these criteria will serve to extend the parameters of the current discussion of this complex issue.

It should be noted that the study to follow is explicitly limited in scope. First, attention will be directed only to the Catholic college or university in the United States. This limitation is necessary to insure that this work remains clear in focus and manageable in size. Moreover, the American college and university differ from their European-style counterparts in terms of structure, and—to an extent—societal function. Hence, the problems of Catholic higher education in the United States are best addressed in light of their limited American context.

Second, the situation of the separate Church-controlled seminary or institute of theology is not the focus of this book, and it should not be assumed that the argument advanced in it is *directly* applicable to such institutions. Seminaries that are independent from universities often exist for unique, denominationally defined purposes that must be considered when discussing the applicability of academic freedom to these institutions.

It should also be noted that throughout this work, the argument advanced is considered equally applicable to the college and the university.

The claim has sometimes been made that the right to academic freedom is truly applicable only to the *university*—particularly its graduate divisions. Colleges, it is argued, are primarily undergraduate teaching institutions whose students are far too immature—intellectually and/or emotionally—to thrive in a free marketplace of ideas.

This claim is being rejected for three reasons. First, it is based upon a specious divorce of teaching from research. Even within the liberal arts college, instruction cannot thrive apart from some contact with contemporary research in the discipline under consideration. Second, the need for academic freedom is rooted in the nature of the scholar's role both as researcher *and* as teacher. Unless one is willing to argue that the content of college instruction should consist of a predetermined body of "givens," this claim makes little sense. If the college instructor's task includes exposing his or her students to the many scholarly approaches to and opinions on a particular issue, then an atmosphere of academic freedom is an essential condition for effective college teaching. Finally, to consider most college students immature is not only an unfair generalization but also a demographically inaccurate one. Indeed, the "nontraditional" adult college student is no longer considered an anomaly in the undergraduate student body.

NOTES

1. Sidney Hook, *Academic Freedom and Academic Anarchy* (New York: Cowles Book Co., 1970), p. 34.

2. Robert M. MacIver, *Academic Freedom in Our Time* (New York: Columbia University Press, 1955), p. 207.

3. See the American Association of University Professors (AAUP), "1915 Declaration of Principles," *AAUP Bulletin* 40 (Spring 1954): 94–97.

4. Charles E. Curran, "Academic Freedom: The Catholic University and Catholic Theology," *The Furrow* 30 (December 1979): 742–43.

5. See the discussions in George A. Kelly, ed., *Why Should the Catholic University Survive?* (New York: St. John's University Press, 1973). Throughout this book, the term *Magisterium* capitalized and italicized will refer to the official hierarchical *Magisterium*.

6. Unless otherwise noted, the phrase *Catholic theologian* will refer not to a theologian of a particular personal faith or denominational affiliation, but to a theologian proficient in a particular type of theology. Hence, the description *Catholic theologian* can be used interchangeably with the description *professor of Catholic theology*.

7. Curran, "Academic Freedom," pp. 748–53; Frederick Walter Gunti, "Academic Freedom as an Operative Principle for the Catholic Theologian" (S.T.D. dissertation, The Catholic University of America, 1969).

ACADEMIC FREEDOM
AND CATHOLIC
HIGHER EDUCATION

1.

The Context of the Problem

Every examination of the problem of academic freedom in the American Roman Catholic university has the potential of becoming an extremely complicated and, at times, a totally unruly undertaking. This fact is due in large part to the multifaceted nature of the problem. First, the term *academic freedom* itself is not unambiguous. As will be discussed, there is fundamental agreement on the framework of the notion as this has been sketched in the major statements of the American Association of University Professors (AAUP).[1] However, the justification of academic freedom and its practical applications remain subject to varying interpretations.[2]

Moreover, the notion of academic freedom as it has developed in the United States has sometimes been interpreted in light of other concepts that are themselves often fraught with ambiguity. The literature on academic freedom is peppered with terms such as *objectivity, neutrality,* and *value freedom,* although these terms are usually unclearly defined by individual authors and are rarely defined similarly by different authors.[3] In addition, some past interpretations of the American notion of academic freedom have included implicit presuppositions concerning the nature of truth.[4] Such conceptions of truth have sometimes been criticized as being far too "empirical" insofar as they tended to limit what was considered "truth" to the products of investigations based upon the scientific method.[5]

Second, when the American notion of academic freedom is applied to the Catholic university, a number of new problems arise. Roman Catholicism is a religion based upon what is commonly called *revelation*: the self-disclosure of God in history through words and deeds.[6] This revelation, the fullness of which is Jesus Christ, is for Catholics transmitted through sacred Scripture and sacred tradition.[7] Moreover, "the task of authentically interpreting the word of God, whether written or handed on, has been entrusted exclusively to the living teaching office of the Church, whose authority is exercised in the name of Jesus Christ."[8] This official teaching authority, or *Magisterium*, is composed of the Pope and the bishops throughout the world in union with the Pope.[9] Hence, for Roman Catholics there are two orders of knowledge—natural and supernatural, with supernatural truth remaining beyond human reach were it not for God's gracious revelation.[10]

From the perspective of some secular scholars, difficulties arise in that Roman Catholicism posits a body of knowledge that is not only beyond human investigation and verification, but is also authoritatively and, at times, infallibly proposed and interpreted by the *Magisterium*. It has often been assumed that when the college or university becomes the locus for the study of Catholic teaching, values vital to academic freedom are necessarily compromised, namely scholarly objectivity, and the autonomy of the institution and its faculty.

In the interest of clarity, this study will commence with an examination of the context of the problem of academic freedom in the Roman Catholic university. Anticipating the examination to be carried out later in this work, a summary definition of the American secular notion of academic freedom will be presented. We will then proceed to an examination of the Catholic context of the problem, briefly exploring the meaning of knowledge, revelation, and *Magisterium* (and its various levels of teaching) from a Catholic perspective. Throughout this chapter, particular attention will be paid to the defining of key terms. For when dealing with a problem of this complexity, defining one's terms is of the utmost importance

ACADEMIC FREEDOM: AN INTRODUCTORY SUMMARY

German Roots

The immediate precursor of the American notion of academic freedom was the model of scholarly freedom developed in nineteenth-century Germany. This German concept of academic freedom was composed of two interdependent ideas—*Lernfreiheit* and *Lehrfreiheit*. *Lernfreiheit*, or the freedom to learn, meant that

German students were free to roam from place to place, sampling academic wares; that wherever they lighted, they were free to determine the choice and sequence of courses, and were responsible to no one for regular attendance; that they were exempted from all tests save the final examination; that they lived in private quarters and controlled their private lives.[11]

Lehrfreiheit, on the other hand, denoted the freedom of inquiry and teaching enjoyed by professors. Friedrich Paulsen of the University of Berlin wrote in 1902 that

it is no longer, as formerly, the function of the university teacher to hand down a body of truth established by authorities, but to search after scientific knowledge by investigation, and to teach his hearers to do the same.... For the academic teacher and his hearers there can be no prescribed and no proscribed thoughts. There is only one rule for instruction: to justify the truth of one's teaching by reason and the facts.[12]

Interestingly, Paulsen qualifies his thoughts on academic freedom. He argues that the professor of religion as well as the professor of political science are bound by the exigencies of the church and state respectively. Moreover, he points out that academic freedom in Germany is *internal* to the university and does not apply to the extramural activities of academic personnel.[13] Thus political partisanship would, in turn-of-the-century Germany, disqualify a professor from his position.

The contemporary American notion of academic freedom differs from its German ancestor in two major ways. First, there never developed in the United States a strong notion of *Lernfreiheit,* or student academic freedom.[14] Second, the earliest statements of the American Association of University Professors are unambiguous in their affirmation of the freedom of extramural utterance and activity as a component of academic freedom.[15] The acknowledgment of these differences should not lead one to belittle the importance of the German notion of academic freedom for the development of its contemporary American counterpart. "It was indeed, in nineteenth-century Germany that the modern conception of academic freedom came to be formulated."[16] As Russell Kirk points out, Americans who studied in Germany in the latter part of the nineteenth century returned to the United States with a conception of academic freedom that, although unclear, was to have a profound effect upon the development of a domestic version of the notion.[17] This effect can be seen in Walter P. Metzger's observation that "from the nineties to the First World War, a good proportion of the leaders and targets in academic freedom cases had studied in Germany," and in his assertion that the German notion contributed to the American conception of academic freedom "the assumption that academic freedom, like academic searching, defined the true university."[18]

Defining the American Notion of Academic Freedom

Although a later chapter will be devoted to a detailed exposition of the concept of academic freedom as it has developed in the United States, it is necessary to offer, from the outset, a working definition of the notion. Turning to the first statement on academic freedom issued by the American Association of University Professors, we see that the American conception is composed of three elements. Hence, the "1915 Declaration of Principles" states that *Lehrfreiheit* includes "freedom of inquiry and research; freedom of teaching within the university or college; and freedom of extra-mural utterance and action."[19]

In harmony with this framework, a number of commentators have developed summary definitions of academic freedom. Among the more noteworthy summaries is that of Arthur O. Lovejoy, a German-trained American scholar who was an active defender of academic freedom and an early organizer of the American Association of University Professors.[20] Lovejoy writes:

> Academic freedom is the freedom of the teacher or research worker in higher institutions of learning to investigate and discuss the problems of his science and to express his conclusions, whether through publication or in the instruction of students, without interference from political or ecclesiastical authority, or from the administrative officials of the institution in which he is employed, unless his methods are found by qualified bodies of his own profession to be clearly incompetent or contrary to professional ethics.[21]

Fritz Machlup, in a well-known 1955 article, defines academic freedom somewhat more broadly in that he acknowledges its application both to teachers and students.[22] In Machlup's view,

> academic freedom consists in the absence of, or protection from, such restraints or pressures—chiefly in the form of sanctions threatened by state or church authorities or by the authorities, faculties, or students of colleges and universities, but occasionally also by other power groups in society—as are designed to create in the minds of academic scholars (teachers, research workers, and students in colleges and universities) fears and anxieties that may inhibit them from freely studying and investigating whatever they are interested in and from freely discussing, teaching, or publishing whatever opinions they have reached.[23]

The Meaning of Freedom in the Academic Context

In what sense is the word *freedom* being employed when modified by the adjective *academic*? Without engaging in a lengthy philosophical discussion, the various meanings of the term freedom may be reviewed. As an abstract concept, freedom is commonly defined both in a positive and a negative fashion. Negatively, it is usually defined as "the absence of restraint," while positively freedom is described as "self-determination" or "self-possession in the exercise of one's activity."[24] In general terms, these common definitions of freedom are in harmony with the use of the term in its academic context: academic freedom denotes the absence of inappropriate restraints upon the scholar as well as the autonomy and self-determination of the scholar and the university as a whole. It is both a freedom *from* and a freedom *for*.

Further analysis yields deeper and more specific meanings of the term freedom. Albert Dondeyne, in an essay entitled "Truth and Freedom: A Philosophical Study," outlines three interrelated dimensions of freedom. First and fundamentally, the author defines freedom as an inexhaustible drive toward self-realization.[25] The second sense of the term *freedom* is identified by Dondeyne as free choice, free will, or self-determination. It is within this sense of the term that the value dimensions of freedom come most clearly to the fore. To act freely means "to act with knowledge of what one is doing and why one is doing it."[26] Every free act is a value choice. Freedom, therefore, should not be confused with haphazardness, but rather should be seen as a principle of order. For freedom invites us to utilize our circumstances to further those values to which we have dedicated our life.[27]

The third dimension of freedom discussed by Dondeyne is freedom in the sociological and political sense. Freedom in this context can be defined as "*the sum total of the economical, social and political conditions* that are necessary for the concrete exercise of freedom and effective liberation of man's personality."[28] Civil liberties, and the removal of the invisible chains of ignorance and poverty, could be cited as examples of freedom in this third sense.

How does our brief overview of these three interrelated meanings of freedom aid in the understanding of the use of the term *academic freedom?* First, it appears that the definitions of academic freedom cited above include elements of what Dondeyne has called freedom in the political and sociological sense. These definitions tend to emphasize (as does much of the literature on the subject) this sense of the term *freedom* insofar as they identify academic freedom with the protection of the scholar from restraints that may originate from various power groups, be these groups religious, governmental, or administrative.

Yet, it would seem that the political and sociological dimension of the notion of academic freedom is not only joined to, but also serves the other dimensions of academic freedom. As Dondeyne states, freedom in the political sense refers to those conditions "necessary for the concrete exercise of freedom."[29] Hence, freedom from external restraint allows the exercise of what might be called scholarly self-determination, which is freedom in Dondeyne's second sense of the term.[30]

Scholarly self-determination ("free-choice" or "freedom of decision") is based upon the notion of competence. As a trained expert, the scholar is free to choose his or her research topics, to investigate those topics, and report his or her conclusions through teaching and publication. The only qualification of this freedom is that the scholar's methods always remain subject to the judgment of his or her professional peers.

Rarely emphasized in discussions of academic freedom is the meaning of freedom as the object of the human drive toward self-realization (freedom in Dondeyne's first sense). But it is precisely the restless drive toward self-realization and the human propensity toward raising questions and reflecting that both ground the common notion of academic freedom and make its protection an important concern.[31] As Dondeyne observes, "among the many occupations which allow man to manifest and realize himself in this world, the unprejudiced search for truth is highest and most specifically human."[32] Therefore, freedom as self-realization is the source of human questioning and of the human pursuit of truth. However, while freedom as self-realization grounds the exercise of freedom as self-determination and freedom in the sociological/political sense, these latter dimensions of freedom remain vital for the fruitful expression of freedom in the first sense. This remains so even when discussing specifically *academic* freedom.

THE THEOLOGICAL CONTEXT OF THE PROBLEM OF ACADEMIC FREEDOM IN THE CATHOLIC UNIVERSITY

When addressing the problem of academic freedom in the Catholic university—and particularly in the theological disciplines—one must be cognizant of the exigencies that arise from the Catholic approach to knowledge and from the nature of the hierarchical *Magisterium*, or teaching authority of the Church. In the sections that follow, we will discuss briefly the Catholic distinction between natural and supernatural knowledge, as well as examine the meaning and structure of the *Magisterium*. The intent within these sections is not to present a comprehensive theological treatment of these subjects, but rather to offer descriptions and definitions that will help to prepare the way for later discussions.

The Teaching of Vatican II on Revelation

The important, indeed fundamental, issue of revelation was addressed by the Second Vatican Council (1962–65) in a document entitled "Dogmatic Constitution on Divine Revelation."[33] As one reflects upon the Council's teaching on revelation, it becomes apparent that this teaching, though sharing continuity with past approaches to the question, represents a noticeable shift in emphasis. This shift is toward a more dynamic, existential view of revelation, and away from an impersonal and rigidly intellectual approach. An appreciation of this change in emphasis, as well as an understanding of the Council's general approach to the question of revelation, requires some familiarity with how the Roman Church addressed this issue in the past. Hence, our examination of the theology of revelation of Vatican II will be prefaced by a brief historical overview of the teaching on revelation reflected in the documents of the First Vatican Council.

Historical Overview

The First Vatican Council (1869–70) "came closer than any previous Church council to setting forth an authoritative Catholic view of revelation."[34] During this Council, the notion of revelation received far more extensive and systematic treatment than during the previous Council held at Trent (1545–63). Moreover, in its "Dogmatic Constitution on the Church of Christ," Vatican I canonized certain teachings concerning revelation that necessarily remain part of Catholic theology to this day.

In chapter 4 of the "Constitution on the Catholic Faith," the Council Fathers affirm that there exist two orders of knowledge—natural and supernatural—which are distinct both in origin and in object.

They are distinct in origin, because in one we know by means of natural reason; in the other, by means of divine faith. And they are distinct in object, because in addition to what natural reason can attain, we have proposed to us as objects of belief mysteries that are hidden in God and which unless divinely revealed, can never be known.[35]

The Council further taught that "although faith is above reason, yet there can never be any real disagreement between faith and reason, because it is the same God who reveals mysteries and infuses faith and has put the light of reason into the human soul."[36]

The second chapter of Vatican I's "Constitution on the Catholic Faith" is devoted entirely to the notion of revelation. Against the extremes of rationalism (and its exaltation of reason) and fideism (with its de-emphasis of the role of reason), the Council affirms that knowledge of God can be arrived at in two ways: the ascendant way of natural knowledge and the descendant way of revelation.[37] The notion of an ascendant way of knowing God is rooted in the Thomistic tradition. In this tradition, as in the teaching of the Council, what is known through natural reason reflecting upon creation is not God in his innermost life, but the fact of God's existence and God's causal relation with the world.[38]

The descendant way of knowing God is founded upon supernatural revelation, which allows humans to know more easily, and with solid certitude, those religious truths accessible to human reason. Yet, as the Council states, it is not for this reason that revelation is necessary. "It is necessary only because God, out of his infinite goodness, destined man to a supernatural end, that is, to a participation in the good things of

God, which altogether exceed the human mental grasp."[39] The great doctrines of redemption cannot be known through reason reflecting upon creation. Knowledge of these doctrines is possible only through God's gracious revelation made manifest in Jesus Christ.

Although when the Council speaks of revelation it speaks in terms of God choosing in his goodness "to reveal *himself* and the eternal decrees of his will," it remains true that the Council conceives of revelation largely in terms of propositions or a body of knowledge.[40] This is reflected in the Council's teaching on faith:

Because man depends entirely on God as his creator and lord and because created reason is wholly subordinate to uncreated Truth, we are obliged to render by faith a full submission of intellect and will to God when he makes a revelation.... By that faith, with the inspiration and help of God's grace, we believe that what he has revealed is true.[41]

Since the Council understands revelation largely in intellectual terms it tends to define faith principally as belief—the intellectual assent to divine truth.[42]

The Theology of Revelation of the Second Vatican Council

The Second Vatican Council's final approved document on revelation was promulgated as *Dei Verbum*—"The Dogmatic Constitution on Divine Revelation." This document, though sharing continuity with statements from previous councils, represents a fresh approach to the Catholic theology of revelation. Roger Schutz and Max Thurian, in their book *Revelation: A Protestant View*, point out that the title of the document is itself an indication of a shift in emphasis.

The first two words of the Dogmatic Constitution on Revelation immediately give the spirit of this important text of Vatican II: *Dei Verbum, The Word of God.* The Council did not intend to speak of Revelation as the transmission of eternal truths by an unchangeable God to an institutional Church. . . . Revelation is considered throughout this magnificent text as the living Word that the living God addresses to a living Church composed of living members.[43]

A shift toward a more relational notion of revelation can be seen in the document's emphasis upon revelation as God's self-disclosure and self-manifestation. For example, in chapter 1 it is written: "God chose to reveal *Himself* and to make known to us the hidden purpose of His will."[44] The notion that revelation is primarily divine self-disclosure can also be perceived in the teaching on the role of Jesus found in the document. The Council Fathers write that "Jesus perfected revelation by fulfilling it through His whole work of making Himself present and manifesting Himself."[45]

It is important to note that this is a broadening of emphasis rather than a change from a previous position. Although revelation is presented primarily as divine self-disclosure, it continues to be associated with a body of revealed truth, a "deposit of faith" that is entrusted to the teaching office of the Church. This ambivalence is apparent in the document's brief discussion of faith. The Council speaks of faith in relational terms, identifying it with the act of freely entrusting one's whole self to God. However, the traditional notion of faith as intellectual assent to truth is also reaffirmed in the same passage: " 'The obedience of faith' ... must be given to God who reveals, an obedience by which man *entrusts* his whole self freely to God, offering 'the full submission of intellect and will to God who reveals,' and freely assenting to the truth revealed by Him."[46]

In the second chapter of the document, the transmission of divine revelation is discussed. The Council reaffirms the notion that the Gospel is transmitted in two ways—through tradition and through Scripture. Tradition is understood in broader terms than in past councils, which tended to equate tradition with *doctrinal* traditions. Here, tradition includes the Church's teaching, life, and worship. The Council underscores the close connection between Scripture and tradition, teaching that both flow from the same "divine wellspring" and, in a sense, merge into a unity in that both transmit the Word of God.[47]

The teachings of the Second Vatican Council also included a more dynamic view of the nature of revealed truth. In the "Constitution on Divine Revelation," the Council Fathers write that the

tradition which comes from the apostles develops in the Church with the help of the Holy Spirit. For there is a growth in the understanding of the realities and the words which have been handed down. This happens through the contemplation and study made by believers, ... through the intimate understanding of spiritual things they experience, and through the preaching of those who have received through episcopal succession the sure gift of truth. For, as the centuries succeed one another, the Church constantly moves forward toward the fullness of divine truth until the words of God reach their complete fulfillment in her.[48]

In a similar vein, the Council Fathers state in the "Pastoral Constitution on the Church in the Modern World" that "theologians are invited to seek continually for more suitable ways of communicating doctrine to the men of their times. For the deposit of faith or revealed truths are one thing; the manner in which they are formulated without violence to their meaning and significance is another."[49]

Although it may appear that Vatican II's tacit acknowledgment of the development of dogma apparent in the above excerpts contradicts the teaching of the First Vatican Council on the permanence of dogma, it does not. Indeed, the Fathers of Vatican I unequivocally affirmed that

the doctrine of faith as revealed by God has not been presented to men as a philosophical system to be perfected by human ingenuity; it was presented as a divine trust given to the bride of Christ to be faithfully kept and infallibly interpreted. It also follows that any meaning of the sacred dogmas that has once been declared by holy Mother Church, must always be retained.[50]

As Bernard Lonergan has persuasively argued, a study of the teaching of the First Vatican Council indicates that the Council Fathers affirmed that "the permanence attaches to the meaning and not to the formula" of a dogma.[51] Hence, Lonergan's now famous dictum: "What permanently is true, is the meaning of the dogma in the context in which it was defined."[52]

Vatican II, recognizing the conditioning influence of cultural, linguistic, and historical factors, was concerned with the more effective communication of divine truth. The Council Fathers acknowledge that communicating the permanent meaning of divine truths in a different cultural or historical context might necessitate their reformulation.[53] Such an approach complements, rather than contradicts, the teaching of Vatican I on the permanence of dogma.[54]

The Nature of the *Magisterium*

Historical Remarks

Yves Congar has observed that from the earliest period of Church history there existed in the Church a ministry of teaching.[55] Congar, as well as Roger Gryson, has characterized this ministry as being more closely akin to our contemporary conception of the ministry of the catechist than to our current conception of the role of the theologian. The teacher provided spiritual nourishment for the Christian community through the instruction of new converts and through teaching directed toward the strengthening and development of the faith of the baptized.[56] Despite the importance and prestige associated with the role of the teacher, during the apostolic and subapostolic age the teacher was not regarded as a member of the ecclesiastical hierarchy.[57] Gryson, distinguishing between the role of pastor and that of teacher in the early church, writes:

On the one hand, the Church was directed by leaders who exercised a jurisdictional power and presided over the assemblies by virtue of their having been vested with the grace of pastors, presumably by that time by an ordination. On the other hand, it counted in its bosom masters who taught the Christian doctrine by virtue of the grace of teachers, which they held directly from the Holy Spirit.[58]

During the second and third centuries, lay teachers established theological schools at Alexandria and elsewhere.[59] Possessing no official ecclesiastical "mission" from pastoral authorities, teachers within these schools taught with an authority based upon their knowledge and reputation and enjoyed relative independence from the hierarchy, which interfered only when the faith was endangered.

Gryson observes that during the third century, pastors found it increasingly difficult to support the independence of teachers. "Although the pastors' function as it appears in the oldest prayers of ordination did not include teaching but only the administration of the community and the liturgical service, they tended to take on the educational function as well and soon would not tolerate its performance by a layperson."[60]

Congar describes this development with a somewhat different emphasis. He points out that by the mid-second century there appeared tension between teachers or "doctors" and "the apostolic witness linked to the succession of ordained ministers."[61] For it was apostolic succession that was thought to insure faithful transmission of teaching. Congar writes:

In this period the *cathedra* (teaching chair) characterizes the bishops. The *cathedra*, the episcopal function, its continuity and succession, and *doctrina* (teaching) are all synonymous. This is especially true of the "Chair of Peter". . . . Thus, for this era *cathedra* largely corresponds to today's magisterium.[62]

Yet Congar claims that there was no real separation between pastors and theologians since both used the same methods and often worked together closely during doctrinal controversies. Moreover, from the fourth century, theologians were for the most part also bishops.[63] This last fact is especially emphasized by Gryson, who claims that during the second century "the function of education was well on the way to being entirely taken over by the hierarchy" and that by the middle of the third century, this "was practically an accomplished fact."[64]

With the founding of the medieval universities, there appeared in the Church an autonomous teaching function, the authority of which was not delegated by or derived from the hierarchy.[65] Indeed, it was during the Middle Ages that there arose in the Western church a distinction between doctoral/scientific and pastoral teaching, and a recognition of a magisterium of theologians. For example,

Thomas Aquinas distinguished between the "magisterium of the pastoral or episcopal chair" and the "magisterium of the teaching chair." The first enjoyed an excellence of power, the second a publicly recognized personal competence. The teaching of the theologian can be a recognized, public office in the Church, but its substance derives from scientific competence. Pastoral teaching, in contrast, derives from the public office of *praelatio*, from authority belonging to a jurisdiction.[66]

The magisterium of the teaching chair exercised considerable authority in doctrinal matters, although preaching—the public proclamation of the Gospel—remained a pastoral act reserved to bishops. Describing the authority of theologians in the recently founded universities, Avery Dulles writes that "the university theology faculties played a normal role in the settlement of theological disputes and in the formulation of official doctrine. Thus the decrees of the Council of Vienne (1311–12) by order of Clement V, were not made official until they had been submitted to the universities."[67]

Following the Counter-Reformation, the authority of the magisterium of the teaching chair declined as the authority of the papal *Magisterium* increased.[68] Congar examines a number of factors in an effort to understand this development. First, despite the fact that theological faculties continued to condemn heretical teachings until the French Revolution, theology was supervised. For example, the establishment of the Index of Forbidden Books in 1564 supplied the papacy with a means of suppressing erroneous positions.[69] Moreover, those theological faculties that were suppressed in France and Germany in the late eighteenth and early nineteenth centuries and eventually restored were for the most part reestablished under papal authority. By the nineteenth century, the independent "teaching chair" had ceased to exist.[70]

Second, by the mid-eighteenth century, there arose a distinction between the "church teaching" and the "church learning," which grew out of an earlier distinction between the infallibility of the body of the faithful and that of the pope and hierarchy.

Third, there appeared an increasing emphasis upon the *means* by which the faith is proclaimed, overshadowing the *content* of faith. Obscured was the fact that the principal task of the *Magisterium* is to witness to the faith, not merely to prepare definitions. As Congar notes, the *Magisterium* tended "to assume an autonomous and absolute value, whereas in fact the *form* of apostolic ministry ought not to be separated from the *content* of tradition."[71]

Fourth, in the "Dogmatic Constitution on the Church of Christ," the Fathers of the First Vatican Council (1869–70) solemnly defined the primacy of jurisdiction of the Pope, rejecting a mere primacy of honor. Basing their argument on this primacy and on the role of the Pope as supreme shepherd and teacher of all Christians, the Fathers of this Council also canonized the dogma of papal infallibility. In chapter 4 of the "Dogmatic Constitution on the Church of Christ," the Fathers state:

faithfully keeping to the tradition received from the beginning of the Christian faith, for the glory of God our Savior, for the exaltation of the Catholic religion, and for the salvation of Christian peoples, We, with the approval of the sacred council, teach and define that it is a divinely revealed dogma: that the Roman Pontiff, when he speaks ex cathedra that is, when, acting in the office of shepherd and teacher of all Christians, he defines, by virtue of his supreme apostolic authority, doctrine concerning faith or morals to be held by the universal Church, possesses through the divine assistance promised to him in the person of St. Peter, the infallibility with which the divine Redeemer willed his Church to be endowed in defining doctrine concerning faith or morals; and that such definitions of the Roman Pontiff are therefore irreformable because of their nature, but not because of the agreement of the Church.

Canon

But if anyone presumes to contradict this Our definition (God forbid that he do so): let him be anathema.[72]

It should be noted that "this definition was the result of prolonged and intense conciliar discussion and debate."[73] Some bishops objected to a treatment of papal infallibility out of the context of the role of the bishops. They felt that the definition gives to the pope a power that is too "personal, separate, and absolute."[74]

In an effort to reassure the bishops who had expressed reservations concerning the definition, Bishop d'Avanzo, speaking on behalf of the Deputation of the Faith—the committee that had composed the definition—explained its meaning. He

stressed that the anti-Gallican expression of the definition *ex sese non autem ex consensu ecclesiae* did not purport to separate the pope from the Church . . . it was the same Holy Spirit who was operative in pope, bishops, and faithful. Secondly, the pope teaching infallibly did not do so in virtue of a new revelation but rather, with the help of the Holy Spirit, his role was to discover the truth already contained in fonts of revelation. Thirdly, it was obvious that the pope did not work privately with the Holy Spirit, but rather that he must seek out the truth in the living witness of the Church.[75]

Hence, in the opinion of d'Avanzo, as well as of Bishop Gasser also of the Deputation, the dogma does not exclude the "essential concurrence and cooperation of the Church."[76]

Contemporary Debate

It does appear that the strictly hierarchical meaning presently ascribed to the term *Magisterium* is a relatively recent development.[77] In light of this, some scholars have called for a revival of the notion of a *magisterium* of theologians. Avery Dulles, for example, entertains such a notion. He writes that "it might be desirable to institutionalize to some degree the participation of theologians in the Church's decision-making processes.

Some interesting models for such institutionalization can be found in the Middle Ages, when the theologian was considered to have quasi-hierarchical status."[78]

On the other hand, William E. May points out that although the contemporary meaning of magisterium is "of relatively recent vintage, the reality to which it refers is not, as Congar . . . notes."[79] Moreover, although May acknowledges that in the Middle Ages the term *magisterium* was used to designate the teaching of theologians, he rejects the use of such a designation today. He argues that the authority of the teachings of theologians

consisted *exclusively* in the nature of the arguments and evidence that they advanced to support their positions, and it thus contrasted sharply with the authority of the teaching given by those who had the *magisterium cathedrae pastoralis* as distinguished from the *magisterium cathedrae magistralis*, that is, by those in whom the *reality* of the magisterium as it is understood today was materially located and formally vested. From this it follows that the term magisterium today cannot be predicated properly of theologians.[80]

In May's opinion, to do so would amount to a rejection of the Church's self-understanding in this area.

The Church's Contemporary Understanding of Its Magisterial Function

In its contemporary theological usage, the term *Magisterium* [81] refers to the official teaching office of the Catholic Church, which is composed of the pope, who is supreme teacher, "Vicar of Christ and pastor of the whole Church," and the bishops, successors of the apostles, who "are authentic teachers . . . endowed with the authority of Christ."[82] It is the responsibility of the *Magisterium* to guard and interpret the deposit of faith. The "Dogmatic Constitution on Divine Revelation" of the Second Vatican Council outlines clearly this responsibility:

The task of authentically interpreting the word of God, whether written or handed on, has been entrusted exclusively to the living teaching office of the Church, whose authority is exercised in the name of Jesus Christ. This teaching office is not above the word of God, but serves it, teaching only what has been handed on, listening to it devoutly, guarding it scrupulously, and explaining it faithfully by divine commission and with the help of the Holy Spirit; it draws from this one deposit of faith everything which it presents for belief as divinely revealed.[83]

Since there are various levels of Church teaching, and varying degrees of engagement of hierarchical teaching authority, a generally accepted terminology is employed to differentiate between these levels. Hence, theologians have come to distinguish between the *ordinary* and *extraor-dinary* exercise of the hierarchical *Magisterium*.[84] "The extraordinary magisterium comprises the *ex cathedra* statements of the pope and the solemn statements of bishops convoked in council in union with the pope to define the faith."[85] Such statements are considered infallible and ir-reformable, and demand the assent of divine faith (without qualification or condition.)[86]

It is important to clarify the precise meaning of the term irreformable in this context. In this regard Juan Alfaro avers that " 'irreformability' makes dogmas, as understood in their original context, lastingly nor-mative for faith."[87] Offering a more developed explanation, Karl Rahner writes:

As regards the definitive decisions of the magisterium, while they are "irre-formable," they are also subject to the created dimensions of human statements and the historicity of human knowledge of the truth. . . . When we say that a doctrine is irreformable, we mean that in its true and proper meaning it can never be rejected as erroneous: it is not revocable as regards the past. The creatureliness and the historicity of dogma mean that it can and must be inter-rogated age by age and confronted with the mental horizons and the knowledge of each age.[88]

To echo Lonergan, what remains permanent is the meaning of the dogma considered in the context in which it was defined.

The object of infallible *Magisterium*—the extraordinary *Magisterium* as well as the infallible ordinary *Magisterium* of bishops which is discussed below—is identified in the "Dogmatic Constitution on the Church." The Council Fathers write that "the infallibility with which the divine Re-deemer willed His Church to be endowed in defining a doctrine of faith and morals extends as far as extends the deposit of revelation, which must be religiously guarded and faithfully expounded."[89] Most theolo-gians consider the object of infallibility—identified as doctrine of faith and morals—to be a twofold object. As Francis A. Sullivan notes, the primary object is the deposit of revelation (either written or handed on) that has been formally revealed, while the secondary object is that which is not formally revealed but which pertains to Christian faith and practice and which is "necessary for the defense and explanation of Gospel truth."[90] According to Sullivan, it is this secondary object that is "intended" in the phrase "which must be religiously guarded and faithfully ex-pounded."[91]

There is much disagreement among theologians over what is contained in the secondary object of infallibility and neither Vatican I nor Vatican II resolved the issue.[92] The types of teachings theologians have often identified with the secondary object of infallibility include condemnations of propositions contrary to revealed truth (e.g., conclusions of science referred to by Vatican I), propositions that necessarily follow (as conclusions of a syllogism) from revealed truth, "dogmatic facts" (e.g., the determination of the ecumenicity of a church council), and the determination of candidates for canonization as saints.[93]

A small number of theologians have argued that *particular applications* of the natural moral law (e.g., the condemnation of artificial contraception as intrinsically evil) are also included within the secondary object of infallibility. Sullivan avers that most Catholic theologians reject this argument. Some of the basic principles of natural law are revealed as well as discoverable through reflection on human experience and, hence, most Catholic theologians would include such principles in the primary object of infallibility.[94] However, Sullivan claims that a majority of theologians would consider *particular applications* of basic principles to complex moral problems neither formally nor indirectly revealed and therefore they constitute a part of neither the primary nor the secondary object of infallibility.[95]

The ordinary *Magisterium* "refers to the normal daily teaching of the bishops throughout the world," and the authoritative noninfallible teachings of the pope (the ordinary papal magisterium).[96] There is a situation within which the ordinary *Magisterium* of bishops is considered infallible. The Second Vatican Council reaffirmed:

Although the individual bishops do not enjoy the prerogative of infallibility, they can nevertheless proclaim Christ's doctrine infallibly. This is so, even when they are dispersed around the world, provided that while maintaining the bond of unity among themselves and with Peter's successor, and while teaching authentically on a matter of faith or morals, they concur in a single viewpoint as the one which must be held conclusively.[97]

As Maguire has noted, this notion of an infallible, ordinary *Magisterium* carries with it certain problems, not the least of which is defining the meaning of concurrence.[98] However, prescinding from a discussion of these difficulties, we will now focus our attention upon the status of noninfallible teachings of the ordinary *Magisterium*.

The Second Vatican Council teaches that the noninfallible teachings of the ordinary *Magisterium* must be adhered to with a religious assent of soul. This teaching is reaffirmed in Canon Law.[99] Yet, what precisely is religious assent of the soul or intellect? Religious assent "does not exclude the possibility that the proposition one affirms might be erroneous," but it does exclude "present doubt as to the truth of what is affirmed."[100] Such assent presumes the truthfulness and reliability of the *Magisterium*. Following the traditional manuals of theology, a more recent textbook states that authentic (authoritative) noninfallible teachings "are to be accepted with an inner assent which is based on the high supernatural authority of the Holy See (assensus internus supernaturalis, assensus religiosus)."[101] Therefore, as Charles E. Curran and Robert E. Hunt note, religious assent is motivated by the authority of the teaching office of the Church.

According to the manuals, "Divine faith is absolutely certain and *super omnia firma*, supremely firm; internal religious assent is not absolutely certain and firm."[102] Therefore, in general, the traditional manuals admitted that *private* dissent from authoritative, noninfallible teaching is possible, although the conditions upon which such dissent is permissible were subject to dispute.[103]

Charles E. Curran and Robert E. Hunt view the "right to dissent" as one aspect of the interpretive function of theology. They write that responsible dissent to noninfallible Church teaching

is merely one way to assure the genuine development of doctrine and to assure that doctrinal vocabulary does not lose its underlying truth-value (as involved with *Mystery*). Such would happen whenever doctrinal formulae become overly clear and distinct and overly literalized or are frozen in an older thought pattern and language structure (the constant temptation of an age with little or no historical sense).[104]

Although most of the traditional manuals of theology taught that one who suspended his or her internal assent must publicly maintain a reverent silence while privately communicating his or her difficulties to the hierarchy, Curran and Hunt argue that, in some instances, *public* dissent may be not only permissible, but also ethically required.

In formulating a judgment about a particular question of public dissent, the theologian must be cognizant of his or her responsibilities and obligations to the hierarchy, to fellow theologians, to individuals affected by the particular teaching, to the university community, to the communication media, and to the public at large.[105] Moreover, the theologian must take into account the nature of the issue at hand—its urgency and its ramifications for the public sphere. "The interpretive possibility of public dissent must be weighed with respect to all the foregoing factors."[106]

William E. May acknowledges that dissent from the teachings of the authentic, noninfallible *Magisterium* "must be recognized as a possibility that at times, . . . can be realized; for the believing subject must, in the inner sanctuary of his conscience where he is alone with God, make his own personal judgments about the meaning of his life and his choices."[107] May cautions that there can never be a "double truth"—one for the teachings of the *Magisterium* and one for the individual's conscience. The faithful Catholic, he argues, not only presumes but anticipates that the truth lies with the magisterium. To conclude that this teaching is erroneous is to reach a judgment that a faithful Catholic ought reach only with the most extreme reluctance; were one to reach this judgment frequently and, as it were almost spontaneously, this would (it seems to me) be a very serious matter. It ought to cause such a person to stop short and begin to reflect quite critically upon his own processes of judging.[108]

Richard A. McCormick criticizes May's position as far too privatized, noting that May does not relate responsible dissent to the development of doctrine.[109] McCormick argues that

if dissent on a particular point is widespread, does this not suggest to us that perhaps the official formulation is in need of improvement? To say otherwise is to say that scholarly (and other) reflection has no relation to the Church's ongoing search for truth and application of her message.[110]

It indeed appears that in the essay under consideration, May limits his discussion of dissent to the realm of conscience, hence precluding consideration of the constructive possibilities of such dissent.

Hierarchical recognition of "licit dissent" to authentic noninfallible Church teaching can be found in a pastoral letter released by the American bishops in 1968.[111] This letter, entitled *On Human Life in Our Day*, outlines clearly those norms which should govern the *public* expression of dissent. The bishops state that dissenting scholars must exhibit a

careful respect for the consciences of those who lack his special competence or opportunity for judicious investigation. These norms also require setting forth his dissent with propriety and with regard for the gravity of the matter and the deference due the authority which has pronounced on it. . . .

When there is a question of theological dissent from non-infallible doctrine, we must recall that there is always a presumption in favor of the magisterium. Even non-infallible authentic doctrine, though it may admit of development or call for clarification or revision, remains binding and carries with it a moral certitude. . . . The expression of theological dissent from the magisterium is in order only if the reasons are serious and well-founded, if the manner of the dissent does not question or impugn the teaching authority of the Church and is such as not to give scandal.[112]

In the matter of responsible dissent, these three norms—serious reasons, protection of Church authority, and the absence of scandal—have become the accepted guides for most American theologians.

A Vatican investigation of the writings of moral theologian Charles E. Curran has raised new questions concerning the legitimacy of public theological dissent to the noninfallible teaching of the hierarchical *Magisterium*. This investigation, initiated by the Sacred Congregation for the Doctrine of the Faith in 1979, led to the issuance in 1985 of a formal request by Cardinal Joseph Ratzinger, current prefect of the Congregation, that Curran "retract his positions on several ethical issues or risk losing his license to teach as a Catholic theologian."[113] Curran—a member of *a pontifical faculty* of the Catholic University of America—responded that "in conscience" he could not and would not change the theological positions he has taken. In a letter dated July 25, 1986, Cardinal Ratzinger informed Curran that the Congregation has judged him no longer "suitable nor eligible to teach Catholic theology."[114] This judgment, approved by Pope John Paul II, means the withdrawal of Curran's *ecclesiastical license* to teach theology and the forfeiture of his position on the pontifical faculty.

In his correspondence with Ratzinger, Curran has consistently emphasized the legitimacy of public dissent if such dissent is responsibly carried out in accordance with the norms developed by the U.S. Bishops in *On Human Life in Our Day*. The Congregation has accused Curran of justifying public dissent "with a defense of personal or private dissent."[115] Labelling this accusation "blatantly false," Curran repeatedly asked the Congregation for further clarification of *its* teaching on public dissent.[116] In his responses, Cardinal Ratzinger merely reaffirmed the Church's teaching that religious assent to the noninfallible teachings of the *Magisterium* is required of all the faithful.[117] However, in his letter of July 25, 1986, Ratzinger *appears* to indicate that the Congregation can envision no conditions under which it would be legitimate for a theologian to dissent *publicly* from the noninfallible teaching of the ordinary magisterium.[118]

CONCLUSION

As a prelude to the discussions that follow, this chapter has sought to define, albeit in a concise manner, the American secular notion of academic freedom and some of its attendant concepts. In particular, we have examined the general idea of freedom so that through such an examination, the dimensions of academic freedom might more easily become apparent.

This chapter has also attempted to introduce the important theological context of the problem of academic freedom in the Catholic university. For Catholic universities, insofar as they are sponsored by a religion based upon a divine revelation guarded and interpreted by an official teaching authority, encounter a fundamental problem: how to reconcile the exigencies arising out of the structure and theology of the Roman Catholic Church with those arising from their status as American institutions of higher learning. This question cannot be dealt with apart from a basic understanding of Catholic teaching on the nature of revelation, and the role of the official teaching authority or *Magisterium*.

It appears that Catholicism is far from the static and authoritarian institution it is sometimes caricatured to be. First, contemporary Catholic teaching on revelation has become much more dynamic. Since Vatican II, the Church has eschewed a rigidly intellectual conception of revelation as a body of truths, recapturing to some degree the more relational notion of revelation as divine self-disclosure. Moreover, recent theological research has placed the model of hierarchical *magisterium* that has developed over the past two hundred years in its historical context, prompting renewed interest in the creative and interpretive functions of theology, and the magisterial function of theologians and indeed of all Christians. Finally, there has appeared, on the part of the hierarchy itself, a recognition of the possibility of licit public dissent from noninfallible teaching (although this is presently being rethought) and an acknowledgment of the conditioned character of the formulations within which permanent dogmas are expressed.

Although mitigating the problem, these developments do not solve it. For there remains the possibility that the infallible meaning of a dogma will conflict with the scholarly pursuit of truth "wherever it may lead," or that the authority of the hierarchical *Magisterium* will collide with the claimed autonomy of the scholarly community.

Definitions of important concepts have been discussed, and the pertinent theological context of the problem has been briefly explored. Attention will now be turned to an examination of the historical and social context of academic freedom in the American Catholic university in the hope of shedding additional light on our problem.

NOTES

1. See the AAUP, "1915 Declaration of Principles," and the "1940 Statement of Principles," *AAUP Bulletin* 45 (Spring 1959): 107–10.

2. Fritz Machlup, "On Some Misconceptions Concerning Academic Freedom," *AAUP Bulletin* 41 (1955): 753.

3. For an interesting categorization of the various meanings of these terms, see Huston Smith, "Objectivity vs. Commitment," in *Colleges and Commitments*, ed. Lloyd J. Averill and William W. Jellema (Philadelphia: Westminster Press, 1971), pp. 38–44.

4. MacIver, *Academic Freedom in Our Time*, pp. 4–5.

5. Germain Grisez, "Academic Freedom and Catholic Faith," *National Catholic Education Association Bulletin* 64 (November 1967): 17–18.

6. Second Vatican Council, "Dogmatic Constitution on Divine Revelation," in *The Documents of Vatican II*, ed. Walter M. Abbott, trans. Joseph Gallagher (New York: The America Press, 1966), no. 2, p. 112.

7. Ibid., no. 8–10, pp. 115–17.

8. Ibid., no. 10, pp. 117–18.

9. Second Vatican Council, "Dogmatic Constitution on the Church," in *The*

Documents of Vatican II, ed. Walter M. Abbott, trans. Joseph Gallagher (New York: The America Press, 1966), no. 23, pp. 47–50.

10. See the First Vatican Council, "Constitution on the Catholic Faith," in *The Church Teaches: Documents of the Church in English Translation*, trans. and ed. John F. Clarkson et al. (Rockford, Ill.: Tan Books, 1973), pp. 32–35.

11. Richard Hofstadter and Walter P. Metzger, *The Development of Academic Freedom in the United States* (New York: Columbia University Press, 1955), p. 386.

12. *The German Universities and University Study*, trans. F. Thilly and W. W. Elwang (1906), pp. 228–31, quoted in Ralph F. Fuchs, "Academic Freedom-Its Basic Philosophy, Function and History," in *Academic Freedom and Tenure*, ed. Louis Joughin (Madison, Wis.: University of Wisconsin Press, 1967), p.249.

13. Ibid., p. 250.

14. The reasons that account for this will be examined in a later chapter.

15. See, for example, AAUP, "1915 Declaration of Principles," pp. 93–94.

16. Fuchs, "Academic Freedom," p. 248.

17. Russell Kirk, *Academic Freedom: An Essay in Definition* (Chicago: Henry Regnery Co., 1955), p. 23.

18. Hofstadter and Metzger, *Development of Academic Freedom*, pp. 396, 393.

19. AAUP, "1915 Declaration of Principles," p. 93.

20. Hofstadter and Metzger, *Development of Academic Freedom*, pp. 396, 476.

21. *Encyclopedia of the Social Sciences*, 1930 ed., s.v. "Academic Freedom," by Arthur O. Lovejoy.

22. Hence, Machlup defers to the dual German notion of academic freedom.

23. Machlup, "Concerning Academic Freedom," pp. 753–54.

24. Albert Dondeyne, "Truth and Freedom: A Philosophical Study," in *Truth and Freedom*, trans. Henry J. Koren (New York: Ad Press Ltd. for Duquesne University, 1954), p. 29. See *Webster's New Twentieth Century Dictionary*, 2nd ed. (1978), s.v. "Freedom."

25. Dondeyne, "Truth and Freedom," p. 30.

26. Ibid.

27. Ibid.

28. Ibid.

29. Ibid.

30. As in every exercise of free choice, implicit and explicit value judgments are inherent in the choices arising from the exercise of scholarly self-determination.

31. Dondeyne, "Truth and Freedom," p. 34.

32. Ibid.

33. Vatican II, "Constitution on Divine Revelation," pp. 111–28.

34. Avery Dulles, *Revelation Theology: A History* (New York: Herder and Herder, 1969), p. 75.

35. Vatican I, "Constitution on the Catholic Faith," chap. 4, p. 32.

36. Ibid., p. 33.

37. Ibid., pp. 27–28.

38. René Latourelle, *Theology of Revelation* (New York: Alba House, 1966), p. 259.

39. Vatican I, "Constitution on the Catholic Faith," chap. 2, p. 28.

40. Ibid., p. 27. Italics mine.

41. Ibid., pp. 28–29.

42. Ibid., p. 29.

43. Schutz and Thurian, *Revelation: A Protestant View*, trans. K. Sullivan (New York: Newman Press, 1968), p. 11. See Gregory Baum, "Vatican II's Constitution on Revelation: History and Interpretation," *Theological Studies* 28 (1967): 51–75.

44. Vatican II, "Constitution on Divine Revelation," no. 2, p. 112. Italics mine.

45. Ibid., no. 2, p. 113.

46. Ibid., no. 5, p. 113. Italics mine.

47. See Ibid., nos. 8–10, pp. 115–17. The Council refrained from judging whether the two vehicles of revelation differ in content.

48. Ibid., no. 8, p. 116.

49. Second Vatican Council, "Pastoral Constitution on the Church in the Modern World," in *The Documents of Vatican II*, ed. Walter M. Abbott, trans. Joseph Gallagher (New York: The America Press, 1966), no. 62, p. 268.

50. Vatican I, "Constitution on the Catholic Faith," p. 34.

51. Bernard Lonergan, *Method in Theology* (New York: Herder and Herder, 1972), p. 323.

52. Ibid., p. 325.

53. Vatican II, "Church in the Modern World," no. 62, p. 268.

54. On the development of doctrine, see Avery Dulles, *The Survival of Dogma* (Garden City, N.Y.: Doubleday, 1971), pp. 171–203; and Lonergan, *Method*, pp. 319–30.

55. Yves Congar, "The Magisterium and Theologians: A Short History," *Theology Digest* 25 (Spring 1977): 15.

56. Roger Gryson, "The Authority of the Teacher in the Ancient and Medieval Church," in *Authority in the Church and the Schillebeeckx Case*, ed. Leonard Swidler and Piet F. Fransen (New York: Crossroad Publishing Co., 1982), p. 177. See also Congar, "Magisterium and Theologians," p. 15.

57. Gryson, "Authority of the Teacher," p. 177.

58. Ibid., p. 178.

59. Congar, "Magisterium and Theologians," p. 15.

60. Gryson, "Authority of the Teacher," p. 179.

61. Congar, "Magisterium and Theologians," p. 15.

62. Ibid., p. 16.

63. Ibid.

64. Gryson, "Authority of the Teacher," p. 179. See John Lynch, "The Magistery and Theologians from the Apostolic Fathers to the Gregorian Reform," *Chicago Studies* 17 (Summer 1978): 208.

65. Gryson, "Authority of the Teacher," p. 182.

66. Congar, "Magisterium and Theologians," p. 16.

67. Dulles, *Survival of Dogma*, p. 104.

68. Congar, "Magisterium and Theologians," p. 18. See Michael D. Place, "From Solicitude to Magisterium: Theologians and Magisterium from the Council of Trent to the First Vatican Council," *Chicago Studies* 17 (Summer 1978): 225–41.

69. Congar, "Magisterium and Theologians," p. 18.

70. Ibid.

71. Ibid.

72. First Vatican Council, "Dogmatic Constitution on the Church of Christ," in *The Church Teaches*, trans. and ed. John F. Clarkson et al. (Rockford, Ill.: Tan Books, 1973), chap. 4, p. 102. Congar points out that the Council's understanding of infallibility as an attribute of papal primacy is rooted "in the strictly modern ideas of political sovereignty. Because of this socio-historical environment, Vatican I must be reexamined, both positively and critically, in the light of careful historical study," "Magisterium and Theologians," p. 19. See T. Howland Sanks, "Co-operation, Co-optation, Condemnation: Theologians and the Magisterium 1870–1978," *Chicago Studies* 17 (Summer 1978): 246–48, and Francis A. Sullivan, *Magisterium: Teaching Authority in the Catholic Church* (New York: Paulist Press, 1983), pp. 90–99.

73. Daniel Maguire, *Moral Absolutes and the Magisterium* (Washington, D.C.: Corpus Papers, 1970), p. 15.

74. Ibid., p. 17.

75. Ibid.

76. Ibid.

77. Congar, "Magisterium and Theologians," p. 17.

78. Dulles, *Survival of Dogma*, p. 104.

79. William E. May, "The Magisterium and Moral Theology," in *Symposium on the Magisterium: A Positive Statement*, ed. John J. O'Rourke and S. Thomas Greenburg (Boston: St. Paul Editions, 1978), p. 75.

80. Ibid., p. 76. For a survey of views on this question, see Richard A. McCormick, *Notes on Moral Theology: 1965 Through 1980* (Washington, D.C.: University Press of America, 1981), pp. 652–68; 778–85. See also Sullivan, *Magisterium*, pp. 203–4.

81. For brief contemporary overviews on the nature of the *Magisterium*, see Karl Rahner and Herbert Vorgrimler, *Dictionary of Theology* (New York: Crossroad Publishing Co., 1981), s.v. "Magisterium"; and *Sacramentum Mundi: An Encyclopedia of Theology*, 1969 ed., s.v. "Magisterium," by Karl Rahner. See Sullivan, *Magisterium*, for a book-length summary.

82. Vatican II, "Constitution on the Church," no. 22, p. 43; no. 25, p. 47. See also Second Vatican Council, "Decree on the Bishops' Pastoral Office in the Church," in *Documents of Vatican II*, no. 2, p. 397; nos. 12–14, pp. 404–406.

83. Vatican II, "Constitution on Divine Revelation," no. 10, pp. 117–18. Here "authentically" implies "authoritatively."

84. Maguire, *Moral Absolutes*, p. 14. See Charles E. Curran and Robert E. Hunt, *Dissent In and For the Church: Theologians and Humanae Vitae* (New York: Sheed and Ward, 1969), pp. 55–56.

85. Maguire, *Moral Absolutes*, p. 14.

86. Vatican II, "Constitution on the Church," no. 25, pp. 47–49. See also *The Code of Canon Law: A Text and Commentary*, ed. James A. Coriden, Thomas J. Green, and Donald E. Heintschel (New York: Paulist Press, 1985), Canon 749, p. 547. Note that Canon 749§3 states: "No doctrine is understood to be infallibly defined unless it is clearly established as such."

87. Juan Alfaro, "Theology's Role Regarding the Magisterium," *Theology Digest* 25 (Fall 1977): 214.

88. *Sacramentum Mundi*, s.v. "Magisterium," p. 356.

89. Vatican II, "Constitution on the Church," no. 25, p. 48.

90. Sullivan, *Magisterium*, p. 129.

91. See Ibid., p. 127.

92. Ibid., pp. 131–34.

93. Ibid., pp. 135–36.

94. No moral principle has ever been solemnly defined.

95. Sullivan, *Magisterium*, pp. 148–52. Germain Grisez and John C. Ford disagree. See their "Contraception and the Infallibility of the Ordinary Magisterium," *Theological Studies* 39 (1978): 258–312.

96. Maguire, *Moral Absolutes*, p. 14. See Curran and Hunt, *Dissent*, p. 42.

97. Vatican II, "Constitution on the Church," no. 25, p. 48. See also Canon 749§2, p. 138.

98. Maguire, *Moral Absolutes*, p. 14. See Sullivan, *Magisterium*, pp. 123–27.

99. Vatican II, "Constitution on the Church," no. 25, pp. 48–49. May points out that such teachings cannot be regarded as merely probable. "Magisterium and Moral Theology," p. 77. See *The Code of Canon Law*, Canons 752 and 753, p. 548.

100. Sullivan, *Magisterium*, p. 161. See also the commentary on Canons 752 and 753 in *The Code of Canon Law*, p. 548.

101. Ludwig Ott, *Fundamentals of Catholic Dogma*, trans. Partrick Lynch (St. Louis: B. Herder Book Co., 1955), p. 10. See the overview of the teachings of the manuals of theology in Curran and Hunt, *Dissent*, pp. 42–47.

102. Curran and Hunt, *Dissent*, pp. 42–43.

103. Ibid., pp.43–44. For example, Ott's textbook states: "The obligation of inner agreement may cease if a competent expert, after a renewed scientific investigation of all grounds, arrives at the positive conviction that the decision rests on an error." In such a case, reverent silence is urged. See *Catholic Dogma*, p. 10.

104. Curran and Hunt, *Dissent*, p. 121.

105. Ibid., pp. 139–43.

106. Ibid., p. 142. See also the discussion in Sullivan, *Magisterium*, pp. 214–16.

107. May, "Magisterium and Moral Theology," p. 81.

108. Ibid., pp. 81–82.

109. McCormick, *Moral Theology*, p. 783.

110. Ibid.

111. National Conference of Catholic Bishops, *On Human Life in Our Day* (Washington, D.C.: United States Catholic Conference, Nov. 1968), reprinted in *Renewing the Earth: Catholic Documents on Peace, Justice, and Liberation*, ed. David O'Brien and Thomas Shannon (Garden City, NY.: Image/Doubleday, 1977), pp. 427–67.

112. Ibid., nos. 49–51, pp. 439–40. See (Bishop) James Malone, "How Bishops and Theologians Relate," and (Archbishop) Daniel Pilarczyk, "Dissent in the Church," *Origins* 16 (July 31, 1986): 169–74 and 175–78 respectively. On Archbishop James Hickey's apparent unilateral repudiation of the 1968 guidelines, see *The National Catholic Reporter*, 5 September 1986, p. 25.

113. "Father Curran Refuses to Retract Views," *Origins* 15 (May 8, 1986): 771. For copies of correspondence between Curran and the Congregation, see *Origins*

15 (March 27, 1986): 665–680. Note especially, "Cardinal Ratzinger's Letter Asking Curran to Retract," pp. 667–68.

114. "Vatican Says Father Curran Can't Teach Theology," *Origins* 16 (August 28, 1986): 201. See Curran's response on pp. 205–6.

115. "Observations of the Doctrinal Congregation," *Origins* 15 (March 27, 1986): 670.

116. See, for example, "August 1984 Response by Curran to Congregation," *Origins* 15 (March 27, 1986): 676.

117. See "Cardinal Ratzinger's Letter Asking Curran to Retract," *Origins* 15 March 27, 1986): 668, and "Congregation Asks Curran to Complete His Response," *Origins* 15 (March 27, 1986): 675.

118. "Curran Can't Teach Theology," pp. 201–3. On early reaction to the Congregation's resolution of the Curran case, see *The National Catholic Reporter*, 5 September 1986. For a reaffirmation of his position, see Curran's "Authority and Dissent in the Church," Origins 16 (November 6, 1986): 375–76.

2.

The American Roman Catholic College and University

The problem of academic freedom in the American Catholic college or university cannot be adequately dealt with apart from a clear understanding of the social and historical context of Catholic higher education in the United States. This chapter will examine a number of factors that have shaped the history of American Catholic higher education and that have influenced, to varying degrees, Catholic theory and practice in the area of academic freedom. In light of the analysis of these historical factors, the contemporary social locus of the American Catholic college and university will be explored.

HISTORICAL FACTORS

In American Roman Catholic educational circles, extensive interest in the subject of academic freedom is a relatively recent phenomenon, one that arose during the past twenty years.[1] Moreover, a review of the limited number of Catholic scholarly discussions of academic freedom during the first half of the twentieth century reveals an approach to the subject often characterized by defensiveness and negativity.[2] To historians of Catholic higher education, these facts are neither surprising nor inexplicable in light of the historical setting of American Catholic higher education. As the historian Philip Gleason has observed, "Academic freedom is a new idea to Catholic educators because they have only recently arrived at the point where it has a vital bearing on the activity of their colleges."[3]

While the presentation of an exhaustive chronological history of American Catholic higher education is not possible within the scope of this study, it is necessary to survey briefly a number of relevant historical factors.[4] These factors, which in part constitute the historical setting of the American Catholic college or university, will be classified and examined under three categories. The first of these groups will be labeled "Educational Goals and Attitudes" and will include factors such as the motivations for founding Catholic colleges in the United States, the evolution of conceptions of the goals of higher education as reflected in curricular developments, attitudes toward research and teaching, and views of the nature of truth. Factors related to "Institutional Structure and Governance" will form the second category. Clerical dominance, traditionally strong presidential authority, and the changing role of the Catholic college faculty are among the factors to be examined within this second category. Finally, conditions relating to the "Historic Social Context of the American Catholic College" will be examined. These include the early isolation of Catholic institutions from the rest of American higher education and the defensiveness of these institutions—in short, elements of the often cited "ghetto mentality" which is said to have characterized American Catholicism well into the twentieth century.[5]

Educational Goals and Attitudes

The birth of Catholic higher education in the United States is associated with the founding of Georgetown Academy—later to become Georgetown University—in 1789.[6] By this date seventeen colleges had been established in what was to become the United States, the first being Harvard, which was founded in 1636.[7] Historian Edward J. Power has offered three factors that account for the delay in the appearance of Catholic higher education in America. First, the failure to establish Catholic higher schools prior to the Revolutionary War is due in part to the small size of the Catholic population in the English colonies. "As late as 1770, probably not more than 22,000 Catholics lived in the colonies along the Atlantic Ocean."[8] Second, Catholics in colonial times faced widespread hostility from their Protestant neighbors. Stephen Steinberg offers this summary description of the anti-Catholic sentiments that characterized the English colonies:

The colonial settlers left England before it had recovered from the scars of the Reformation. Not only did these settlers carry with them a deep-seated anti-Catholicism, but once in America they were removed from the liberal currents that gradually diminished anti-Catholic feeling in Europe (Billington, 1964, p. 4). Furthermore, many of the Protestant settlers were themselves refugees from religious persecution and sought to establish religious colonies in the New World where they could pursue their religious doctrines without interference or competition from others. This combination of religious fervor and native anti-Catholicism resulted in the persecution of Catholics, frequently under the sanction of law.[9]

Indeed, in some colonies, Catholic religious exercises were proscribed and the establishment of schools by Catholics forbidden.[10] A 1704 Maryland law, for example, threatened deportation to any Catholic who established a school.[11] As Power observes, "To suppose that Catholics in the colonies could have followed in the footsteps of their non-Catholic countrymen to establish schools and affirm a strong official policy toward education under Catholic control would be to expect the impossible."[12]

Power offers a third reason for the relatively late appearance of American Catholic institutions of higher learning. In his view, the attitudes of Catholics—lay and clerical—toward higher education were not conducive to the development of institutions of higher studies.[13] A number of Catholic elementary schools were established in the English colonies from 1640 onward, though the goals of these schools were primarily religious.[14] However, in the area of advanced education, there failed to appear among colonial Catholics a clear commitment to higher learning—a commitment that was exhibited by many of the Protestant denominations.[15] Power argues that even among the leaders of colonial Catholics, there seemed to be an indifference to advanced education apart from that necessary to prepare candidates for seminary studies.[16] This latter goal was to play a large role in the later establishment of Catholic higher schools.

As Steinberg and Power point out, the position of Catholics improved somewhat with the dawn of the national period. "With independence, confidence grew that the political and religious destiny of the nation had been established and most legal restrictions on Catholics were abrogated."[17] However, it would be incorrect to assume that bigotry and persecution disappeared completely. Nevertheless, it was in the early years of the national period that the establishment of Catholic higher schools began. It should be noted that the description "higher schools" is used with some reservations, for the curriculum of early Catholic colleges combined elementary and secondary studies and only gradually were collegiate level studies added.[18]

In his two influential works on the history of Catholic higher education, Power has convincingly argued that three principal motives lay behind the founding of Catholic colleges through 1850. Colleges were established

to offer a preparatory or preliminary education for boys aspiring to the seminary; to create a center for missionary activities from which the good offices of religion might diffuse the message of the Church to unconverted people or to supply the benefits of religion to Catholics in sparsely-settled and far-flung dioceses of a wilderness America; and to conduct a Catholic house of study and discipline where boys and young men might live in a controlled environment and thus cultivate moral and religious virtue.[19]

Although the motives were emphasized to different degrees depending upon the individual institution, Power argues that every Catholic college during the formative period reflected these motives in their founding.

In Power's view, intellectual development was a motive always present in the founding of Catholic higher schools, though it was rarely emphasized. According to his assessment of the evidence, "Before 1850 no Catholic college was established with the purpose of intellectual development, a commitment to the intellectual life or liberal learning, uppermost in the minds of its founders."[20] Andrew M. Greeley argues that the early Catholic colleges were, indeed, founded to provide preseminary training for future clerics as well as to enable lay Catholics to pursue higher studies without endangering their faith. However, he cautions that it would be a mistake to assume that these were the only motivations for establishing Catholic colleges. He claims that the American bishops' "respect for learning as an element in Catholic life" was also a factor.[21] While he is not in disagreement with Power on this point, it would appear as though Greeley places somewhat more emphasis upon intellectual development as a motive behind the establishment of early Catholic colleges.

Agatho Zimmer, in a 1938 dissertation, alludes to four motivating factors behind the establishment of Catholic colleges, although he does not explore their comparative importance.[22] The four motives cited by Zimmer—the propagation of the faith, the development of moral character, the dissemination of the arts and sciences, and seminary preparation—are virtually identical to those identified by Power, though Power certainly questions the strength of the early Catholic college's commitment to the dissemination of liberal culture.[23]

Evidence does seem to support the contention that the motivation behind the founding of Catholic colleges was, until the late nineteenth century, primarily religious and/or moral in character. The earliest manifestation of this motivation is the founding of Georgetown in 1789. John Carroll, Apostolic Prefect from 1784 and first bishop of Baltimore from 1790, recognizing that the young American nation faced a critical shortage of priests, sought to remedy that shortage through the development of a body of native clergy.[24] At the November 1785 meeting of Maryland clergymen, Carroll proposed the establishment of a preparatory school where candidates aspiring to the priesthood could receive training and where Catholic youth could be safely educated. By this time Carroll had come to recognize that Catholic youth could not utilize existing non-Catholic institutions without serious challenges being made to their faith.[25] Carroll's proposal was approved and Georgetown Academy was established.

The religious motivation for establishing higher Catholic schools continued to be paramount into the second part of the nineteenth century.[26]

Power and John D. Donovan have pointed out that when a bishop sought to establish a college, or when he invited or allowed a religious community to found a higher school in his ecclesiastical jurisdiction, it was often because he viewed the college as a pastoral instrument through which Catholicism could be strengthened and extended.[27] The bishop

could lend support to a school wherein religious objectives were paramount and thus hope to serve the Catholic people of his diocese; in other words, few bishops aimed at creating citadels of learning capable of attracting students the country over. Their commitment to higher education was too narrow for such academic idealism; they wanted, instead, a community college which would function as an educational arm of the Church.[28]

It was the strongly pastoral conception of Catholic higher education, a conception that emphasized religion and morals, that irritated the great nineteenth-century Catholic educational commentator Orestes Brownson. In 1857, Brownson wrote that "while our schools, colleges, and universities abate nothing in the ascetic discipline, or their religious training, . . . they should pay more attention to the secular learning and science of the day."[29]

By the late nineteenth century, however, intellectual goals had grown in importance as motivating factors in the founding of Catholic colleges. "The seminary and missionary motives or moral development *as primary objectives* were not stressed."[30] Nonetheless, religious and moral goals were by no means abandoned by Catholic educational leaders.[31] For example, as recently as 1955, John Tracy Ellis discussed the "overemphasis which some authorities of the church's educational system in the United States have given to the school as an agency for moral development" to the detriment of intellectual pursuits.[32] And in a 1970 article, he observed that the strengthening and defense of the student's faith were—until recent years—the principal purposes of Catholic colleges and universities.[33]

The moral and religious motivation behind the founding and continuing of Catholic colleges into the late nineteenth century is also reflected in the curriculum of these colleges. "Prior to 1870 all Catholic colleges began their academic history as combinations of elementary and secondary schools."[34] The elementary curriculum was composed of the rudiments—reading, grammar, arithmetic—while the secondary course of studies was largely classical in content. It has been argued that while it was not identical with them, the classical curriculum of early Catholic higher schools exhibited the influence of the *Ratio Studiorum*—the European Jesuit classical course of studies—and the European classical schools.[35]

As the early colleges matured, elementary studies were gradually eliminated and collegiate courses added. What developed was a program consisting of both preparatory secondary studies—for example, basic grammar—and collegiate level classical courses including Latin grammar, rhetoric, and humanities. This program was usually spread over six (or seven) years with three years devoted to secondary studies and three years devoted to collegiate courses.[36] Georgetown, the leader among Catholic institutions well into the nineteenth century, instituted the six-year course leading to the bachelor of arts degree in 1820.[37] It is important to note that the six-year curriculum, "with only slight modification and some internal reorganization, dominated Catholic college degree programs for the next half century."[38]

Power has pointed out that the emphasis upon classical studies in early Catholic colleges was due in part to their importance as preparation for seminary training.

Yet Catholic colleges, despite their determination to keep intact an affiliation with seminaries, adopted somewhat broader goals which included the preparation of secular youth who, in time, came to the colleges in pursuit of para-professional and professional credentials. In a word, Catholic colleges could ill afford the luxury of a classical preparatory curriculum; and when this became clear they added to the classical curriculum courses in English studies, as well as commercial and scientific subjects.[39]

Nonetheless, classical studies remained central theoretically, if not actually, through the greater part of the nineteenth century.

Stephen Steinberg has suggested a further rationale for the Catholic emphasis upon classical education. He writes that from the Catholic perspective,

the purpose of education was to cultivate moral virtue and pursue religious truths. Given these attitudes, it is not surprising that Catholics were strongly committed to a classical education. Studies in the humanities, classics, and philosophy were viewed as bringing students closer to God and therefore consistent with the Church's educational ideals. In contrast, science and vocational training seemed spiritually vacant, and came dangerously close to substituting a base materialism for high moral purpose.[40]

As the end of the nineteenth century approached, it became clear that changes were necessary in the inflexible undergraduate curriculum of Catholic colleges.[41] While some Catholic educators were claiming that the Catholic college curriculum was superior to its secular counterpart, the value of classical studies was being questioned by a public that was placing increasing emphasis upon mathematics, the physical sciences, and other branches of practical knowledge. Moreover, Catholic colleges, adhering to a six- or seven-year curricular model, not only found themselves out of step with most other American institutions, but also faced the unwillingness of the newly founded regional accrediting agencies to endorse their programs.

While never an unadulterated classical course of studies, the Catholic college curriculum was gradually enriched by the inclusion of other programs of study, including more commercial and scientific courses. This process, which began slowly in the years following the Civil War, was accelerated after the turn of the century. Increasingly, Catholic colleges "keeping pace with other institutions of higher learning in the United States, were prepared to offer curricula leading to any recognized degree."[42]

Until the 1880s, Catholic institutions held tenaciously to the six- or seven-year college program. In Power's view, the reason for this tenacity becomes clear if one considers

the indelibly religious nature of the Catholic college and the fact that it was first an instrument of the Church and only afterwards a school. The high school years . . . were the most fertile years for cultivating vocations to the religious life as priest, brother, or in the case of Catholic women's colleges, sisters. With demonstrations of this fact always at hand, Catholic college managers were horrified by the thought that the principal source of clerical supply might be allowed to escape their control; so they made every effort to rescue their preparatory departments from the spiritual erosions of the American college way of life.[43]

Nevertheless, St. Louis University took the lead among Catholic institutions and organized the first four-year college curriculum in 1880–81. In many Catholic colleges, however, a *complete* break with the high school course did not occur until the 1940s.[44]

The transformation of Catholic colleges into universities usually occurred, not through the development of research-oriented doctoral programs, but by the addition of professional schools.[45] This pattern is—to a limited degree—similar to that detectable in the development of many non-Catholic universities. For instance,

writing in the 1880s, President Frederick A. P. Barnard distinguished three stages in the history of Columbia University. His classification may well be applied to all the older collegiate foundations of the East which were gradually transforming themselves into universities during this period. The first period, as Barnard saw it, was that of the college. The second was dominated by the adding of various professional schools. The final period was that of the true university, when a comprehensive program of graduate studies was developed.[46]

Most Catholic universities never progressed to Barnard's third stage—the stage of developing a comprehensive program of graduate studies. Although the "establishment of the Catholic University of America in

1889 was an early response to the need for a graduate level institution,"[47] the development of extensive graduate programs has been limited in Catholic universities. Moreover, doctoral programs at Catholic universities have not always been of the highest quality. Problems arising from the isolation of Catholic institutions, financial pressures, faculty quality, and lack of adequate facilities have been barriers to greater success.[48] There have also been what might be termed ideological barriers to greater success in graduate education, including the attitudes of many Catholic educators toward research and the nature of truth. Commenting upon the static philosophy of education widespread in Catholic circles in the past, Andrew M. Greeley writes:

It was assumed that the Catholic Church had an organic "integrity of vision" about the meaning of the world and of life, and it was the purpose of the college to pass on this vision of meaning to the student. . . . The goal of Catholic higher education was then considered to be "the development of the whole man" (a cliché repeated consistently in Catholic college catalogs even today). The schools were not so much concerned with the pushing back of the frontier of truth as with passing on a given tradition of truth in which little in the way of addition or alteration was necessary.[49]

In the past it was often assumed that research, considered vital to the American university, was incongruous with the Catholic worldview. As recently as 1938, for example, George Bull of Fordham University affirmed that "research cannot be the primary object of a Catholic graduate school, because it is at war with the whole Catholic life of the mind."[50] For Catholic education, in his view, should not be concerned with the pursuit of truth, but rather with "deeper penetration into the velvety manifold of reality as *Catholics possess it.*"[51] Such an attitude was not conducive to the successful accomplishment of graduate education as it had developed in the United States, nor was it congruous with American conceptions of what a university is or should be. In what sense then could Catholic institutions claim to be universities?[52] In part, the response of many institutions to this question consisted of the claim that Catholic colleges were primarily *teaching* institutions dedicated to the needs of their students.[53]

Over the past three decades, there has been a gradual erosion of the narrow conceptions of education and of the nature of truth and, correspondingly, a greater emphasis has been placed upon research-oriented graduate study.[54] As Philip Gleason has observed, now "the leading Catholic institutions are dedicated to the *discovery* of truth, and Catholic educators have lost the old assurance in their grip on truth."[55]

Within this historical survey of Catholic "Educational Goals and Attitudes," certain factors have been examined that have militated against the development of a conception of academic freedom. These include the largely religious motivation for establishing and continuing Catholic colleges, the inflexibility of the Catholic college curriculum into the twentieth century, and the rigid approach to the nature of education and the narrow conception of truth that characterized Catholic higher education until after the Second World War. Gleason's summary is worth quoting at length:

When the present century opened, Catholic colleges were small places which saw it as their function to introduce to students and to inculcate in them a previously-arrived-at synthesis of secular knowledge, intellectual skills, ethical values, and religious truth. Free investigation or independent research played virtually no role in this process, and because they did not academic freedom was a negligible concern. It was also a negligible concern because Catholic educators were in practically universal agreement that they understood the knowledge, skills, values, and religious truth that collegians needed to learn.[56]

For Catholic colleges and universities, the past thirty-five years have brought change, the past twenty quite rapid change. To paraphrase Gleason's comment quoted at the commencement of this chapter, academic freedom *now* has an important bearing on the activity of Catholic colleges. However, prior to turning our attention to how Catholic theorists have handled the concept of academic freedom in recent years, the two other categories of pertinent historical factors will be examined.

Institutional Structure and Governance

Catholic attitudes toward academic freedom were conditioned by the patterns of structure and governance that developed in American Catholic colleges and universities. Chief among these patterns are clerical control, the traditionally extensive authority of the Catholic college president, and the evolution of the position of the faculty—particularly the lay faculty—in Catholic institutions.

Catholic higher education in America has a long and generally continuing history of clerical control. As was noted earlier, Catholic colleges were usually founded by a bishop or by a religious community with the permission of a bishop. "Another type of foundation was the lay private-venture college, although no college before 1850 or after 1860 was founded by laymen."[57] It is interesting to note that none of the three colleges founded or conducted by laymen between 1850 and 1860 was successful.[58]

Edward Power has offered two reasons for the lack of success of lay ventures into higher education. From the perspective of most Catholics, a Catholic education was synonymous with being taught by religious. A

Catholic education supplied by laymen was to many inconceivable.[59] This is certainly understandable if one takes account of the fact that the moral and religious goals of Catholic higher education remained important, if not paramount, into the twentieth century. As Gleason observes, lay persons were usually considered less competent than clerics concerning religious matters.[60] "Throughout American Catholic history the accepted view was that if an activity was religious, a priest, or at least a religious, should be in charge of it; and education was viewed as such an activity."[61]

The suspicion with which the clergy and hierarchy viewed the schools and colleges under lay control is also cited by Power as a reason for their lack of success. According to Power, the hierarchy offered less than enthusiastic support to the few lay ventures into Catholic education.[62] The attitudes of the hierarchy toward these ventures were informed by their conceptions of the goals of Catholic colleges, goals which were primarily religious in nature.[63] No doubt, the prevailing attitude among the hierarchy was that religious matters were best left in clerical hands.

Direct clerical control characterized Catholic higher education into the 1960s. Although from early times all incorporated Catholic colleges had legally mandated boards of trustees, these boards were usually composed of members of the religious community sponsoring a particular college, or other clerics.[64] Moreover, despite their legal status, the boards of Catholic colleges rarely exercised real policy making authority. Such authority was actually vested in the president and, indirectly, in the religious superior of the sponsoring order or the bishop.[65]

The vital role played by religious orders in the development of Catholic higher education is well known.[66] Indeed, "nearly all of the Catholic colleges were founded and maintained by religious orders." This is part of the reason why clerical control of Catholic institutions remained strong into contemporary times. As Gleason has observed, religious orders "as self-perpetuating bodies with a natural disinclination to organizational hara-kiri, have simply retained in their own hands control of the institutions they established."[67] It was not until 1967 that formal ownership of a Catholic college was transferred to a lay board of trustees.[68] Since then, there has been a shift by a number of colleges toward lay or mixed control.[69] It has been suggested that among the major motivations for this shift was a desire on the part of Catholic colleges and universities to qualify for public funds.[70]

Historically, Catholic higher education has been characterized by strong presidential authority.[71]

Until very recently neither faculty consultative bodies nor boards of trustees provided any limitation on the power of the president. If, in addition, the president is the superior of the religious community, or at least its local branch on the college campus (as [was] true with most Jesuit presidents), his power becomes even more substantial.[72]

Power argues that although a strong president was not unique to Catholic colleges, the model of Catholic presidential authority was borrowed not from the practice of other American colleges, but from the patterns of government that prevailed in European secondary schools and seminaries.[73]

A capsulized description of the Catholic college president of the nineteenth century would begin with the observation that he was a cleric, usually a priest.[74] Bishops and religious superiors tended to appoint a president not on the basis of academic qualifications, but rather on the basis of his status as a cleric with "unblemished moral and sacerdotal credentials."[75] The president was expected to be a priest-pastor, an administrator, a fundraiser, an educator, and a disciplinarian.[76] Although his power over the operation of the college went unchallenged internally, the president remained accountable to his bishop and, in the case of colleges controlled by religious orders, his superior.[77]

The presidents of Catholic colleges continued to exercise extensive authority throughout the nineteenth and into the twentieth century.[78] However, following World War II, Catholic college governance entered a transition period.[79] As faculties and trustees began to exercise increasing power and influence, the role of the Catholic college president changed. Yet, as Power points out, presidents "were neither forced to relinquish their authority, in which charters and statutes sustained them, nor were they tricked out of it by the cunning of professors; it was gratuitous action on the presidents' part that delegated some academic authority to the faculty."[80]

Turning to an examination of the evolution of the nature and position of the faculty of Catholic colleges, it becomes clear that in early Catholic colleges, the faculty was largely clerical. As Power writes, "The Catholic college was . . . determined to be a religious agency first and a school second; thus, the usual qualifications for a teacher in a Catholic college began by demanding clerical status."[81] The academic qualifications of the faculty of Catholic colleges into the mid-nineteenth century were, for the most part, unimpressive. There were some truly able teachers; however, most of these were among the large number of teachers imported from Europe, and their success was often impeded by language barriers.[82]

Early Catholic colleges experienced a shortage of priest-teachers and, hence, seminarians were often given teaching assignments.[83] Laymen were associated with Catholic colleges from earliest times, though their numbers were few and their status was quite low.[84] Sebastian Erbacher reported that there were 26 laymen out of 240 college teachers in 1850,

55 out of 313 in 1855, 63 out of 303 in 1860, and 104 out of 385 in 1865, while the 1872 report of the United States Commission of Education listed 80 laymen out of 677 faculty members.[85] Power has warned that the title "faculty member" is to be used quite loosely when dealing with lay teachers in early Catholic colleges. He writes:

They were employees and they were treated as such. Their status was probably little better than that of grade school boys. Laymen were bound by regulations quite as firmly as were the religious: cleric, priests, or monks; and though laymen had taken no vows they were required to live on their college grounds and conform to all religious exercises.[86]

During the first hundred years of Catholic higher education in America, laymen were at best marginal members of the academic community. Part of the unreceptiveness of Catholic colleges to lay faculty was rooted in the prevailing attitudes toward higher education. Colleges were viewed as primarily religious institutions while teaching was seen as an extension of the pulpit.[87] This view was reflected in the types of teaching positions held by laymen. Rather than teaching the classically oriented curriculum considered central by Catholic educators of the nineteenth century, laymen were employed to teach the deprecated commercial and English courses.[88] It was only with the admission of commercial courses to full collegiate status in the late 1800s that laymen rose to true faculty status.[89]

As Greeley points out, "By the time of World War II, there were large numbers of lay faculty members in Catholic colleges and universities."[90] Unlike their predecessors who rarely held advanced degrees, lay professors since World War II have been characterized by more extensive academic qualifications and a more intellectual, rather than religious, orientation.[91] Moreover, since the mid–1950s, Catholic faculty members have exercised an increasing amount of control over the functioning of their colleges. "Faculty participation in college control" has been "evidenced in a number of ways, such as the implementation of policies on academic freedom, appointments to the faculty, tenure arrangements and tenure decisions, salaries, curricular renovation and innovation, admissions practices and policies, and the determination and supervision of academic standards."[92]

Over the past thirty-five years, there has been significant improvement in the quality and status of the faculty of Catholic colleges.[93] Greeley's 1967 National Opinion Research Center study of Catholic higher education found surprising progress in areas such as compensation, teaching load, and academic freedom, and some improvement "in developing faculty participation, professional standards, and faculty research competence, although the progress here was frequently much less than satisfactory."[94]

The historical characteristics of the institutional structure and governance of Catholic colleges and universities have had a negative impact upon the development of any operative notion of academic freedom. The history of clerical control in Catholic institutions, traditional presidential authoritarianism, and the slow rise of faculty power have forestalled, until recent decades, the evolution of an atmosphere of freedom on Catholic campuses.

Clerical control of colleges, particularly control by a religious order, has often meant control by persons extrinsic to the academic community, namely a bishop or more often, a religious superior. In the past (and in some institutions today), the religious superior of the controlling religious community appointed key administrative personnel.[95] This practice has often resulted in the appointment of obedient, unimaginative, "safe" individuals. Greeley writes:

The religious community can traditionally be expected to emphasize obedience, discipline, loyalty, order, and respect for familiar, diffuse, particularistic, and descriptive values. The higher educational institution, insofar as it tries to imitate typical American institutions, will be more likely to emphasize initiative, imagination, creativity and specific achievement, and universal values. A man can have all the talents necessary to be an extraordinarily effective college administrator and yet the provincial, as a representative of the religious community, may think that he cannot safely be trusted with power and responsibility.[96]

Moreover, individuals appointed to administrative positions frequently did not hold proper credentials for those positions. For example, in his 1967 study, Greeley has noted that many important administrative offices in Catholic colleges have often been held by "amateurs."[97] Judged qualified by standards of a religious community, these administrators possessed neither the talent nor the training for the positions they held. The rationale behind the appointing of "safe" community members or amateurs to important positions is to insure continuing control, and to preserve the institution from change. Such a policy has often been, and continues to be successful.[98]

Clerical control has also tended to stratify college faculties along lay-clerical lines. As discussed earlier, lay teachers in Catholic colleges were at best tolerated as practical necessities during most of the nineteenth century. Catholic colleges were religious institutions first, and educational institutions only secondarily, and the role of lay teachers reflected this outlook.[99] Although faculty status—especially lay faculty status—began to rise toward the end of the nineteenth century, lay faculty power became a reality only during the past three decades.[100] Yet it is interesting to note that as late as 1964, Donovan's sociological study of Catholic College professors indicated that approximately fifty percent of the lay faculty sample "felt that they were 'second class citizens,' 'necessary evils,' or 'without any significant voice.' "[101]

The particular administrative tone set by clerical control also militated against an earlier development of a theory of academic freedom on the Catholic campus. Donovan argued that until recent decades,

the college administration and the faculty were priests or brothers, and these roles defined their first and most powerful loyalties. They were not independent professional persons but subordinate officers in a bureaucratic organization. Obedience to the authority of religious superiors was a primary expectation and this, not because of their technical claims to competence and authority, but because they were the ecclesiastically appointed religious superiors.[102]

Hence, for many years, the government of Catholic colleges was, in essence, patterned after, if not an extension of, the government of a religious order or other religious structure. Professional patterns of governance were eclipsed by those of the religious organization.[103] Since the additon of large numbers of lay faculty members following World War II, the approach to the governance of Catholic colleges has been in a process of transition.[104]

Turning to the strong, ecclesiastically-based presidential authority that characterized Catholic higher education into the 1960s, two major ramifications of this authority became apparent, neither of which encouraged an atmosphere of freedom in the Catholic college.[105] First, during the nineteenth and early twentieth centuries, "Catholic college presidents tended to form an image of themselves as custodians of a *status quo* rather than as innovators or reformers."[106] This conservatism was, in part, related to the ecclesiastical basis of presidential power. For the authority of the president "was not assumed; it was bestowed on him, or on his office, by bishops and religious superiors who believed that a house of studies should be ruled without interference from other members of the college community."[107] As discussed above, most persons appointed to administrative positions by religious superiors were "safe" individuals, or at least individuals who understood the source of their power and governed accordingly.

Second, strong presidential authority sometimes developed into authoritarianism.[108] Particularly in the nineteenth century, obedience to presidential authority was demanded. Although changes have occurred over the past twenty-five years, Power wrote in 1958:

From their origin to the present, with few exceptions, the colleges have been administered as if they were extensions of parochial activities engaged essentially and primarily in moral development. It has been difficult for college presidents to realize, for example, that a vow of obedience and an appointment to teach at a Catholic college are not the same.[109]

Strong presidential authority was coupled with a lack of faculty—especially lay faculty—power. Power points out that during the formative period of Catholic higher education, that is until approximately 1870, even a rudimentary notion of academic freedom was absent.[110] The curriculum was rigid, the teaching texts were prescribed, and the instructor was closely supervised.[111] Although toward the end of the nineteenth century lay faculty status began to improve, Catholic college faculties by no means became bodies of self-governing disinterested scholars.[112] Active Catholic opponents of intellectual freedom were few, not because of a prevailing Catholic liberalism, but "because of the almost universally docile acceptance in Catholic circles of not only the teachings of the Church, but too, of the authoritarian regimes that governed the Church's colleges."[113]

As we have seen, the period following World War II saw an influx of large numbers of lay faculty members, and an elevation of the qualifications and professional outlook of Catholic college professors. By the late 1950s, faculty members began to have input into the governance of their colleges in areas such as faculty appointments, curricular legislation, academic standards, and tenure policies.[114] This liberalization was strengthened and augmented by the spirit of freedom and openness which characterized the Second Vatican Council.[115]

Most Catholic colleges have endorsed the "1940 Statement of Principles on Academic Freedom and Tenure" of the American Association of University Professors, and commentators such as Andrew Greeley have pointed to the relatively few *reported* violations of academic freedom in Catholic colleges in recent years.[116] However, the demand for faculty freedom, if pressed, might cause problems in some institutions.[117] As Power wrote in 1972, "conservatism is almost indigenous to Catholic college faculties, and it may be some time before the fundamental issues in academic freedom are put to the ultimate test."[118]

Historic Social Context of the American Catholic College

The rather late manifestation of Catholic interest in a notion of academic freedom is also attributable to the social posture assumed by Catholic colleges and universities until recent times.[119] As Greeley observed in a 1967 study, "The Catholic population is an immigrant population only now entering the mainstream of the social and economic life of the country and, hence, only now are its colleges and universities turning aside from the posture of an immigrant religious group and taking on the posture of a typically American educational institution."[120]

Historian Philip Gleason has examined two recent social changes which have had an influence upon Catholic attitudes toward academic freedom. First, Gleason has pointed to the gradual cultural assimilation of American Catholics as well as to the corresponding decrease of anti-Catholic sentiments in American society.[121] The anti-Catholic bias that characterized the English colonies prior to the Revolutionary War is well known.[122] Although few in number, Catholic colonists were subject to social discrimination, as well as to severe legal restrictions on religious practice and educational endeavor.[123] With the dawn of the national period, however, came greater acceptance of Anglo-American Catholics.[124] Nevertheless, this early tendency toward the assimilation and acceptance of Catholics was to be frustrated. From the late 1820s onward, large numbers of Catholic immigrants—at first Irish and German—began entering the United States.[125] The wave of immigrants continued throughout the century with German and Irish immigrants being joined in America by the waves of southern and eastern Europeans that constituted the "New Immigration" following the Civil War.[126] With massive immigration came a drastic change in the character of the American Catholic population. To quote Gleason, "Catholics became almost overnight a throng of foreigners who were poor, uncultivated, and sometimes aggressive in demanding that their religious rights be respected."[127]

Anti-Catholic bigotry in the United States was exacerbated by this massive immigration. American prejudice against the foreign born came to be directed with particular vehemence against foreign-born Catholics and, indeed, toward the Catholic Church in general.[128] The onset of immigration left the Catholic Church in the precarious position of being not only religiously dissimilar from American society, but socially (and sometimes linguistically) divergent as well. Hence, there developed within American Catholicism a "ghetto (or siege) mentality," a defensiveness often characteristic of a "deviant" group living in the midst of a larger society inimical to its interests.[129] The establishment of a comprehensive network of Catholic schools—from elementary schools through colleges—was in part a reaction to the position of Catholics who found themselves in a hostile land.[130] It may be recalled that the motives for founding Catholic colleges into the twentieth century included the desire to establish institutions wherein young Catholics might safely pursue their studies and receive the moral and religious training necessary to enable them to withstand the challenges to their faith emanating from the larger culture.[131]

So long as the Church and its schools continued to maintain a defensiveness vis-à-vis a hostile environment, academic freedom in Catholic colleges could not germinate. In recent decades, however, there has been a positive change in the position of Catholics in American society, and correspondingly, this has influenced the atmosphere of the Church's institutions of higher learning. Gleason comments that a

combination of Catholic acculturation and declining external hostility has reduced the need for a defensive and apologetical orientation at all levels of

Catholic education. As the barriers of suspicion and ill-will are removed, the pressure to close ranks in a rigidly defensive posture diminishes; the horizons of Catholic education are correspondingly enlarged, and the demand for greater freedom to launch out in new directions is a natural consequence.[132]

The second social change identified by Gleason as influencing Catholic attitudes toward academic freedom is related to the first. Cultural assimilation or "emergence from the ghetto" has been accompanied by an improvement in the socio-economic status of Catholics.[133] As the socio-economic status of Catholics has advanced, the demand for higher education has increased. Hence, in 1930 there were 102,000 students enrolled in American Catholic colleges, while in 1940 the number had risen to 162,000. By the late 1960s, enrollment hovered around 400,000.[134] The great increase in enrollment has necessitated the hiring of large numbers of lay professors, many of whom have had some experience in non-Catholic universities.[135] Gleason has convincingly argued that the recent "demands for more academic freedom and lay participation in academic policy-making are a natural consequence of their experience and of the position they now occupy in the system."[136]

The rise in the socio-economic status of Catholics has also resulted in a greater congruity between the educational values and expectations of Catholics and those of the general population.[137] This change has meant that in recent years a greater emphasis has been placed upon academic freedom and similar values by students and the general Catholic population. Gleason writes:

Today, more than at any earlier time, the Catholic population resembles the general American population in terms of wealth, social status, educational background, and acceptance of the prevailing democratic and anti-authoritarian spirit. Hence the demand that is transmitted upward is for a college education characterized by those qualities associated with the finest secular institutions of American higher learning. Among those qualities, academic freedom is conspicuous.[138]

The social context of Catholic higher education throughout the nineteenth and into the twentieth century was not conducive to an atmosphere of freedom and openness on the Catholic campus. Catholicism, viewed as a dangerous foreign force during much of the colonial period, came to be increasingly distrusted as large numbers of poor, uncultivated Catholic immigrants reached America's shores in the nineteenth century. Finding itself in a hostile environment, American Catholicism developed a defensive "ghetto mentality" that kept its colleges and universities intellectually isolated from the rest of American higher education through the first half of the twentieth century.[139] This defensive mentality impeded the development of a notion of academic freedom on Catholic campuses.

In the decades following the Second World War, the American Catholic population entered the final stages of its acculturation process. "Catholic higher education, therefore, is also definitively departing from its original position within the walls of the immigrant ghetto, attempting to become part of the broader American higher educational enterprise."[140]

CONTEMPORARY AMERICAN CATHOLIC HIGHER EDUCATION

A General Description

Presently, Catholic higher education consists of a collection of 223 colleges and universities spread across forty of the fifty states. This group includes twenty-four two-year colleges, a number of small liberal arts colleges, and large universities with thousands of students and extensive graduate and professional programs. Most Catholic colleges are coeducational, though forty colleges are for women only or primarily for women, while two remain for men alone.[141]

Commentators have consistently emphasized the diversity of American Catholic higher education.[142] Greeley, for example, has remarked that "there is neither organizational nor ideological unity within Catholic higher education, and the outside observer who expects that he will be able to generalize about this helter-skelter aggregation of schools soon realizes that he is skating on very thin ice."[143] Indeed, Catholic colleges differ not only in size, but in such areas as faculty quality, student clientele, degree programs, financial resources, facilities, and educational aspirations.[144]

It is important to recognize that this great diversity is not systematized through any type of direct, centralized control. The extensive role religious orders have played in the development of American Catholic higher education is, in part, responsible for this relative independence of Catholic colleges. Most Catholic colleges are presently operated by—or, prior to independent control, were related to—"teaching orders, which are free to define their mission and clientele as they wish."[145] As Jencks and Riesman have observed, the consequence has been "pluralism verging on anarchy."[146]

What all Catholic colleges have in common is "some kind of commitment to the Roman Catholic faith, though the nature of this commitment varies from school to school, both in theory and practice."[147] Moreover, all Catholic colleges and universities fall under the jurisdiction of the Vatican through the Sacred Congregation for Catholic Education, although practically speaking, intervention by this Congregation into the affairs of American colleges has been quite rare.[148] It should be noted, however, that on April 15, 1985, the Congregation released a proposed schema for a Pontifical document on Catholic universities and invited "an examination in full freedom and frankness."[149] This working draft, which in its norms reflects relevant sections of the 1983 Code of Canon Law, has been criticized on legal, theological, and educational grounds.[150]

The new Code of Canon Law of the Roman Church, which became operative on November 27, 1983, reaffirms and strengthens the bishops' role of vigilance over Catholic higher schools. As Power points out, historically "both permission and fundamental encouragement to establish colleges derived from them—especially after 1850—for the canonical structure of the Church admitted of no such initiative without the bishop's approval."[151] According to the new Code, the title "Catholic university" can be used only with permission of an ecclessiatical authority—usually the local ordinary or bishop.[152] In addition to specific directives that will be discussed in detail in a later chapter, bishops are given a general mandate in Canon 810§2:

The conference of bishops and the diocesan bishops concerned have the duty and the right of being vigilant that in these universities the principles of Catholic doctrine are faithfully observed.[153]

While direct intervention of bishops in the internal affairs of Catholic colleges has been quite infrequent, the potential for such involvement remains.[154]

It is clear that American Catholic higher education is a manifold entity. As a group, Catholic colleges are not guided by a "master plan" nor can they be regarded as a "system" except in the very broadest sense of the term.[155] Despite indirect Church jurisdiction over them, Catholic colleges are not subject to direct, centralized governance. Their diversity as educational institutions is even mirrored in the colleges' varying interpretations of their single common characteristic—a commitment to the Roman Catholic faith.

A Typology of Catholic Colleges and Universities

Although generalizations about Catholic colleges and universities are difficult to make, some degree of categorization is possible and, for our purposes, necessary. One attempt at categorizing American institutions has been made by Robert J. Henle for the International Federation of Catholic Universities.[156] Henle has proposed three classifications of Catholic colleges, which, with the addition of the category of universities with Pontifical faculties, constitute the basis of the typology that will be employed here.

The first type of American Catholic university is the university with ecclesiastical or canonically erected faculties. As Charles E. Curran has pointed out, "Almost all American colleges and universities are not canonically erected except for some faculties at The Catholic University."[157] These faculties differ from other non-canonical faculties in that they maintain a direct juridical relationship with the Apostolic See through the Sacred Congregation for Catholic Education.

In the 1979 *Apostolic Constitution Sapientia Christiana*, ecclesiastical faculties are described as "those which have been canonically erected or approved by the Apostolic See, which foster and teach doctrine and the sciences connected therewith, and which have the right to confer academic degrees by the authority of the Holy See."[158] The Apostolic Constitution requires that members of canonically-erected faculties who teach sacred disciplines receive from the Chancellor a canonical mission to teach, while other teachers must receive permission to do so.[159] All professors appointed to permanent posts must receive a declaration of *nihil obstat* from Rome.[160]

The second category of Catholic universities is the model of Catholic exclusivity.[161] Colleges within this category perceive themselves as Roman Catholic educational communities, most of whose members share the same faith. The academic programs offered by such institutions present knowledge and truth exclusively within a Catholic framework.[162] As Henle points out, colleges adopting this model are, in effect, attempting to withdraw from the pluralism that characterizes American society and its educational institutions. Their goal is "the development of a thoroughly Catholic character and mind."[163]

While some Catholics may hail such an approach to higher education as a return to a truly *Catholic* higher education, others might consider this model a regression to the Catholic intellectual ghetto, a ghetto that isolates Catholic education and hinders the Church in its encounter with culture.[164] Predictably, very few colleges represent this model in a highly pure fashion. One that does is Newman College in St. Louis.[165] Henle has observed that although few colleges fall into the "exclusive" category absolutely, a number of institutions—the University of Dallas, for example—exhibit characteristics of this model. Such schools "have insisted on canonical control as essential for a Catholic university and have maintained a high degree of Catholic exclusivity and a measure of sectarian isolation."[166] It should be noted that although some colleges within this category continue the pattern of direct religious control, others such as Newman are governed by an independent board of trustees.[167]

Our third "type," the Catholic pluralistic university, rejects the narrow defensive sectarianism of the model of Catholic exclusivity.[168] Colleges and universities that fall into this category seek to embody in their institutional life the openness that has characterized the relation between the Church and culture since the Second Vatican Council.[169] These institutions have come to recognize that "they could best serve the church by being good institutions of higher learning and holding on to their autonomy."[170]

The evolution of the Catholic pluralistic university began in the years following World War II.[171] The large numbers of new students—Catholic as well as non-Catholics—entering Catholic colleges in the late 1940s triggered the expansion of facilities and faculties in a number of institutions.[172] As discussed earlier, large numbers of lay persons, many with non-Catholic academic experience, were added to Catholic faculties. Moreover, a new emphasis upon academic excellence and the intellectual goals of Catholic higher education was developing. As federal and corporate research grants became increasingly available some Catholic universities utilized the opportunity to expand scholarship and research on their campuses.[173] These institutional changes, together with the theological renewal of the Second Vatican Council and the social assimilation of the Catholic population, contributed to the development of the Catholic pluralistic university.[174]

The universities that fall into this category—Georgetown, Fordham, and Notre Dame, for example—share a number of characteristics. First, these institutions share a Catholic commitment although the practical implications of it will vary from institution to institution. This commitment has its origin in "the intention of the founders, the intention of the donors and supporters, the expectancies of traditional constituencies (alumni, parents, students), and the will of contemporary supporters and administrators."[175] It is incorporated by the governing board, which, in the pluralistic university, is usually independent. Second, as an institution dedicated chiefly to academic excellence, the pluralistic university counts among its members a number of highly qualified lay teachers as well as many non-Catholic scholars—both students and faculty members.[176] Finally, the pluralistic university seeks to extend the frontiers of knowledge through scholarship in the autonomous academic disciplines, while allowing a pluralism of ideas to reign.[177]

The final type of American Catholic college Henle calls the "Catholic secular college."[178] Institutions of this type have abandoned any specific Catholic character. These are independently governed, lay-controlled colleges that consider education a "temporal work of mercy" for which only "the motivation remains distinctively Christian."[179] Webster College in St. Louis, Missouri, would fall into this category insofar as it has become officially a secular college.[180] It was in 1967 that Jacqueline Grennan, the president of Webster, "left the religious life but remained as head of the college and formal ownership was transferred from the Sisters of Loretto to a lay board of trustees."[181] At the time, Grennan argued that "the very nature of *higher* education is opposed to juridical control by the church."[182] Yet as Henle has observed, the movement toward complete secularization of Catholic institutions was never wide-spread and, in fact, seems to have ceased completely.[183]

Thus, a fourfold typology can be employed in an effort to categorize Catholic colleges and universities. In general, the typology presented above is based upon differences in educational philosophy and institutional goals, as well as relevant variations in the relation of Catholic colleges to the Church. No actual institution purely and absolutely conforms to a particular type.[184] Moreover, what was presented above is only one of many possible typologies that could be constructed to better study and understand Catholic higher education.

CONCLUDING SUMMARY

Until the 1960s there was "very little Catholic discussion of academic freedom, and the little that did occur was often quite negative in tone."[185] As Gleason has acknowledged, this is due in part to the fact that prior to the past three decades, the notion of academic freedom had almost no bearing on what was being done in Catholic colleges.[186] It is hoped that the foregoing historical survey of the educational goals, patterns of governance, and historic social context of American Catholic higher education clarifies and supports Gleason's observation.

As Catholic colleges and universities underwent institutional and social changes, the issue of academic freedom became increasingly relevant to Catholic intellectual life. Since the early twentieth century, intellectual goals have become increasingly important, while curricular developments since that time have largely reflected similar developments in non-Catholic institutions. Catholic educational philosophy has, in general, broadened since the 1950s, abandoning its narrow conception of truth and distrust of research. The past three decades have brought a number of institutional changes to Catholic institutions. Expansion of many Catholic schools has meant an increased number of well-trained lay faculty members. Moreover, faculty power has increased, while in a number of schools clerical control has been replaced by lay or mixed lay-clerical governance through an autonomous board of trustees. Finally, the social assimilation of large sectors of the American Catholic population and the related decrease in the "defensiveness" of the Catholic population have been reflected in the social stance of American Catholic institutions, including the Catholic college and university.

It is clear, however, that contemporary Catholic institutions have not uniformly experienced nor uniformly responded to these changes. As noted above, Catholic higher education is characterized by great diversity. Our typology of Catholic institutions reflects the fact that institutional response to society, the Church, and the educational mission continues to vary.

NOTES

1. Philip Gleason, "Academic Freedom: Survey, Retrospect and Prospects," *National Catholic Education Association Bulletin* 64 (August 1967): 67–68.

2. Ibid., p. 68.

3. Philip Gleason, "The Crisis in Catholic Universities: An Historical Perspective," *Catholic Mind* 65 (September 1966): 52. See John Tracy Ellis, "A Tradition of Autonomy?" in *The Catholic University: A Modern Appraisal,* ed. Neil G. McCluskey (Notre Dame, Ind.: University of Notre Dame Press, 1970), p. 226; Edward J. Power, *Catholic Higher Education in America: A History* (New York: Appleton-Century-Crofts, 1972), pp. 420–21; and Gleason, "Academic Freedom," pp. 70–73.

4. For detailed studies see Edward J. Power, *A History of Catholic Higher Education in the United States* (Milwaukee: Bruce Publishing Co., 1958) and Power, *Catholic Higher Education.* This section is particularly dependent upon these important works.

5. See, for example, Philip Gleason, "Immigration and American Catholic Intellectual Life," *Review of Politics* 26 (1964): 147–73.

6. Historian Edward J. Power cites 1786 as the founding of Georgetown. See his discussion in *History of Catholic Higher Education,* pp. 28–31, and *Catholic Higher Education,* pp. 36–42.

7. See Power, *Catholic Higher Education,* pp. 49–50, and Richard Hofstadter and C. Dewitt Hardy, *The Development and Scope of Higher Education in the United States* (New York: Columbia University Press, 1952), pp. 3–4.

8. Power, *History of Catholic Higher Education,* p. 25. See also Andrew M. Greeley, *The American Catholic: A Social Portrait* (New York: Basic Books, 1977), p. 34.

9. Stephen Steinberg, *The Academic Melting Pot: Catholics and Jews in American Higher Education,* Carnegie Commission Studies (New York: McGraw-Hill, 1974), p. 34.

10. Power, *Catholic Higher Education,* p. 9. Rhode Island was an exception and by 1700 afforded Catholics full civil and religious rights. Steinberg, *Melting Pot,* p. 34.

11. Power, *Catholic Higher Education,* p. 9. See also Francis X. Curran, *Catholics in Colonial Law* (Chicago: Loyola University Press, 1963), p. 82.

12. Power, *Catholic Higher Education,* p. 9.

13. Ibid., p. 7.

14. See Ibid., p. 3, and Power, *History of Catholic Higher Education,* pp. 27–28.

15. Power, *Catholic Higher Education,* p. 7.

16. Ibid., p. 46.

17. Steinberg, *Melting Pot,* pp. 34–35. See Power, *History of Catholic Higher Education,* p. 33, and *Catholic Higher Education,* pp. 9–10.

18. See Power, *Catholic Higher Education,* pp. 122–41, and Andrew M. Greeley, *From Backwater to Mainstream: A Profile of Catholic Higher Education,* Carnegie Commission Studies (New York: McGraw-Hill, 1969), p. 11.

19. Power, *Catholic Higher Education,* p. 48. See also Power, *History of Catholic Higher Education,* pp. 33–37.

20. Power, *Catholic Higher Education*, pp. 47–48. On the debate concerning the motives behind the establishment of early non-Catholic colleges, see Power, *Catholic Higher Education*, pp. 48–53; *History of Catholic Higher Education*, pp. 34–36; and Hofstadter and Hardy, *Higher Education*, p. 3.

21. Greeley, *Backwater to Mainstream*, pp. 10–11.

22. Agatho Zimmer, *Changing Concepts of Higher Education in America Since 1700* (Washington, D.C.: The Catholic University of America Press, 1938), pp. 97–99, 120.

23. See Power, *Catholic Higher Education*, pp. 47–48.

24. Ibid., p. 18.

25. Ibid., pp. 47–48.

26. John D. Donovan, *The Academic Man in the Catholic College* (New York: Sheed and Ward, 1964), p. 18.

27. See Power, *Catholic Higher Education*, p. 43; and Donovan, *Academic Man*, p. 18.

28. Power, *Catholic Higher Education*, pp. 43–44.

29. Orestes Brownson, "Present Catholic Dangers," *Brownson's Quarterly Review* 2 (July 1857): 363, repr. in *American Catholicism and the Intellectual Ideal*, ed. Frank L. Christ and Gerard E. Sherry (New York: Appleton-Century-Crofts, 1961), p. 18.

30. Power, *History of Catholic Higher Education*, p. 47. Italics mine.

31. See Donovan, *Academic Man*, p. 18, and Power, *Catholic Higher Education*, p. 62.

32. John Tracy Ellis, *American Catholics and the Intellectual Life* (Chicago: Heritage Foundation, 1956), p. 46. See also Power, *Catholic Higher Education*, p. 392.

33. Ellis, "Tradition of Autonomy?" p. 226.

34. Power, *Catholic Higher Education*, p. 122.

35. See Ibid., pp. 123–24. The degree of influence is disputed. See Power, *History of Catholic Higher Education*, pp. 54–57; Andrew M. Greeley, *The Changing Catholic College* (Chicago: Aldine Publishing Co., 1967), p. 25.

36. See Power, *Catholic Higher Education*, pp. 128–32.

37. Ibid., p. 139.

38. Ibid., p. 132.

39. Ibid., p. 125.

40. Steinberg, *Melting Pot*, p. 52.

41. Power, *History of Catholic Higher Education*, p. 81.

42. Power, *Catholic Higher Education*, p. 251.

43. Ibid., pp. 244–45.

44. Ibid.

45. Greeley, *Backwater to Mainstream*, pp. 13–14. For example, Marquette University in Milwaukee was founded by the Jesuits as Marquette College in 1864. A college curriculum was organized in 1881. In 1907 Marquette became affiliated with Milwaukee Medical College and in 1908 established a law school. In 1907 the name of the institution was changed to Marquette University. See Power, *History of Catholic Higher Education*, chaps. 8 and 9 and Appendix A.

46. John S. Brubacher and Willis Rudy, *Higher Education in Transition: A History of American Colleges and Universities, 1636–1968* (New York: Harper and Row, 1968), p. 183.

47. Philip Gleason, "American Catholic Higher Education: A Historical Perspective," in *The Shape of Catholic Higher Education*, ed. Robert Hassenger (Chicago: University of Chicago Press, 1967), p. 36.

48. See Power, *Catholic Higher Education*, pp. 368–72. On the quality of Catholic graduate education, see pp. 451–52. It would appear that the level of quality of graduate programs in Catholic universities continues to be a problem. See Andrew M. Greeley, "Why Catholic Higher Learning is Lower," *National Catholic Reporter*, 23 September 1983.

49. Greeley, *Backwater to Mainstream*, p. 11. See also Gleason, "Higher Education," pp. 47–50.

50. George Bull, "The Function of the Catholic Graduate School," *Thought* 13 (September 1938): 378, repr. in *Intellectual Ideal*, ed. Christ and Sherry, pp. 114–15.

51. Bull, "The Function of the Catholic Graduate School," quoted in Gleason, "Higher Education," p. 48.

52. Power, *Catholic Higher Education*, p. 404.

53. Ibid.

54. Greeley, *Catholic College*, p. 31

55. Gleason, "Academic Freedom," p. 71.

56. Ibid.

57. Power, *History of Catholic Higher Education*, p. 32.

58. Ibid., pp. 32–33.

59. Ibid.

60. Gleason, "Higher Education," p. 31.

61. Ibid. See also Power, *Catholic Higher Education*, p. 70.

62. Power, *History of Catholic Higher Education*, p. 33.

63. Power, *Catholic Higher Education*, pp. 43–44.

64. Ibid., p. 77.

65. Ibid., pp. 82, 442.

66. See Ibid., pp. 42–45, and Power, *History of Catholic Higher Education*, pp. 31–33.

67. Gleason, "Higher Education," p. 31.

68. Christopher Jencks and David Riesman, *The Academic Revolution* (Garden City, N.Y.: Doubleday, 1968), p. 346; Greeley, *Backwater to Mainstream*, p. 17. That institution was Webster College in Missouri.

69. On the shift in the makeup of boards, see Jencks and Riesman, *Academic Revolution*, p. 346, and Power, *Catholic Higher Education*, p. 442. A few schools—The University of Dallas and Sacred Heart University, for example—have even appointed lay presidents.

70. Power, *Catholic Higher Education*, p. 442. For a discussion of the laws and regulations governing the use of federally funded facilities on church-related campuses, see Edward McGlynn Gaffney, Jr. and Philip R. Moots, *Government and Campus: Federal Regulation of Religiously Affiliated Higher Education* (Notre Dame, Ind.: University of Notre Dame Press, 1982), chap. 4. A state by state discussion of eligibility requirements for state aid to church related colleges and universities can be found in Fernand N. Dutile and Edward McGlynn Gaffney, Jr. *State and Campus: State Regulation of Religiously Affiliated Higher Education* (Notre Dame, Ind.: University of Notre Dame Press, 1984).

71. Greeley, *Backwater to Mainstream*, p. 127; Power, *Catholic Higher Education*, pp. 70–71. As Power points out, strong presidential authority was not unique to Catholic institutions, though it existed in Catholic campuses to a greater degree. See Power, *History of Catholic Higher Education*, p. 149.

72. Greeley, *Backwater to Mainstream*, p. 127.

73. Power, *Catholic Higher Education*, p. 71.

74. Ibid., p. 73. In colleges founded by communities of brothers, the presidency was usually held by a brother, and later in women's colleges, by a sister. See Power, *History of Catholic Higher Education*, p. 197.

75. Power, *Catholic Higher Education*, pp. 71–72, 85. Clergymen occupied most college presidencies in American colleges into the second half of the nineteenth century. See Brubacher and Rudy, *Higher Education in Transition*, p. 364.

76. Power, *Catholic Higher Education*, pp. 74, 80.

77. Ibid., pp. 75–76, 81.

78. Ibid., p. 419.

79. See Greeley's summaries in *Backwater to Mainstream*, pp. 15–17, 127–28.

80. Power, *Catholic Higher Education*, p. 419. On the revitalization of boards of trustees, see pp. 441–42, and Jencks and Riesman, *Academic Revolution*, pp. 346–51.

81. Power, *Catholic Higher Education*, p. 91.

82. Ibid., pp. 94–96.

83. Power, *History of Catholic Higher Education*, p. 92.

84. Ibid., p. 95.

85. Ibid. Power is reluctant to accept the precision of these figures.

86. Ibid.

87. Power, *Catholic Higher Education*, p. 197.

88. Ibid., pp. 105–6.

89. Ibid., p. 106.

90. Greeley, *Catholic College*, p. 105. Greeley points out that as of 1967, approximately two-thirds of Catholic college faculty members were laypersons.

91. Donovan, *Academic Man*, pp. 24–25.

92. Power, *Catholic Higher Education*, p. 420.

93. See Greeley, *Backwater to Mainstream*, pp. 45–53 for relevant statistics.

94. Greeley, *Catholic College*, p. 140. See pp. 109–40 for the results of Greeley's study.

95. Ibid., p. 141.

96. Ibid., p. 8.

97. Ibid., p. 144. See also Power, *Catholic Higher Education*, p. 68.

98. Greeley, *Catholic College*, pp. 144–46.

99. Power, *Catholic Higher Education*, p. 68.

100. Ibid., pp. 106, 419–20, 429.

101. Donovan, *Academic Man*, p. 183.

102. Ibid., p. 198.

103. Ibid.

104. See, for example, Power, *Catholic Higher Education*, pp. 420–28, and Greeley, *Backwater to Mainstream*, pp. 14–17. The increasing acculturation of American Catholicism has also contributed to this process. See the discussion of this below.

105. Both are adapted from Power's work.

106. Power, *Catholic Higher Education*, p. 84.

107. Power, *History of Catholic Higher Education*, p. 149.

108. Ibid. See also Ellis, "Tradition of Autonomy?" pp. 227–28.

109. Power, *History of Catholic Higher Education*, pp. 149–50.

110. Power, *Catholic Higher Education*, p. 111.

111. Ibid.

112. See Ibid., pp. 285–86, and Ellis, "Tradition of Autonomy?" pp. 228–84.

113. Ellis, "Tradition of Autonomy?" p. 254.

114. Power, *Catholic Higher Education*, p. 420.

115. Ellis, "Tradition of Autonomy?" pp. 228–84. See also Curran, "Academic Freedom," p. 747.

116. Greeley, *Backwater to Mainstream*, pp. 117–18; *Catholic College*, pp. 11–15. See, for example, the list of administrations censured by the AAUP (1930–67) found in *Academic Freedom and Tenure*, ed. Louis Joughin (Madison, Wis.: University of Wisconsin Press, 1967), pp. 143–46. For an account of the 1965 St. John's University (New York) case, see John Leo, "Some Problem Areas in Catholic Higher Education: The Faculty," in *The Shape of Catholic Higher Education*, ed. Robert Hassenger (Chicago: University of Chicago Press, 1967), pp. 193–201. The issues raised by the dissent to the 1968 encyclical *Humanae Vitae* expressed by a number of professors at the Catholic University of America are explored in John F. Hunt and Terrence R. Connelly, *The Responsibility of Dissent: The Church and Academic Freedom* (New York: Sheed and Ward, 1969). On recent incidents involving the issue of abortion, see "Academic Freedom and the Abortion Issue," *Academe* 72 (July-August 1986): 1a–13a.

117. Greeley, who defends the record of Catholic colleges on academic freedom, admits "we rather suspect that there will be more problems in the future than there are at the present time . . . as the quality of the faculty improves and as faculty members become more sensitive to their rights." *Catholic College*, p. 112.

118. Power, *Catholic Higher Education*, p. 421.

119. See Gleason, "Immigration," pp. 149–54 on the Catholic Church as an "institutional immigrant."

120. Greeley, *Catholic College*, p. 23.

121. Gleason, "Crisis," p. 46.

122. John Tracy Ellis, *American Catholicism* (Chicago: University of Chicago Press, 1956), p. 19. See also Steinberg, *Melting Pot*, p. 34.

123. See Francis X. Curran, *Colonial Law*, passim.

124. Gleason, "Higher Education," p. 20.

125. Ellis, *American Catholicism*, pp. 61–62.

126. Ibid., p. 101.

127. Gleason, "Higher Education," p. 20.

128. See Ellis, *American Catholicism*, pp. 62–64.

129. Gleason, "Immigration," p. 153. See also James W. Trent, *Catholics in College* (Chicago: University of Chicago Press, 1967), p. 14.

130. See Steinberg, *Melting Pot*, pp. 33–50.

131. A Catholic clergyman wrote in 1907: "We will not have any educated layman twenty years from now if non-Catholic universities are selected for the education of our Catholic youth." R. H. Meyer, "The Catholic Chaplain at the

Secular University," *Catholic Educational Association Bulletin* 4 (November 1907): 170, quoted in Steinberg, *Melting Pot*, p. 49.

132. Gleason, "Crisis," pp. 46–47.

133. See Andrew M. Greeley, *The American Catholic: A Social Portrait* (New York: Basic Books, 1977), chap. 3, and Gleason, "Crisis," p. 47.

134. Greeley, *Backwater to Mainstream*, p. 15. See Philip Gleason, "Freedom and the Catholic University," *National Catholic Education Association Bulletin* 65 (November 1968): 22.

135. Gleason, "Catholic University," p. 22.

136. Ibid., p. 23.

137. Gleason, "Crisis," p. 47. See also Greeley, *Catholic College*, pp. 33–54.

138. Gleason, "Crisis," p. 47.

139. Trent, *Catholics in College*, p. 14. Relevant, though tangential to the present project, is the examination and critique of Catholic intellectual life carried out by some Catholic scholars into the 1950s. See Power's summary in *Catholic Higher Education*, pp. 388–94; Ellis, *American Catholics and the Intellectual Life*; Gustave Weigel, "American Catholic Intellectualism: A Theologian's Reflections," *Review of Politics* 19 (July 1957): 275–307 reprinted in *Catholic Education: A Book of Readings*, ed. Walter B. Kolesnik and Edward J. Power (New York: McGraw-Hill Book Co., 1965), pp. 65–89.

140. Greeley, *Backwater to Mainstream*, p. 19.

141. These are 1982 figures based upon John R. Crocker, *The Student Guide to Catholic Colleges and Universities* (Wilmington, N. C.: McGrath Publishing, 1982). These numbers do not include seminaries. Note the comment of Jencks and Riesman: "No two enumerations of Catholic colleges arrive at the same total." *Academic Revolution*, p. 343.

142. For example, Greeley, *Backwater to Mainstream*, pp. 1–4; and Jencks and Riesman, *Academic Revolution*, pp. 343–46.

143. Greeley, *Backwater to Mainstream*, p. 2.

144. This is apparent from studies such as that carried out by Greeley. See *Backwater to Mainstream* and *Catholic College*.

145. Jencks and Riesman, *Academic Revolution*, p. 343. Note that some colleges have been transferred to the control of independent boards, with the original sponsoring order serving the colleges in various ways.

146. Ibid.

147. Greeley, *Backwater to Mainstream*, p. 4.

148. Ibid., pp. 115–16.

149. Sacred Congregation for Catholic Education, "Proposed Schema for a Pontifical Document on Catholic Universities," *Origins* 15 (April 10, 1986): 706.

150. See "Catholic College and University Presidents Respond to Proposed Vatican Schema," *Origins* 15 (April 10, 1986): 698, 699–704. See also George Kelly, "Vatican's Proposed Higher Education Schema Supported," *Origins* 15 (April 10, 1986): 704–5.

151. Power, *Catholic Higher Education*, p. 43.

152. *Code of Canon Law*, Canon 808, p. 572.

153. Ibid., Canon 810§2, p. 574.

154. Greeley, *Backwater to Mainstream*, pp. 116–17.

155. Ibid., p. 1.

156. See Robert J. Henle, "The Pluralism of North America and the Catholic University of Today," in *The Catholic University: Instrument of Cultural Pluralism to the Service of Church and Society* (Paris: International Federation of Catholic Universities, 1979), pp. 54–72.

157. Curran, "Academic Freedom," note 25, p. 754. The Catholic University of America has Pontifical or ecclesiastical faculties of canon law, theology, and philosophy.

158. John Paul II, *The Apostolic Constitution Sapientia Christiana on Ecclesiastical Universities and Faculties* (Washington, D.C.: United States Catholic Conference, 1979), Article 2.

159. Ibid., Article 27.1.

160. Ibid., Article 27.2.

161. Henle, "Catholic University of Today," p. 59.

162. Ibid., p. 57.

163. Ibid.

164. Ibid., p. 59.

165. See the description of the function of a Catholic college in the *Cardinal Newman College Catalogue*, 1977, p. 7.

166. Henle, "Catholic University of Today," p. 59.

167. Ibid., pp. 58–59.

168. Ibid., pp. 64–68.

169. Vatican II, "Pastoral Constitution on the Church in the Modern World," no. 40, p. 238. See also Henle, "Catholic University of Today," p. 65.

170. Curran, "Academic Freedom," p. 746.

171. Henle, "Catholic University of Today," p. 62.

172. Greeley, *Catholic College*, pp. 29–30.

173. See Power, *Catholic Higher Education*, pp. 404–6; and Henle, "Catholic University of Today," pp. 63–64.

174. Henle, "Catholic University of Today," p. 64.

175. Ibid., pp. 65–66.

176. Ibid., p. 63.

177. Ibid., p. 66.

178. Ibid., p. 60.

179. Ibid.

180. See John Cogley, "The Future of an Illusion," in *The Catholic University: A Modern Appraisal,* ed. Neil G. McCluskey. (Notre Dame, Ind.: University of Notre Dame Press, 1970), p. 297; Greeley, *Backwater to Mainstream*, p. 17; and Trent, *Catholics in College*, pp. 262–63.

181. Greeley, *Backwater to Mainstream*, p. 17.

182. Robert Hassenger, "What Makes a College Catholic?" *Commonweal* 99 (November 1973): 181.

183. Henle, "Catholic University of Today," p. 60.

184. On the limitations of typologies, see H. Richard Niebuhr, *Christ and Culture* (New York: Harper and Row Publishers, Harper Colophon Books, 1975), pp. 43–44.

185. Gleason, "Academic Freedom," p. 68.

186. Gleason, "Crisis," p. 52.

3.

Academic Freedom and the Catholic Campus: The Current State of the Discussion

Since the early 1960s, the problem of academic freedom in the Roman Catholic college and university has been the subject of ongoing discussion by Catholic scholars. Moreover, the notion of academic freedom has been treated both directly and indirectly in various pronouncements of the *Magisterium*. The first part of this chapter will survey the teaching of the *Magisterium* on academic freedom since the Second Vatican Council. Included for examination will be the documents of the Council, occasional statements of Pope Paul VI and Pope John Paul II, *The Apostolic Constitution Sapientia Christiana* on ecclesiastical faculties, the 1983 Code of Canon Law, and relevant statements of the American Catholic Bishops.

The second part of the chapter will be devoted to a descriptive examination of current models of academic freedom as these have been developed by Catholic theorists. These models will be examined under two categories: Restrictive Models and Revised Secular Models. Throughout this section, special attention will be given to the sensitive area of university theology. Finally, a brief examination of pertinent organizational statements on academic freedom will be presented.

THE TEACHING OF THE *MAGISTERIUM* ON ACADEMIC FREEDOM SINCE VATICAN II: A DESCRIPTIVE SURVEY

The teaching and general tone of the Second Vatican Council (1962–65) have certainly contributed to a heightened interest among Catholics in the subject of academic freedom.[1] Although a developed or comprehensive treatment of this subject is absent from the Council's documents, brief references to academic freedom, as well as the general theological shift represented by the Council's teachings, have contributed to the acceptance of academic freedom on Catholic campuses.[2] The changing theological emphasis evidenced in the Council's teaching include such factors as a broader understanding of the Church and the role of the laity within it, a renewed emphasis upon the freedom and dignity of the human being, and an affirmation of the autonomy and value of the arts and sciences and human culture in general.

In the "Dogmatic Constitution on the Church," the Council Fathers avoided a narrow overemphasis upon the institutional and hierarchical aspects of the Church, and defined the Church in more communal terms as the people of God.[3] Section 12 of this document acknowledges:

It is not only through the sacraments and Church ministries that the same Holy Spirit sanctifies and leads the People of God and enriches it with virtues. Allotting His gifts "to everyone according as he will" (1 Cor. 12:11), He distributes special graces among the faithful of every rank. By these gifts He makes them fit and ready to undertake the various tasks or offices advantageous for the renewal and upbuilding of the Church. . . .[4]

The "Decree on the Apostolate of the Laity" also emphasizes the part played by the laity in the mission of the Church. The decree states that "the laity, too, share in the priestly, prophetic, and royal office of Christ and therefore have their own role to play in the mission of the whole People of God in the Church and in the world."[5]

Peter Lyons observes that while the Council reaffirmed the central place of the hierarchical *Magisterium*, it

created a new theological context for understanding the role of the hierarchy in the Church. While the old and new teachings are not perfectly reconciled, the main stress of the *Constitution on the Church* is on the Church's new self-understanding as a community and on the active, responsible role of the Catholic people.[6]

This new self-understanding has influenced all areas of the Church's life, including its colleges and universities. Greeley, for example, considers the Council's teaching on the laity one reason for the move toward the laicization of the boards of trustees of some Catholic colleges.[7]

The Council also fostered a strong sense of the freedom and dignity of the human being.[8] In the "Pastoral Constitution on the Church in the Modern World," human dignity is said to be based upon the creation of the human being in the image of God.[9] Moreover, the Council Fathers state in the document that "authentic freedom is an exceptional sign of the divine image within men."[10] They observe that

God has willed that man be left "in the hand of his own counsel" so that he can seek his Creator spontaneously, and come freely to utter and blissful perfection through loyalty to Him. Hence man's dignity demands that he act according to a knowing and free choice. Such a choice is personally motivated and prompted from within. It does not result from blind internal impulse nor from mere external pressure.[11]

This emphasis upon the dignity and freedom of every human being is particularly evident in the Council's "Declaration on Religious Freedom" where the principles discussed above are expanded and given practical application.[12] Within the declaration, religious freedom is presented as a human right founded upon human dignity. It is argued that while human beings are "impelled by nature and also bound by moral obligation to seek the truth, especially religious truth" and "to adhere to the truth, once it is known," no one is to be coerced into acting against his or her beliefs or restrained from acting in accordance with those beliefs.[13] Furthermore, the very nature of religious truth precludes coercion in matters religious. For "truth cannot impose itself except by virtue of its own truth, as it makes its entrance into the mind at once quietly and with power."[14]

The Council's teaching on religious liberty is limited in scope, with three doctrinal tenets being proposed:

the ethical doctrine of religious freedom as a human right (personal and collective); a political doctrine with regard to the functions and limits of government in matters religious; and the theological doctrine of the freedom of the Church as the fundamental principle in what concerns the relations between the Church and the socio-political order.[15]

There is no consideration of the applicability of the principles declared to other areas, for example, freedom within the Church, or academic freedom in the theological disciplines.[16] However, as John Courtney Murray observes,

The conciliar affirmation of the principle of freedom was narrowly limited—in the text. But the text itself was flung into a pool whose shores are wide as the universal Church. The ripples will run far.[17]

Specific affirmations of the freedom of inquiry are made in the "Pastoral Constitution on the Church in the Modern World" and in the "Declaration on Christian Education." While reaffirming the distinction between the two orders of knowledge—faith and reason—the Council Fathers, in the "Pastoral Constitution on the Church in the Modern World," declared the legitimate autonomy of the human arts and sciences.[18] They further declared that "within the limits of morality and the general welfare, a man be free to search for the truth, voice his mind, and publicize it; that he be free to practice any art he chooses; and finally that he have appropriate access to information about public affairs."[19]

A true freedom of inquiry for those engaged in research and teaching in Catholic colleges and universities was also affirmed by the Council. In the "Declaration on Christian Education," the Fathers state that in Catholic institutions of higher learning, the Church

seeks in a systematic way to have individual branches of knowledge studied according to their own proper principles and methods, and with due freedom of scientific investigation. She intends thereby to promote an ever deeper understanding of these fields, and as a result of extremely precise evaluation of modern problems and inquires, to have it seen more profoundly how faith and reason give harmonious witness to the unity of all truth.[20]

In the "Pastoral Constitution on the Church in the Modern World," this freedom of inquiry is even extended to those engaged in scholarly work in the sacred sciences. The bishops state in section 62:

In order that such persons may fulfill their proper function, let it be recognized that all the faithful, clerical and lay, possess a lawful freedom of inquiry and of thought, and the freedom to express their minds humbly and courageously about those matters in which they enjoy competence.[21]

This passage is certainly subject to varying interpretations. The key phrase is "*lawful* freedom of inquiry," for upon one's definition of the adjective *lawful* will rest one's overall interpretation of the sentence. Later Church pronouncements which contain references to academic freedom (for example, *Sapientia Christiana*), tend to reveal a narrow interpretation of this conciliar text.

It should be noted that the Council Fathers' teachings on the freedom of inquiry are complemented by their tendency to view the nature of truth in a new way. In the "Declaration on Religious Freedom," the manner in which truth is sought is described as a quest:

The inquiry is to be free, carried on with the aid of teaching or instruction, communication, and dialogue. In the course of these, men explain to one another the truth they have discovered, or think they have discovered, in order thus to assist one another in the quest for truth.[22]

This statement illustrates a departure from the static notion of "truth as fully possessed" that tended to characterize Roman Catholic theology in years past. As Frederick Gunti has observed, while the existence of truth is not denied, "the truly human processes by which truth becomes the possession of man is acknowledged."[23] Furthermore, while reaffirming the reality of the "sure gift of truth" given to the Church and received through episcopal succession, the Council recognized the dynamic process by which "the Church constantly moves forward toward the fullness of divine truth until the words of God reach their complete fulfillment in her."[24]

The teachings of Vatican II, characterized by a more positive and open approach to culture, greater attention to the role of the laity, and a greater emphasis upon human freedom and dignity, have encouraged interest in the subject of academic freedom in the Catholic university.[25] Moreover, the Council's specific endorsements of the freedom of inquiry of the scholar have been excellent resources for those who champion academic freedom on the Catholic campus. However, statements by the *Magisterium* since the Council have not interpreted conciliar teaching in the broadest fashion. It is to these statements that we now turn our attention.

The occasional statements of Pope Paul VI on Catholic higher education emphasize two central and related characteristics of the Catholic college or university. First, the Catholic institution of higher learning is distinguished by the spirit of faith that should pervade all its undertakings. Addressing the professors and students of the Pontifical Gregorian University in 1972, Paul VI stated that "an atmosphere of faith must invisibly but firmly guide every personal and collective scholarly effort and all free, honest scientific research."[26] In an address to the delegates of Catholic universities assembled in Rome in November 1972, the Pope concretized this notion and applied it to every Catholic college and university. Referring to the Catholic institution, the Pope said:

Faithfulness to the message of Christ, as it is transmitted by the Church, is the reason for the university's continual reflective effort and for its institutional commitment. In the service of the People of God, it is thus in a position to approach the incessant conquests of human knowledge in the light of faith and to manifest the transcendent purpose which alone gives life its full meaning.[27]

Of particular importance in this passage is the phrase "Faithfulness to the message of Christ, *as it is transmitted by the Church*." The faith perspective that characterizes the Catholic university is rooted in the "deposit of faith" transmitted, safeguarded, and interpreted by the *Magisterium*.[28] Hence, the second distinguishing characteristic of the Roman Catholic college or university, as found in the statements of Pope Paul VI, is the relation of the institution to the hierarchical *Magisterium*. Directing his comments to the assembled delegates of Catholic universities in 1969, the Pope states: "The magisterium remains the authentic guarantee of your inspiration, in freely accepted fidelity to the living tradition received from the Apostles."[29]

In his statements on the Catholic university, Paul VI continually emphasized that the faith commitment of the Catholic institution and its relation to the *Magisterium* do not hinder, but rather enhance its scholarly work.[30] Vital links with the Church's tradition do not bridle research.[31] Rather, the divine authority of revelation guides research and increases its possibilities.

Revealed dogma, authoritatively defined by the Church, offers us God's truth and infuses into us the sense of God whose action we must see shining through human problems, muddled though they may be. It guides us to the discovery of "all the truth," in order to direct us to sure points, in which the premise of the revealed datum can exercise all its beneficial influence on the development of a harmonious and stimulating synthesis of human knowledge.[32]

In the Pope's view, the Catholic university is the "ideal place for carrying out fully scientific research in the honest freedom of God's sons."[33]

In a 1971 statement, the Pope reemphasized the Church's respect for culture, endorsed scholarly research, and rejected "*a priori* systems that mortgage the authentic analysis and synthesis of which men are so much in need."[34] To those standing outside the Catholic context, the Pope's words might appear contradictory, for it could be argued that what the Pope considers an aid to the scholarly endeavor is precisely an example of the type of *a priori* system that he so forcefully rejects. The key to understanding his position is found in the distinction between natural and supernatural knowledge. In the context of the pursuit of knowledge on the natural plane—knowledge accessible to all humans through reason—the Pope strongly rejects the imposition of *a priori* systems that inhibit the scholar's quest. However, from a Catholic perspective, supernatural truth remains above natural knowledge. Moreover, there can never exist a real conflict between reason and revelation, since both have God as a common source.[35] In the Pope's view, revelation does not frustrate the scholar's pursuit of truth, but rather aids, guides, and corrects it.

Pope Paul VI explored the specific status of university theology in a 1972 address to the professors and students of the Gregorian University, which, it should be emphasized, is a Pontifical university with direct ties to the Vatican. In his statement, the Pope affirmed that theology must be at the service of faith, for theology is, by his definition, faith expressed conceptually. Because of this role of service, theology is profoundly linked to the *Magisterium*, which guarantees the orthodoxy of faith.[36]

Paul VI affirms that, historically, the relations between theology and the *Magisterium* have been mutually helpful and complementary, and he rejects the mentality that would set the two "against each other artificially."[37] He states: "Following this line of mutual understanding, confidence and cooperation—which does not interfere with the *legitimate* rights of research and freedom, as We said above—theology fulfills an irreplaceable function in the Church."[38] The *"legitimate* rights of research and freedom" spoken of by the Pope do not, however, include the right to depart from orthodoxy. Paul's words on this subject to the students and faculty of Gregorian University are worth quoting at length:

Every doctrine incompatible with faith or difficult to reconcile with it, must feel it impossible to exist in a university such as yours, just as . . . no teacher could exist there whose thinking is not perfectly faithful to the mind of the Church. Hence the necessity for an orthodoxy jealously guarded and taught by the professors. Unity of will and thought must be harmonious in an academic body which cannot admit divisions in fundamental questions.[39]

Although the Pope was speaking in the context of a Pontifical university, it would appear that his words would be equally applicable to theology in the non-canonical Catholic university, in light of his implicit and explicit notions concerning the nature of university theology. In his view, university theology is ecclesiastically-centered, holding a "midway position between the faith of the church and the Church's magisterium."[40] Moreover, in his statements, the Pope was unequivocal in his affirmation of the fundamental and vital links between theology and the *Magisterium*.

Despite the absence of a comprehensive treatment of academic freedom in the statements of Paul VI, the direction of his views on this subject is clear. The Pope's statements exhibit the openness to culture and the human arts and sciences which characterized the teachings of the Second Vatican Council. Hence, Paul VI affirms the legitimate autonomy and freedom of the scholar in the human disciplines, and rejects *a priori* systems that bridle the pursuit of truth.[41] Paul asserts that divine revelation—guarded and interpreted by the *Magisterium*—remains the inspiration, guide, and corrective of every pursuit of truth in the Catholic institution of higher learning.[42] Moreover, in his view the rights of research and freedom in the theological disciplines must always be exercised with respect for the nature of theology as the "science of God" and the vital relationship between theology and the *Magisterium*.[43]

The teachings of Pope John Paul II on academic freedom have thus far been similar in tone and content to those of Paul VI, his predecessor. In an address to representatives of American Catholic higher education at the Catholic University of America in Washington, D.C., the Pope outlined three aims of the Catholic college or university. Briefly stated, they are first, contributing to the Church and society through scientific research and the study of human problems; second, the training of knowledgeable individuals with an integrated vision of faith and culture for service to society; and third, the establishment of a community of Christian witness among faculty members and students.[44] The Pope reminded his audience that the Catholic college or university shares in the Church's overall mission of evangelization and service. It would appear that his conceptions of the role of the Catholic institution are pastoral as well as academic. It is within this context that John Paul II addresses the question of academic freedom.

As a former university professor, the Pope expressed a deep appreciation of the university as a center of research and instruction dedicated to the pursuit of truth. Eschewing any hint of anti-intellectualism, John Paul exhorted his listeners to strive toward the highest standards of scholarship.[45] Moreover, he endorsed unequivocally freedom of investigation and scholarly objectivity as academic values. However, in his view, these values must be interpreted differently in the area of theological scholarship due to the nature of that discipline. John Paul points out that insofar as Catholic colleges and universities are institutionally committed to the Christian message and to the Church's mission of evangelization, "they have an essential relationship to the hierarchy of the church."[46] This relationship is particularly important for fruitful theological scholarship.

From the perspective of John Paul II, theological scholarship is directed toward a deeper understanding of the God who has revealed himself—who has issued an initiating call to which the human being must respond.[47] This call, God's spoken word, is contained in the Scriptures and the tradition of the Church as interpreted by the *Magisterium*.[48] The Pope argues that the human "can reach a certain understanding of the supernatural mysteries, thanks to the use of his reason, but only to the extent to which the latter rests on the unshakable foundation of faith. . . ."[49] Therefore, faith is "necessary for all theological research worthy of the name"[50] and this response of faith on the part of the theologian will necessarily bring him or her into direct encounter with the *Magisterium*, which guards and interprets God's self-revelation. Hence, John Paul stated at the Catholic University of America:

true theological scholarship, and by the same token theological teaching, cannot exist and be fruitful without seeking its inspiration and its source in the word of God as contained in sacred scripture and in the sacred tradition of the church, as interpreted by the authentic magisterium throughout history.[51]

Academic freedom, then, will be qualified by this relationship with the *Magisterium* and, more fundamentally, by the nature of this discipline which is directed toward the study of God's self-revelation and the human being as a natural being called to a supernatural end. John Paul argued:

True academic freedom must be seen in relation to the finality of the academic enterprise which looks to the total truth of the human person.

The theologian's contribution will be enriching for the church only if it takes into account the proper function of the bishops. . . . It devolves upon the bishops of the church to safeguard the Christian authenticity and unity of faith and moral teaching. . . . [52]

The academic freedom of the theologian must also be limited by the right of "the faithful" not to be troubled, confused, or led astray "by theories easily simplified or manipulated by public opinion for ends that are alien to the truth."[53] The precise way in which the right of the theologian to academic freedom is weighed against the right of "the faithful" not to be troubled is not explored.

In general, the words of Pope John Paul II demonstrate a positive openness to the university and its mission. The Pope endorses the contemporary values of freedom and objective research. However, his extremely pastoral interpretations of the aims of the Catholic college or university and particularly the nature of university theology lead him to adopt extensive limitations on the freedom of the university theologian. Concluding his address to American Catholic educators, the Pope said:

It behooves the theologian to be free, but with the freedom that is openness to the truth and the light that comes from faith and from fidelity to the church.[54]

The question that is raised by this statement is: Has the reality to which the Pope is referring been so qualified as to no longer constitute anything approaching freedom of investigation as this is understood in the American context?

New norms governing ecclesiastical universities and faculties were issued by Pope John Paul II on April 15, 1979. These norms, which are found in *The Apostolic Constitution Sapientia Christiana*, have a bearing upon academic freedom in ecclesiastical or canonically-erected universities and faculties and, hence, are of interest here—albeit tangential.[55] It should be emphasized that these norms apply only to ecclesiastical universities and faculties that grant Pontifical degrees.

The norms outlined in *Sapientia Christiana* must be seen in the context of the specialized purposes of the ecclesiastical university or faculty. Those purposes, as presented in the Apostolic Constitution, are scholarly, educational, and pastoral.[56] First, ecclesiastical faculties contribute to the advancement of knowledge in their disciplines through scientific research. They particularly strive toward a deepening of the knowledge of Christian revelation. Second, these faculties train students "in their own disciplines according to Catholic doctrine."[57] Finally, the ecclesiastical university participates in the Church's work of evangelization.

Because of their specialized functions and close relationship with the hierarchy (with which they have juridical ties), ecclesiastical faculties and universities are subject to a number of controls that emanate from authorities external to the academic community. In the area of university governance, the statutes of each ecclesiastical university or faculty must be approved by the Sacred Congregation for Catholic Education.[58] Moreover, the same Congregation names, or at least confirms, the Rector and President of such universities.[59] Finally, the Chancellor of the university is always the Prelate Ordinary—the local bishop—unless otherwise established by the Holy See.[60]

The norms of the Apostolic Constitution require that faculty selection be based not only upon scholarly competence, but also upon other, unrelated criteria. Teachers "must be marked by upright life, integrity of doctrine, and devotion to duty," and those that "teach matters touching on faith and morals are to be conscious of their duty to carry out their work in full communion with the authentic Magisterium of the Church. . . ."[61] Moreover, according to the norms, the judgment of faculty competence is not left solely in the hands of academic peers. Articles 27 and 28 state:

> Those who teach disciplines concerning faith or morals must receive, after making their profession of faith, a canonical mission from the Chancellor or his delegate, for they do not teach on their own authority but by virtue of the mission they have received from the Church. The other teachers must receive permission to teach from the Chancellor or his delegate.
>
> All teachers, before they are given a permanent post or before they are promoted to the highest category of teacher, or else in both cases, as the Statutes are to state, must receive a declaration of *nihil obstat* from the Holy See.[62]

Hence, ecclesiastical authorities external to the academic community are made ultimate judges of competence. Implicit in these norms is the assertion that theological competence is not merely scholarly in nature. Other criteria—moral rectitude and doctrinal orthodoxy—are also to be considered. Therefore, in view of this approach to theological competence, it is understandable (although perhaps not defensible) that those competent to judge adherence to these non-scholarly criteria be included in the determination of a theologian's competence.

A specific reference to academic freedom is made in Section VI of the document. It is admitted that a "just freedom" in research and teaching is necessary for true progress in theological scholarship.[63] However, it is stated that

> (a) true freedom in teaching is necessarily contained within the limits of God's Word, as this is constantly taught by the Church's Magisterium;
> (b) likewise, true freedom in research is necessarily based upon firm adherence to God's Word and deference to the Church's Magisterium, whose duty it is to interpret authentically the Word of God.[64]

It would appear that the adjectives *true* and *just* used to modify the noun *freedom* impose extensive limitations upon the concept.

The particular aims of the ecclesiastical university or faculty as outlined in the document help to explain the Constitution's norms. Apparently, the goal of such a university or faculty is not the disinterested search for truth. Rather, the university is presented in a strictly ecclesiastical context, with theology being viewed as an extension or "a continuation of the teaching function of the hierarchical magisterium."[65] Therefore, it is not surprising that "judgments about competency are not made by peers, and promotion and tenure depend on judgments made by church authority."[66] Although critical commentary on these norms will be presented in a later chapter, it seems safe to conclude that the notion of academic freedom presented in the document has undergone so many qualifications that its viability can be legitimately questioned.

On January 25, 1983, a new Code of Canon Law for the Latin Rite Roman Catholic Church was promulgated by Pope John Paul II. This new set of laws, the first since 1917, became operative on November 27, 1983—the first Sunday of Advent and the beginning of the Church year.[67] In Book III of the new Code, canons governing Catholic universities and other institutions of higher studies are presented.[68] In Canon 807, the Church's right to erect and regulate universities is affirmed. Interestingly, the reasons cited for the establishment of these universities are quite broad. The canon states that such universities are established to advance human culture and the development of the human person, and to complement the Church's teaching office.[69] Hence, from the outset, the new Code follows the Second Vatican Council in avoiding a narrow definition of the purposes of Catholic colleges and universities.

Specific reference to intellectual freedom is made not in the section that deals with Catholic universities, but in the section of Book II that considers the rights of all Christ's faithful. There, Canon 218 affirms the theological scholars' "lawful freedom of inquiry and of prudently expressing their opinions on matters in which they have expertise, while observing a due respect for the Magisterium of the Church."[70] Within the section dealing with Catholic universities, a partial deference is made to scholarly autonomy in the university. Hence, Canon 809 states that in Catholic universities, "the various disciplines are to be investigated and taught with due regard for their academic autonomy, and with due consideration for Catholic doctrine."[71]

Particularly noteworthy are those canons that deal with scholarly competence. As in some of the statements and documents examined above, the new Code injects non-scholarly criteria into the notion of scholarly competence.

It is the responsibility of the authority who is competent in accord with the statutes to provide for the appointment of teachers to Catholic universities who besides their scientific and pedagogical suitability are also outstanding in their integrity of doctrine and probity of life; when those requisite qualities are lacking they are to be removed from their positions in accord with the procedure set forth in the statutes.[72]

Therefore, "integrity of doctrine" and "probity of life" are made criteria by which to judge the fitness of a scholar and defects in these areas constitute a basis upon which to dismiss a professor. This canon presents a notion of competence quite different from that which is commonly accepted in American higher education.

The new Code gives to bishops considerable authority over Catholic universities, and particularly over theological faculties. In Canon 810§2, the conference of bishops and diocesan bishops are given the duty and the right of vigilance over Catholic colleges and universities so that "principles of Catholic doctrine are faithfully observed."[73] It should be emphasized that the bishops are given the right of vigilance, not governance, control, or intervention.[74] Nonetheless, the canon can create a situation in which an ecclesiastical authority external to the scholarly community becomes involved in the strictly academic affairs of the university.

Perhaps the most potentially troublesome canon is 812: "It is necessary that those who teach theological disciplines in any institute of higher studies have a mandate [*mandatum*] from the competent ecclesiastical authority."[75] It should be pointed out that this canon does not apply to present appointments, non-Catholics, Oriental Catholics, or part-time professors. In essence, the mandate represents a juridical commission to teach granted by the Apostolic See, the local bishop, or his delegate. It is not to be confused with the canonical mission required in ecclesiastical universities, which implies direct participation in the teaching mission of the Church.[76] The necessity of a mandate to teach raises serious problems in the areas of academic freedom, the nature of scholarly competence, juridical competence—judging scholarly fitness, and university autonomy.[77]

Prior to concluding this section on *Magisterial* teaching on academic freedom, two statements of the American hierarchy merit brief mention. *To Teach As Jesus Did*, a pastoral message on Catholic education, was issued by the National Conference of Catholic Bishops in 1972. In this statement is found an approach to academic freedom similar to those encountered in the documents and statements examined thus far. On the one hand, the American bishops acknowledge that Catholic colleges and universities serve the Church "by deep and thorough study of Catholic beliefs in an atmosphere of intellectual freedom and according to canons of intellectual criticism which should govern all pursuit of truth."[78] Hence, they will be "strongly committed to academic excellence and the responsible academic freedom required for effective teaching and research."[79] On the other hand, however, the bishops remind their readers that academic freedom in the area of theological scholarship must be understood in the context of the nature of the theological disciplines. The bishops state:

For a Catholic institution, there is a special aspect to academic freedom. While natural truth is directly accessible to us by virtue of our innate ability to comprehend reality, the datum or raw material from which theological reflection arises is not a datum of reality fully accessible to human reason. The authentic Christian message is entrusted by Jesus Christ to His community, the Church. Theological research and speculation, which are entirely legitimate and commendable enterprises, deal with divine revelation as their source and material, and the results of such investigation are therefore subject to the judgment of the magisterium.[80]

Therefore, the bishops affirm the necessary freedom and autonomy of the Catholic college or university, but insist that this autonomy be balanced against fidelity to the Christian message as transmitted by the Church.[81]

A similar position is taken in the 1980 statement entitled *Catholic Higher Education and the Pastoral Mission of the Church.*[82] In this statement, the American bishops assert that "academic freedom and institutional independence in pursuit of the mission of the institution are essential components of educational quality and integrity; commitment to the Gospel and the teachings and heritage of the Catholic church provide the inspiration and enrichment that make a college fully Catholic."[83] Furthermore, they argue that the autonomy of the university and the responsibilities of the hierarchy should not conflict, for theologians and the *Magisterium* have different yet mutual responsibilities to the Church, and both render service to the truth.[84] However, the precise way in which these two realities are to be reconciled is not explored. Merely stating the absence of conflict does not resolve the difficulty of making harmony a reality.

The teaching of the Second Vatican Council constitutes an important resource useful in the development of a theory of academic freedom for the Catholic college or university. The Council recognized a broader ecclesiology—emphasizing the role of the laity in the mission of the Church. Moreover, its overall emphasis upon the freedom and dignity of the human being, its affirmation of the autonomy and value of the human arts and sciences, and its acknowledgment of the value of a "lawful" freedom of inquiry have buttressed the cause of freedom on Catholic campuses.

However, *Magisterial* statements on academic freedom and related subjects since Vatican II have not always interpreted the Council's teachings in the broadest fashion. This is particularly true of *Sapientia Chris-*

tiana and the 1983 *Code of Canon Law*. In addition, despite their insistence on the autonomy of the university, recent Popes and the American bishops have failed to offer ways to reconcile that autonomy with the type of "institutional commitment" and the conception of university theology that they insist upon.

ROMAN CATHOLIC MODELS OF ACADEMIC FREEDOM

The discussion of academic freedom among Catholic scholars during the past twenty years has given rise to a number of theoretical models developed for the Catholic educational context.[85] The second part of this chapter will be devoted to a descriptive examination of these models, which will be classified under two categories: restrictive models and revised secular models.[86] Implied in this categorization is the use of the secular formulation of academic freedom as a standard of measurement. It should be noted that it is being used as such not because it is accepted uncritically by the author, but because it is the basic formulation regarded as valid by most of American higher education. These categories are not intended as valuational classifications, nor is the claim being made that they represent a developed and tested typology. They are, in effect, merely organizational aids.

In general, those models of academic freedom that can be included within the restrictive category qualify to varying degrees the American secular formulation, particularly when applied to the theological disciplines.[87] This qualification is considered necessary insofar as the Catholic college or university, as well as its theology department, has a special relation to the *Magisterium* which guards and interprets divine revelation. Perhaps a more important characteristic of restrictive models is the rejection of what are considered the necessary philosophical foundations of the secular formulation of academic freedom. These foundations, which are said to be rooted in the perspective of the Enlightenment, have been variously labeled as liberal-humanistic, secular-rationalistic, and positivistic by some Catholic scholars.[88]

The revised secular formulations of academic freedom developed by Catholic scholars tend to accept the basic validity of the secular model. These formulations advocate the application of the accepted American principles of academic freedom to all college and university disciplines, including theology. In most of these models the application of the principles of academic freedom to theology necessitates the modification or revision of the notion of scholarly competence.[89] Revised secular models tend to justify academic freedom by demonstrating its importance to the proper functioning of the discipline of theology and its positive contribution to the life of the Church.

Restrictive Models of Academic Freedom

In a paper presented at a 1973 symposium on the character of Catholic higher education, S. Thomas Greenburg sketched an approach to academic freedom based upon what he considers a necessary distinction between the Catholic college or university as a university, and the Catholic college or university as one level of Catholic education. According to Greenburg, the problems and confusions surrounding the issue of academic freedom in the Catholic institution are due principally to a failure to recognize this distinction between what he calls two different frames of reference.[90]

Within the first frame of reference, the Catholic institution of higher learning is viewed in the context of the totality of Catholic education.[91] In this perspective, Catholic higher education is merely one level of all Catholic education. As such, the Catholic institution of higher learning shares the goal of all Catholic education, which is "the formation of the person with regard to his ultimate destiny."[92] The Catholic institution, then, does not possess a unique purpose. Rather, it merely represents Catholic education at an advanced level of operation.

From within the second frame of reference, the Catholic university has a unique purpose.[93] Like secular universities, its goal is the free pursuit of truth. Its status is that of "an independent and autonomous entity, distinct from the total educational process and the proper goals of all Catholic education."[94] In Greenburg's view, this second frame of reference is derived from the European tendency to identify the university with graduate study and research. He argues that such a frame of reference is foreign to the American situation, where the college and university are defined primarily as educational institutions that are subsumed under the heading of "post-secondary" education and that constitute a part of the overall American educational system.[95]

Greenburg points out that one's conception of academic freedom will be conditioned by one's frame of reference. If the Catholic institution of higher learning is seen as one part of the Church's overall educational system, then commonly accepted principles of scholarly freedom and academic autonomy, which are based on a different frame of reference, will be rejected. A close relationship between the college and the *Magisterium* will not be viewed as a violation of scholarly autonomy since "an educational institution that is directed toward the formation of the person with regard to his ultimate destiny must be inextricably related to the guarantee of that Christian message which identifies the content of the person's ultimate destiny."[96]

Greenburg offers a somewhat similar argument in a later writing, though here it is presented in a more developed and nuanced fashion.[97] Greenburg claims that there exists in some sectors of Catholic higher

education an "unchallenged Platonism" that confuses the abstractly conceived nature of the university with the development of the nature in
reality.[98] This "Platonistic" position,

> which bases itself on the 'nature' of the university, considered qua university,
> recognizes *only* those commitments which follow from the "imperatives" of the
> abstractly conceived nature of the university. It recognizes no *authority* external
> to the nature of the university, holding that the only "real authority" to be
> identified and followed is that which is related to the interior imperatives of the
> nature of the university itself.
> This method is *essence-based* rather than *existence-based*. It hypostasizes the na-
> ture of the university and makes it its own independent initiator of its own
> activity. It is Platonistic in its roots and it results in a concretization of an ab-
> straction which inverts the order of reality itself.[99]

It is this "Platonistic" perspective that undergirds the secular notion of
academic freedom.

In Greenburg's view, this perspective is a distortion insofar as the
nature of the university, to exist outside the mind, "needs an existent
source, external to itself: either the Church, the State, or a group of
private persons, which gives it its existence, accompanied by certain
commitments and certain existential conditions of being which determine the manner in which the potential of the nature will be developed
in the concrete world."[100] The existent source, the commitments, and
the existential conditions of being of the university will determine the
definitions of academic freedom and autonomy normative for it.[101] Although the same university nature is shared by Catholic, state, and private universities, the existential conditions and commitments of each
type will differ and, hence, academic freedom will be defined differently
in each.[102]

Greenburg argues that the condition of being and the existential commitments of the Catholic university are such that academic freedom must
recognize the university's fidelity to the Christian message and to the
hierarchical *Magisterium*, which guards and interprets that message.[103]
Similarly, in the Catholic Ecclesiastical university, academic freedom must
also recognize the university's canonical erection and its particular relation with the Apostolic See.[104] What Greenburg has sketched is a model
of academic freedom that is based not upon the nature of the university,
the nature of truth-seeking, or the common good, but upon the university in (what he terms) its existential condition of being.

Philosopher Germain Grisez has also contributed to the ongoing discussion of academic freedom in the Catholic context.[105] Grisez argues
that the notion of academic freedom generally accepted in the United
States "reflects the humanistic and liberal faith that human goods are
most likely to be achieved by unrestrained human effort."[106] Grisez fur-

ther claims that while the secular colleges and universities with which this notion finds its most comfortable home profess ideological neutrality, they embody a particular worldview and a set of nonsectarian values.[107] This worldview, the roots of which extend to the Enlightenment, rejects supernatural revelation and reduces religion to human experience. Values, according to this perspective, have no transcendent source but are merely "a function of the relation of man to his natural environment, express subjective feelings, or at best express requirements of a certain state of culture."[108] This perspective also precludes the acceptance of an unalterable truth known with certitude. Truth is attained through methodological research and remains subject to revision in light of subsequent discoveries. Finally, according to Grisez, this worldview includes what might be termed a secular soteriology based upon knowledge: increasing control over nature and the resolution of human problems will be achieved as knowledge increases. Scientific research, therefore, becomes the "principle of man's salvation."[109]

Grisez points out that this worldview is totally incongruous with Catholic faith. Nevertheless, some Catholic institutions have attempted to imitate the nonsectarian model, while some Catholic faculty members have at least implicitly accepted the secularist worldview. One sign of this is the degree to which the American notion of academic freedom finds acceptance among Catholic faculty members—even in departments of theology.[110] In Grisez's view, this is problematic. He argues that while from the secular perspective freedom is the primary condition for attaining truth, it is not so in the Catholic worldview. For the believer, freedom—though necessary—is secondary. *"The primary condition for attaining truth is humility and the obedience of faith,* because the First Truth gives Himself to man gratuitously in the divine revelation."[111]

According to Grisez, faith is not a restriction on intellectual freedom, but rather makes available to the human intellect transcendent truth that would otherwise remain inaccessible.[112] "The truth of faith makes an incontrovertible demand on the intellect of the believer" (although "faith requires freedom of acceptance").[113] The unbeliever is unaware of this demand because of his or her incapacity to recognize it, not because he or she enjoys any greater freedom.

Grisez rejects any attempt to harmonize faith and academic freedom through recourse to a theology that views faith as something indefinite and subject to rearticulation. Although the substance of faith is not identical with its expression,

that substance is uniquely expressed by definitive articles which are proposed (and disputes concerning which are adjudicated) by the living *magisterium.* . . . This authority, which is "external to the academic community itself," cannot be set aside by Catholics. Acceptance of this authority, and all of its implications, is the most distinctive mark—though not the most fundamental characteristic—of truly Catholic intellectual life.[114]

Even within areas of faith subject to rearticulation and discussion, the formulations of the *Magisterium* remain absolutely normative.

It is not surprising that Grisez rejects conceptions of university theology that preclude a direct relation and subordination of the discipline to ecclesiastical authority. In his estimation, "genuine theology" is possible only when the principles of faith are accepted by theologians in a way similar to the acceptance of natural facts by scientists. "Theologies are falsified when anathematized, just as scientific theories are falsified when the results of experiments go against them."[115]

Although Grisez does not present a developed procedural model of academic freedom, he presents the philosophical basis of his model quite clearly. He rejects the philosophical basis of the secular notion of academic freedom and redefines the concept in terms of the exigencies of the Catholic college or university, particularly as they are manifested in the theological disciplines.

Grisez does offer some practical suggestions for the Catholic institution. Included among these is his endorsement of the AAUP "1940 Statement of Principles" as a *procedural norm*.[116] He is not entirely clear on the exact meaning of this. He is clear, however, in his insistence that the Catholic college or university must make clear to its prospective members that faith is the first principle of its intellectual effort and that it is therefore institutionally committed to the ecclesiastical *Magisterium*. During a 1973 conference, Grisez went as far as to suggest that it might be desirable to grant permanent faculty positions only to committed Catholics.[117] When queried on the criteria by which a scholar's "Catholic commitment" would be ascertained, he replied:

a Catholic university philosophy or theology department ought to know how to select people it wants to select. The main criterion for a department is the actual status of the Church's teaching at a given time. For example, if I had my choice in selecting members for a Catholic university, I would not accept anyone who cannot accept *Humanae Vitae*. The teaching of the Church is where it stands. Conversations are always possible. . . . But anyone who rejects the central position of *Humanae Vitae* and who says this is an open question is not a Catholic I want in my institution.[118]

Grisez affirms that according to a "Catholic concept" of academic freedom, lay faculty members do have a right to participate in the government of their institutions, though this right never includes the freedom to reject the authority of the *Magisterium*.[119] Grisez rejects the model of religious obedience which often characterized the faculty-administration relationship in years past, and argues that the faculty should have "authentic academic freedom," including the freedom to legislate in academic affairs according to the principle of competence.[120]

Grisez also exhorts Catholic boards of trustees to exercise their power without timidity. Most boards have final authority (or at least veto power) over faculty decisions concerning faculty appointments, promotions, and tenure. Grisez argues that the preservation of Catholic institutions is dependent upon the ability of boards to exercise their authority wisely and firmly.[121]

Bishops, too, are encouraged to exercise their teaching authority. In Grisez's estimation, clear teaching is the most effective response to the challenges of theologians to Church authority and doctrine.[122] Grisez does not refer to any further involvement of bishops in the faculty disciplinary processes of Catholic universities. There seems to be implicit in his argument a recognition that disciplinary action against faculty members would be handled internally, by an administration committed to the Church's *Magisterium*.[123]

The approach of Augustine Rock presented in a 1968 paper is perhaps more nuanced than that of Grisez in that Rock's model includes important distinctions often overlooked.[124] These include the distinction between the ordinary and extraordinary *Magisterium* (and the varying levels of assent required of the believer), and the differing contexts represented by the undergraduate college, the full university, and the seminary.

Rock characterizes the university as an institution where students are mature enough to judge the validity of a professor's teaching, where extensive scholarly research is carried out, and where teaching and research are subject to the judgment of competent professional peers.[125] It is to such a full academic community that academic freedom properly belongs. However, such freedom does not exempt the Catholic university scholar from adherence to the teachings of the extraordinary *Magisterium*. The infallible teaching of a pope or general council demands the full assent of faith.[126]

Rock argues that the freedom of the Catholic scholar is not curtailed by the demand that the full assent of faith be given to truth proclaimed by the Church as revealed.[127] This is because assent to a revealed truth is a free decision "to which we are sweetly moved by grace." Moreover, such revealed truth is supernatural truth and not directly "the property of academe."[128] Full assent to revealed truth is particularly vital for the theologian, for in Rock's estimation, to be a Christian theologian, one must accept the Christian revelation that constitutes the principles of the discipline.[129] The *Magisterium*, as guardian and interpreter of revelation, falsifies or certifies theologies just as in physics facts are verified or falsified via the scientific method.[130] Moreover, the authority of the *Magisterium* cannot be circumvented by questioning the eternal validity of a particular formula. "The point is that *right now* the belief of the Church can be articulated validly or invalidly. It is the prerogative of the magisterium to ensure that it is done validly."[131]

In cases where university teaching is judged contrary to revealed truth, Rock exorts the local ordinary to make firm but gentle correctives.[132] When a major university is involved, the local ordinary may refer the case to the Holy See for its intervention.[133] Rock does not clarify what form such intervention would take, nor whether such intervention would override the internal processes of the university in question.

Rock's model of academic freedom is broad enough to allow a measure of liberty to theologians dealing with the noninfallible teaching of the ordinary *Magisterium* in a university context. Rock acknowledges that "in this area the theologian is free responsibly to question and investigate." However, Rock emphasizes that "the manner in which he publishes the results of his questioning and research pertains to the responsibility which goes with his academic freedom."[134]

Rock affirms that the theologian remains dependent upon the *Magisterium* in two ways. The *Magisterium* judges the results of theological research, while it keeps the theologian in touch with the historic patrimony of the Church.[135] However, it is permissible for a university theologian to reach a conclusion that is not in harmony with the teaching of the ordinary *Magisterium*, if the requirements of academic fairness are fulfilled: that both sides of the question be presented, that the conclusion reached is the result of competent scholarly research, and that it be published in a responsible fashion.[136]

When applied to the college or small university context, Rock's model of academic freedom includes additional restrictions. Rock exhorts bishops to be particularly vigilant in protecting orthodoxy in this context. The ordinary must exercise his authority if a theology professor is "proposing anything contrary to the infallible magisterium or even consistently making light of the ordinary magisterium."[137] For the faith of students must be protected.[138] Rock is quite vague in his description of what form episcopal intervention might take.

Rock addresses briefly the seminary context. In his view, diocesan seminary professors have no clear title to academic freedom insofar as such a seminary was founded by an ordinary for a particular purpose, and that purpose "is obviously not the pursuit of learning."[139]

Rock's approach to academic freedom is a highly nuanced one. Indeed, when applied to the "full university" his model exhibits elements of the revised secular models of academic freedom. Nonetheless, we have chosen to include his framework in the present category for two major reasons. First, his model as applied to the undergraduate college and small university tends to fall into the restrictive category. Second, his model in all its applications allows intervention by episcopal authority, though it fails to specify the nature of that intervention, or to provide functional safeguards against the violation of the proper autonomy of the university or the discipline of theology.[140]

Revised Secular Models of Academic Freedom

Varying approaches can be subsumed under the category "revised secular models of academic freedom." What these models have in common is the acceptance—with certain revisions—of the notion of academic freedom as it has been developed and made normative in American higher education.[141] Unlike theorists whose models fall into the restrictive category, the scholars whose work will be examined below generally accept (though not uncritically) the basic vision of the nature of the scholar's task implicit in the secular notion of academic freedom.[142]

John Walsh, for example, constructs a model of academic freedom based upon a view of the Catholic university as a manifestation of the Church learning.[143] Although Walsh recognizes the manifold nature of academic freedom, he argues that its most important dimension is the freedom to teach.[144] It is teaching at its highest level that distinguishes the college or university from all other institutions.

Walsh points out that the right to teach is an acquired right contingent upon one having become a knower. The primary obligation of the teacher, he avers, is intellectual honesty—a scholar's honesty with him or herself as well as his or her students. This involves following an argument wherever it may lead—even to conclusions that are unpopular. Acting as a spokesperson for the ideas of another—as a "mouthpiece," if you will—is dishonest, and destroys the true meaning of teaching.[145]

Walsh insists that the right to teach means the same on the Catholic campus as it does on any other. "The Catholic university is a true university and those who teach in it lay full claim to academic freedom."[146] Is full academic freedom reconcilable with the aims of a Catholic university? In Walsh's estimation it is, if the erroneous identification of the Catholic university with the teaching function of the Roman Catholic Church is abandoned. Walsh claims that "to think of the Catholic university as an instrument of the Church for the carrying out of its teaching mission leads . . . both to serious misunderstandings of the Church's teaching mission in itself and to profound distortions of the nature of a university."[147] The university, rather than being a locus of the Church teaching, is a manifestation of the Church learning.[148]

Genuine and fruitful learning in all disciplines, including theology, requires freedom of inquiry. Walsh writes that "academic freedom is so essential because it makes it possible for all of us to pursue the highest and deepest learning . . . without fear of any kind of recrimination, provided only that we never confuse academic freedom with shabby and superficial scholarship."[149] Thus, within the Catholic university, the demands of learning—including freedom of inquiry in all disciplines—must be adhered to.[150]

Ladislas M. Orsy advances the thesis that "no school of theology incorporated into a university can function without academic freedom—in the broadest and best sense of the expression as it is understood in American academic circles."[151] In his view, such freedom is possible both in theory and in practice if the respective roles of the theologian and the Church's teaching authority are understood properly.

While all members of the Church constitute the teaching Church (ecclesia docens), the Pope as the head of the episcopal college, and his brother bishops, have a unique God-given teaching authority.[152] They have been entrusted with the task of preserving the Word of God from all corruption and the responsibility of leading the People of God "toward the Kingdom without letting them lose their way."[153] The bishops, therefore, have the authority (given to them through their consecration) to judge whether a particular doctrine or teaching is faithful to God's revelation [154]

On the other hand, theology is the intellectual exploration of God's revelation. The charism of the bishops and that of theologians need not conflict, but must complement one another. Orsy argues that in order to pursue his or her mission in the Church fruitfully and effectively, the theologian requires an atmosphere of trust, confidence, and freedom.[155] The task of the theologian is not to restate the facts of revelation, but rather to explore revelation more fully and to gain greater insights into it.[156] It is through the theologian that the Church's quest for a deeper understanding of the truth continues. Therefore, bishops must jealously guard the academic freedom of theologians.

Orsy outlines some of the practical implications of his argument. First, colleges and universities should not be under the jurisdiction of the local ordinary since one bishop does not possess "the full charism of the authentication of the Christian doctrine."[157] Orsy does affirm the authority of the Pope and the full episcopal college over a university, though the exercise of episcopal authority would be extremely rare—especially apart from an ecumenical council.[158] It *appears* as though the exercise of authority to which Orsy refers would consist of a clarification of the Church's teaching on a particular question, rather than direct intervention into the affairs of a college or university to correct or discipline a theologian.

This assessment is supported by Orsy's analysis of a theoretical case within which a qualified and dedicated theologian, after being appointed to a chair of Catholic theology at a Catholic university "persistently professes and teaches a doctrine that cannot be accepted as one representing the Catholic tradition or its legitimate development."[159] Orsy rejects the traditional solution of condemnation and removal. Rather, he advises that professional criticsms from other theologians be requested. Hence, the problem would be addressed internally by the theologian's scholarly peers. If such an action were ineffective, the bishops could declare that the teaching of this particular theologian on the issue at hand differs from Catholic doctrine. In this manner, the official teaching of the Church would be reaffirmed, and the position of the theologian would be understood as a private opinion.[160] The problem could therefore be resolved without intrusions into the academy by authorities external to it.

Robert E. Hunt, Frederick W. Gunti, and Charles E. Curran have addressed the problem of academic freedom on the Catholic campus in similar ways.[161] All advocate the extension of full academic freedom (as it is commonly understood in American academia) to Catholic university scholars in all disciplines, including theology.[162]

Gunti views the academic freedom of theologians "as a basic human right, flowing from their human dignity and their responsibility to perform their theological ministry for the Church."[163] Curran claims that society is best served by a university characterized by academic freedom. Turning specifically to theology, he argues that such freedom is necessary in light of the nature of the discipline (which requires freedom to properly exercise its function) and the relationship between theologians and the hierarchical *Magisterium*. He adds that academic freedom is beneficial to theology, to the Catholic university, and to the entire Church.[164]

What precisely is the nature and function of the theologian that justifies the extension of academic freedom to him or her? Gunti views the theologian as exercising a charism (in the Pauline sense)—a charism of learning—the aim of which is the building up of the Body of Christ.[165] He further characterizes the theologian as a mediator between the *Magisterium* and the community of faith.[166] Hunt expresses a similar position. In his view, "Theologians hold a sort of midway position between the faith of the Church and the teaching office of bishops."[167] They aid the *Magisterium* in arriving at a deeper understanding of the faith it guards and teaches. Without academic freedom, theologians cannot develop "good" Catholic theology, and only good theology serves the Church and the world.[168]

In a similar vein, Curran emphasizes the interpretive function of theology. He defines theology as "a scientific discipline, a human activity that presupposes faith."[169] Reminding his readers that faith is not merely directed toward revealed propositions or truths, but rather primarily toward the God who reveals Himself, Curran points out that human knowledge of the mystery of God will never be complete in this present life. Moreover, human linguistic and symbolic expression of faith will always be imperfect due to "the historically and culturally conditioned nature of our knowledge and of our verbal and symbolic expression of this knowledge."[170] Hence, the importance of theology. Curran writes:

Theology has the never ending task of trying to interpret better and understand more adequately the mystery of faith in the light of contemporary realities. No longer is theology understood in the light of a science seeking certitude based on a deductive methodology. Interpretation of the sources of revelation and of the teaching of the hierarchical magisterium in the light of the signs of the times is theology's function.[171]

According to Curran, it is this interpretive function of theology that establishes the need for academic freedom in the theological disciplines.[172] For "part of the theological function of interpretation of the hierarchical teaching involves the possibility of dissent from authoritative, non-infallible church teaching."[173]

Hunt, Gunti, and Curran agree that the American notion of academic freedom can and should be applied to the study of Catholic theology.[174] No limitations on the freedom of the theologian are necessary insofar as the theologian, like all scholars, is bound by the duties of professional responsibility and competence.[175] These duties make academic freedom a self-limiting principle. Defining Catholic theological competence, Gunti writes:

A scholar who is competent does not exceed the principles of his science. Thus, for a theologian to merit the name of "Catholic theologian" and to be competent within that field, it is demanded that he theologize within the context of a Catholic faith-commitment. If he does otherwise, he is not a Catholic theologian. His right to alter his faith-commitment is not challenged, but should he do so he can no longer be considered a Catholic theologian. In theology as in other disciplines, the jury of peers is the only competent tribunal which can decide whether a scholar is acting responsibly and within the canons of his discipline.[176]

Gunti includes among the criteria of scholarly theological competence both theologizing within and adhering personally to a Catholic faith-commitment. He tends to link these two together, apparently assuming that one who "does" Catholic theology will have such a faith-commitment.

Like Gunti, Hunt and Curran consider the notion of competence a key notion when arguing for the applicability of the principle of academic freedom to the Catholic theological fields. However, unlike Gunti, they do not specifically include holding a Catholic faith-commitment among the criteria of Catholic theological competence. Hunt writes that the teachings of the hierarchical *Magisterium* constitute "part of the total data which the Catholic theologian must integrate into his work. He must be aware of them, evaluate them, and give them their proper weight and place in his work. If he does not, the problem is professional qualification and competency."[177] Hunt does not explain the precise meaning of the phrase "proper weight and place."

In a similar vein, Curran has written that "competency requires that one be true to the presuppositions, sources and methods of the discipline." This means that "the theologian should distinguish between the data of revelation and theories or hypotheses that have been proposed," specify official Church teaching and interpret it "in accord with accepted hermeneutical principles," and label personal hypotheses as such. "If the Roman Catholic theologian is not competent, then the professor can be dismissed for cause just as an incompetent physicist or anthropologist can be dismissed for cause in accord with the principles of academic due process."[178].

Upon a first reading, it does appear that Curran's description of theological competence is quite broad. It seems that Curran gives the theologian freedom to develop and propose *personal* theories and hypotheses so long as they are labeled as such, and so long as official church teaching is clearly set forth and properly interpreted. Yet, there is some ambiguity surrounding the principle of competence in Curran's model. In the course of an interview, Professor Curran made it clear that the professor of Catholic theology is *not* free to advance conclusions that are clearly in opposition to (and not merely reinterpretations of) matters of divine faith—including infallible statements of the *Magisterium*. Such conclusions can very well be indicative of a lack of competence.[179]

It should be pointed out that Hunt, Gunti, and Curran argue that the judgment of a theologian's competence can only be made by his or her peers within academic due process. Under no circumstances should Church authorities intervene in the internal affairs of the college or university. Such intervention would be a violation of the Catholic university's necessary autonomy. "Church teaching authority can point out for the good of the church that the theory of a particular theologian is erroneous, but the judgment about dismissal must be made by academic peers giving due weight to official church teaching."[180]

Hunt, Curran, and Gunti have argued that full academic freedom, as it is understood and applied in the American academy, can and must be applied to the Catholic institution, including the discipline of theology. Such an application becomes theoretically possible in light of these scholars' similar understandings of Roman Catholic theological competence. Questions can be raised concerning the adequacy of these notions of competence. For example, Gunti's approach to theological competence seems reminiscent of that advanced by Charles Donahue in the mid–1950s.[181] Donahue argues that the theologian has a dual commitment: a commitment to the science of theology, and a sacral commitment to one's religious tradition. A violation of or change in a Catholic's sacral commitment, evidenced perhaps by the proposal of a particular theological position, would be a violation of the theologian's position as a Catholic theologian.[182] The issue that will be addressed is whether the notion of competence advanced by Gunti contains within it an implicit conception of a "dual commitment" and, if so, whether this limits the acceptability of his model.

ACADEMIC FREEDOM IN PERTINENT ORGANIZATIONAL STATEMENTS

The position paper entitled "The Catholic University of Today"—commonly called the "Land O'Lakes Statement"—was the result of an invitational seminar convened at Land O'Lakes, Wisconsin, in July 1967.[183] Participating in this seminar, sponsored by the International Federation of Catholic Universities, North American Region, were twenty-six distinguished leaders of Catholic higher education, including the presidents of six major Catholic institutions.[184]

From the outset, the "Land O'Lakes Statement" affirms that the Catholic university, like all universities, must have a true autonomy and academic freedom. Article 1 states:

The Catholic university today must be a university in the full modern sense of the word, with a strong commitment to and concern for academic excellence. To perform its teaching and research functions effectively the Catholic university must have a true autonomy and academic freedom in the face of authority of whatever kind, lay or clerical, external to the academic community itself. To say this is simply to assert that institutional autonomy and academic freedom are essential conditions of life and growth and indeed of survival for Catholic universities as for all universities.[185]

Also affirmed specifically by the seminar participants was the academic freedom of the student. In their view, "the whole world of knowledge and ideas must be open to the student; there must be no outlawed books or subjects."[186]

At the Eighth Triennial Congress of the International Federation of Catholic Universities held in September 1968 in Kinshasa, Republic of the Congo, "the ideas in the Land O'Lakes Statement regarding autonomy and academic freedom were considered by many as outlandish and dangerous."[187] Some participants who held a more traditional philosophy of Catholic higher education warned against false autonomy and argued in support of a necessary dependence of the Catholic university on the *Magisterium*.[188] Because of the impossibility of reaching an agreement on the meaning of academic freedom and autonomy in the Catholic context, these subjects were not treated in the statement that arose from this meeting.[189]

In January 1969, the Congregation for Catholic Education, under its Cardinal Prefect Gabriel-Marie Garrone, invited the Catholic universities of the world to elect representatives who would meet with the Congregation in Rome.[190] On April 25, 1969, "thirty-nine delegates and observers from twenty-two countries assembled in Rome for the week-long congress."[191] The position paper adopted by this congress—"The Catholic University and the Aggiornamento"—addresses in detail the problem of academic freedom in the Catholic university.[192]

This position paper outlines clearly the delegates' views on the nature of Catholic institutional autonomy. While affirming that "the Catholic university must have a true autonomy and academic freedom," the delegates point out that this does not "imply that the university is beyond the law: the university has its own laws which flow from its proper nature and finality."[193] That proper nature is the "pursuit of truth without conditions." A university does remain accountable to society and is subject to "the legitimate exigencies of the society which sustains it."[194] Yet, no limitation on university freedom and autonomy that conflicts with the unconditional pursuit of truth should be tolerated.

However, the position paper does highlight the unique nature of the Catholic university. The delegates write:

In the Catholic university there is a special element in the domain of academic autonomy including freedom of teaching and research. Though all natural truth is directly accessible to us through the exercise of our innate ability to grasp and to understand reality, the authentic Christian message is not available to us except with a guarantee of doctrinal authority, which is the magisterium of the church. The datum from which theological reflection arises is not a datum of reality fully accessible to the human intelligence, but a revealed message entrusted to the Church. The freedom of the theological researcher, at the risk of basic self-destruction, rests on the foundation of revelation.[195]

Nevertheless, the delegates assert that Catholic university scholars, including theologians, must be accorded full academic freedom. The theologian must be free to research, hypothesize, and publish, subject to evaluation by peers.[196]

The Catholic theologian also has a number of responsibilities: "As an individual he is bound to accept the authentic teaching of the Church and to submit to its legitimately exercised authority. As a theological scholar he is bound by the nature of his discipline to take into proper account the pronouncements of the Church."[197] In those cases when the teaching of a theologian is open to serious questioning, the *Magisterium* can intervene if the "truth of the revealed message is at stake."[198] The delegates affirm that within "a university without statutory relationships with ecclesiastical or religious superiors, these authorities may deal with the theologian as an individual member of the Church."[199] They may warn the faithful. However, "any juridical intervention in university affairs must be excluded."[200] In institutions with a direct relation to ecclesiastical authorities, the intervention of such authorities must respect the statutes of the institution and the procedures of academic due process.

The forty-three cardinals and eight bishops of the Sacred Congregation for Catholic Education met in October 1969. The results of that session, approved by Pope Paul VI on November 13, 1969, include conceptions of academic freedom and university autonomy that stand in stark contrast to those presented in the position paper of the Rome Congress.[201]

First, the Congregation reaffirmed the centrality of ecclesiastical authority in the Catholic university. Insofar as the Catholic university exists in the context of the Catholic community it must be "related to those who preside over the Catholic community: the Catholic hierarchy."[202] Second, the Congregation rejected the notion that the mission of the *Magisterium* to safeguard Catholic doctrine is opposed to scientific freedom. In its view, the guidance of the *Magisterium* "protects and assists" rather than hinders higher studies. Finally, responding to the position paper of the Rome Congress, the members of the Congregation expressed the following doubts:

1. that research in the field of theology can be conducted with the same freedom as in any other field;
2. that the judgment about the value of a doctrine in theology can be normally left to fellow theologians;
3. that a critical attitude towards the truths of the faith can be assumed;
4. that a diverse relationship with the Magisterium can exist depending upon the various types of Catholic universities.[203]

Moreover, the Congregation asked that the following principles be adhered to:

1. that the competence of the Magisterium extends not only to the truths of faith, but also to those matters connected with the truths of faith;
2. that freedom in doing research be distinguished from freedom to teach or diffuse the fruits of research, to avoid confusing and bewildering the minds of the faithful.[204]

In light of the doubts and objections expressed by the Congregation, Cardinal Garrone invited the International Federation of Catholic Universities (IFCU) to prepare a revised text of the position paper.[205] In view of this end, four regional meetings of the IFCU were convened; the North American meeting was held in September, 1971. The result of the conference of American and Canadian educators was a report that not only reaffirmed the principles presented in the original position paper of the Rome Congress, but also contained an appendix that re-emphasized the need for institutional autonomy and academic freedom in the North American context.[206] The conference participants based their assertions on the fact that the American Catholic college or university is an institution independent of the pastoral mission of the Church and not subject to "ecclesiastical-juridical control, censorship, or supervision." They argued that "a question of orthodoxy in a classroom ought not be dealt with through the board, the president, or the deans of the university. Nor should the administration of the university be used to impose sanctions for violation of church laws."[207] Such procedures, according to the participants, would constitute violations of the nature of universities.

This North American report, together with the reports of the other regional meetings, was reviewed at a preparatory meeting which was held at Grottaferrata in February 1972.[208] That meeting gave rise to a revised text of the IFCU position paper, which was sent to the Catholic universities of the world, together with an invitation to choose delegates for the Second Congress, scheduled for November, 1972.[209]

Forty delegates from twenty-three countries participated in the Second Congress, which was held in Rome from November 20 to 29, 1972.[210] This Congress finally approved the statement that is now known as "The Catholic University in the Modern World."[211] In this document, a specific section is devoted to the delicate questions surrounding the relations of the university with the Catholic hierarchy. Despite certain additions and expansions, the principles contained in the revised document do not differ substantially from those found in the document that arose from the First Congress.

In "The Catholic University in the Modern World," the delegates state:

Even at the level of civil society, public order and interest can entail limitations to the self-government of the university, provided that the requirements of the unconditioned research for the truth are respected. *A fortiori* that community which is the Church will have its rights vis-à-vis Catholic universities.[212]

Yet, this concessionary statement is not given full application later in the document where the principles of freedom and autonomy presented in the position paper of the First Congress are simply restated. In a similar manner, the document outlines the respective roles of the theologian and the *Magisterium*, emphasizing their interdependence.[213] In this section, the theologian is described as recognizing the right of the *Magisterium* "to judge the value of his theology, its authentic catholicity, and its conformity with divine revelation."[214] However, while bishops have "the right to judge and declare whether a teaching that is publicly proposed as Catholic is in fact such, still the judgment concerning the product of a theologian's scholarly research will normally be left to his peers."[215] Hence, the position paper of the Second Congress could be interpreted either as being more nuanced than that of the First Congress, or basically a restatement of the same principles utilizing a rhetoric more palatable to the hierarchy.

In any event, the principles on academic freedom of theologians presented in "The Catholic University in the Modern World" are clear. In summary they are as follows:

1. When teaching Catholic theology, theologians must present the authentic doctrine of the Church.
2. The teaching role of the theologian is inseparable from his or her scholarly research.
3. "Theologians must be able to pursue their discipline in the same manner as other research scholars, keeping in mind, as every researcher must, the particular nature of their own discipline. They must be free to question, to develop their hypotheses, to search for more adequate interpretations and formulations, to publish and defend their views on a scholarly level, and to study theological sources, including pronouncements of the teaching Church, with the full freedom of scholarly research."[216]
4. The hierarchy may intervene only when the truth of the Christian message is at stake.
5. Any intervention by the hierarchy must respect the statutes of the university and accepted academic procedures.[217]
6. The form of intervention will vary, but in institutions without a statutory relationship with Church authorities, such authorities "will deal with the individual involved only as a member of the Church."[218]
7. The judgment of the results of scholarly research is normally made by a theologian's academic peers.
8. If it is apparent that the faith of those to whom they minister is being threatened, bishops "have the right and duty to intervene, by advising the person involved, informing the administration, and in an extreme case, declaring such a teaching incompatible with Catholic doctrine. However, unless statutory relationships permit it, this will not involve a juridical intervention, whether direct or indirect, in the institutional affairs of the university. . . ."[219]

The entire document was examined and considered by the Plenary Assembly of the Sacred Congregation for Catholic Education, which met on April 2–3, 1973.[220] The Congregation found this document to be a considerable improvement over that of the 1969 Congress. Yet, the Fathers of the Congregation considered it to be "valid but needing improvement."[221] First, the document is not sufficiently clear on the necessity for each Catholic university to state explicitly and formally its commitment as Catholic, and the necessity of developing instruments of self-regulation in the areas of faith, morality, and discipline.[222] Moreover, it was emphasized that the absense of formal statutory bonds between some Catholic universities and ecclesiastical authorities "in no way means that such institutions are removed from those relationships with the ecclesiastical hierarchy which must characterize all Catholic institutions."[223] Finally, the Congregation stated that the document must be considered as a whole to avoid the misinterpretation that would result from taking certain elements out of context, "especially regarding the treatment given to autonomy of teaching and research."[224]

The 1972 Rome document represents only the position of the Second Congress of Delegates of the Catholic Universities of the World. Yet, it remains significant in that despite the Congregation's reservations, and despite the obvious differences in implicit educational philosophy between the Congregation and the Congress, the document was accepted by the Plenary Session as valid—albeit with certain qualifications.

This chapter has surveyed the implicit and explicit models of academic freedom found in Church pronouncements, scholarly studies, and organizational statements. The foregoing descriptive account is hardly exhaustive, although it does serve as a basic introduction to the major approaches to the problem of academic freedom that have been developed in the Catholic context.

The reader might have noticed that recent discussions of the issue of academic freedom in the Catholic college and university have focused almost exclusively upon the area of theology. There are a number of reasons for this. First, most of these discussions have been carried on by theologians. It is understandable that they would be particularly attentive to potential problems in their own discipline. Moreover, the Catholic Church's present understanding of its hierarchical structure and magisterial function, and the variety of understandings in the Church of the nature of the Catholic university and of the discipline of theology make theologians in Catholic universities quite vulnerable and their freedom precarious. Put simply, theology remains the area within which difficulties related to academic freedom are most likely to arise.

Finally, implicit in much of the literature on academic freedom in the Catholic university is the assumption that the freedom of scholars in "secular" disciplines is no less secure on the Catholic campus than it is on any other. Their assumption is, in part, the result of the endorsement by the Second Vatican Council and by recent popes of the legitimate autonomy of the human arts and sciences and the just freedom ("within the limits of morality and the general welfare") of scholars working in these areas.[225] It is also based upon the Catholic view of the complementary relation between faith and reason, and the Catholic confidence that conflict between the two "orders of knowledge" is not possible since they are directed to different aspects of the same reality.[226]

Challenges to the academic freedom of secular disciplines *specifically related to the Catholic nature of the institution* are rather unlikely to arise. Catholicism eschews literalist interpretations of scripture that might lead to "creation vs. evolution" type difficulties. Moreover, in general, theological imperialism is avoidable in that faith is not considered by Catholics to be a source of "scientific" information. It is true that some theologians have argued that the secondary object of infallibility includes condemnations of propositions contrary to revealed truth (e.g., conclusions of science referred to by Vatican I). There is a potential for difficulty in this area. Other theologians have averred that particular applications of the natural moral law are also included within the secondary object of infallibility, though these scholars are in a very small minority.

Nevertheless, the freedom of scholars in the human arts and sciences is not entirely secure on the Catholic campus. It is never entirely secure on any campus. In light of this, perhaps Catholic theorists have been remiss in not devoting greater attention to the potential challenges to the academic freedom of scholars in the non-theological disciplines on Catholic campuses.

NOTES

1. Peter A. Lyons, "Academic Freedom at Catholic Universities," *The Ecumenist* 10 (May-June 1972): 61; Curran, "Academic Freedom," pp. 747–48.

2. Curran, "Academic Freedom," p. 747.

3. Vatican II, "Constitution on the Church," no. 9, pp. 24–26.

4. Vatican II, "Constitution on the Church," no. 12, p. 30.

5. Second Vatican Council, "Decree on the Apostolate of the Laity," in *The Documents of Vatican II*, ed. Walter M. Abbott, trans. Joseph Gallagher (New York: The America Press, 1966), no. 2, p. 491.

6. Lyons, "Academic Freedom," p. 61.

7. Greeley, *Backwater to Mainstream*, p. 17.

8. Curran, "Academic Freedom," p. 747.

9. Second Vatican Council, "Church in the Modern World," no. 12, pp. 210–11.

10. Ibid., no. 17, p. 214.

11. Ibid.

12. Second Vatican Council, "Declaration on Religious Freedom," in *The Documents of Vatican II*, ed. Walter M. Abbott, trans. Joseph Gallagher (New York: The America Press, 1966), pp. 675–96.

13. Vatican II, "Declaration on Religious Freedom," no. 2, p. 679.

14. Ibid., no. 1, p. 677.

15. John Courtney Murray, "Religious Freedom," in *The Documents of Vatican II*, ed. Walter M. Abbott, trans. Joseph Gallagher (New York: The America Press, 1966), pp. 672–73.

16. See Peter Hebblethwaite, "Human Rights in the Church," in *Authority in the Church and the Schillebeeckx Case*, ed. Leonard Swidler and Piet F. Fransen (New York: Crossroad Publishing Co., 1982), pp. 190–201. In his notes on the

Declaration, Murray points out that for the Catholic, the truth subsists in the Church. He states that "no man may say of the religious truth which subsists in the Church: 'It is no concern of mine.' Once given by Christ to His true Church, the true religion remains the one way in which all men are bound to serve God and save themselves." In "Religious Freedom," note 3, p. 676.

17. Murray, "Religious Freedom," p. 674.

18. Vatican II, "Church in the Modern World," no. 59, p. 265.

19. Ibid., pp. 265–66.

20. Second Vatican Council, "Declaration on Christian Education," in *The Documents of Vatican II*, ed. Walter M. Abbott, trans. Joseph Gallagher (New York: The America Press 1966), no. 10, p. 648.

21. Vatican II, "Church in the Modern World," no. 62, p. 270.

22. Vatican II, "Declaration on Religious Freedom," no. 3, pp. 680–81.

23. Gunti, "Academic Freedom as an Operative Principle," p. 234.

24. Vatican II, "Constitution on Divine Revelation," no. 8, p. 116.

25. See Gleason, "Catholic University," p. 23.

26. Paul VI, "The Mission of a Catholic University," *The Pope Speaks* 17 (1972): 134.

27. Paul VI, "New Tasks for Catholic Universities," *The Pope Speaks* 17 (1972): 355–56.

28. See Vatican II, "Constitution on Revelation," no. 10.

29. Paul VI, "To the Delegates of Catholic Universities," *L'Osservatore Romano* (English) 8 May 1969, p. 4.

30. Ibid.

31. Paul VI, "Mission of a Catholic University," p. 135.

32. Ibid.

33. Ibid.

34. Paul VI, "Vitality of the Mission of Catholic Universities," *L'Osservatore Romano* (English) 20 May 1971, p. 10.

35. First Vatican Council, "Constitution on the Catholic Faith," chap. 4, p. 33.

36. Paul VI, "Mission of a Catholic University," p. 136.

37. Ibid., p. 137.

38. Ibid. Italics mine.

39. Ibid., p. 138.

40. Ibid., p. 137.

41. Paul VI, "Vitality of the Mission of Catholic Universities," p. 10.

42. Paul VI, "Mission of a Catholic University," p. 135.

43. Ibid.

44. John Paul II, "Excellence, Truth and Freedom in Catholic Universities," *Origins* 9 (November 1979): 307.

45. Ibid.

46. Ibid.

47. See John Paul II, "Ideal Ascent Towards Truth," *L'Osservatore Romano* (English), 19 November 1979, p. 112.

48. John Paul II, "Truth and Freedom," pp. 307–8.

49. John Paul II, "Ascent Towards Truth," p. 12.

50. Ibid.

51. John Paul II, "Truth and Freedom," pp. 307–8.

52. Ibid., p. 308.

53. Ibid.

54. Ibid.

55. John Paul II, *Sapientia Christiana*, Article 39.

56. Ibid., Article 3.

57. Ibid.

58. Ibid., Article 7.

59. Ibid., Article 18.

60. Ibid., Article 16.

61. Ibid., Article 26.

62. Ibid., Articles 27–28.

63. Ibid., Article 39.

64. Ibid.

65. Curran, "Academic Freedom," p. 753.

66. Ibid.

67. John Paul II, "Apostolic Constitution Sacra Disciplinae Leges," in *The Code of Canon Law*, pp. xxiv–xxvi.

68. *The Code of Canon Law*, Canons 807–14. Ecclesiastical universities are treated in Canons 815–21.

69. Ibid., Canon 807, p. 572.

70. Ibid., Canon 218, p. 151.

71. Ibid., Canon 809, p. 573.

72. Ibid., Canon 810§1, p. 574.

73. Ibid., Canon 810§2, p. 574.

74. See James A. Coriden's commentary on Canon 810§2 in *The Code of Canon Law*, p. 574. Coriden notes that an earlier draft of this canon gave to bishops the authority to remove teachers for reasons of faith or morals.

75. *Code of Canon Law*, Canon 812, p. 575. On the storm of opposition to this canon, see Coriden's commentary on pp. 575–76.

76. See Ladislas Orsy, "The Mandate to Teach Theological Disciplines: Glosses on Canon 812 of the New Code," *Theological Studies* 44 (1983): 480, and Coriden's commentary in *The Code of Canon Law*, p. 576.

77. If a dispensation from the law is not granted, serious legal—and financial—ramifications for American Catholic universities may result.

78. National Conference of Catholic Bishops, *To Teach As Jesus Did* (Washington, D.C.: United States Catholic Conference, 1972), par. 68, p. 18.

79. Ibid., par. 74, p. 21.

80. Ibid., par. 75, p. 21.

81. Ibid., par. 73, p. 20.

82. National Conference of Catholic Bishops, *Catholic Higher Education and the Pastoral Mission of the Church* (Washington, D.C.: United States Catholic Conference, 1980).

83. Ibid., p. 4.

84. Ibid., pp. 7–8.

85. Our primary focus will be upon those models developed since the Second Vatican Council.

86. The label "restrictive" has been chosen because the practical application

of the models within this category would result in the restriction of academic freedom and scholarly autonomy as these are understood in the literature of the AAUP.

87. See, for example, Augustine Rock, "The Catholic University and Academic Freedom," *Proceedings of the Catholic Theological Society of America* 23 (1968): 245–60.

88. Germain Grisez, "American Catholic Higher Education: The Experience Evaluated," in *Why Should the Catholic University Survive?* ed. George A. Kelly (New York: St. John's University Press, 1973), pp. 47–48.

89. See Gunti, "Academic Freedom As An Operative Principle," pp. 262–64.

90. S. Thomas Greenburg, "The Problems of Identity in Catholic Higher Education: The Statement of the Question," in *Why Should the Catholic University Survive?* ed. George A. Kelly (New York: St. John's University Press, 1973), pp. 14–18.

91. Ibid., p. 17.

92. Ibid.

93. Ibid.

94. Ibid., p. 18.

95. Ibid., pp. 18–19.

96. Ibid., p. 23.

97. S. Thomas Greenburg, *Sapientia Christiana: Impediments to Implementation From the Catholic Universities* with a Foreword by John Cardinal Krol (San Antonio: The Institute of Catholic Higher Education, 1979), pp. 11–45.

98. Ibid., pp. 11–16.

99. Ibid., pp. 13–14.

100. Ibid., p. 19. On p. 25, Greenburg defines the nature of the university as "an academic community which pursues truth through the teaching of, and research into, the various academic disciplines."

101. Ibid., pp. 20–21.

102. Ibid., pp. 32–33.

103. Ibid., p. 25. See also p. 33.

104. Ibid., p. 23. In the same place, Greenburg states that "in a state university, academic freedom must recognize 'neutrality in religion.' "

105. See Grisez, "Catholic Higher Education," pp. 41–44; "Academic Freedom and Catholic Faith," *National Catholic Education Association Bulletin* 64 (December 1967): 15–20.

106. Grisez, "Academic Freedom," p. 16.

107. Grisez, "Catholic Higher Education," p. 47.

108. Ibid., p. 48.

109. Ibid.

110. Ibid., p. 49.

111. Grisez, "Academic Freedom," p. 17.

112. Ibid.

113. Ibid.

114. Grisez, "Academic Freedom," p. 18. Grisez does not refer specifically to the various levels of required assent to the teaching of the *Magisterium*. See Curran and Hunt, *Dissent*, chaps. 2–6.

115. Ibid.

116. Ibid.

117. Grisez, "Catholic Higher Education," p. 51. This would apply to all disciplines.

118. "Summary of Discussion," in *Why Should the Catholic University Survive?* ed. George A. Kelly (New York: St. John's University Press, 1973), p. 97. *Humanae Vitae* is Pope Paul VI's 1968 encyclical on the regulation of birth.

119. Grisez, "Academic Freedom," p. 18.

120. Ibid., p. 19.

121. Ibid., p. 18.

122. Ibid., p. 19.

123. Ibid., p. 18.

124. Rock, "The Catholic and Academic Freedom," p. 251.

125. Ibid., p. 260.

126. Ibid., pp. 255–56.

127. Ibid., p. 251.

128. Ibid.

129. Ibid., p. 258.

130. Ibid., p. 252.

131. Ibid., p. 253.

132. Ibid., p. 259.

133. Ibid., p. 257.

134. Ibid., p. 251.

135. Ibid., p. 253.

136. Ibid., p. 256.

137. Ibid., p. 257.

138. Ibid., p. 259.

139. Ibid., p. 257.

140. The foregoing survey is by no means an exhaustive one. See also Paul Beutenmuller, "Truth, Freedom and a University," *Social Justice Review* 59 (July-August 1966): 121–22; and Charles Donahue, "Freedom and Education III: Catholicism and Academic Freedom," *Thought* 29 (1955): 555–75.

141. See, for example, Curran, "Academic Freedom," pp. 742–48.

142. Most Catholic scholars who accept the basic principles of academic freedom, recognize the excesses often associated with the model in the past, e.g., certain interpretations of scholarly neutrality.

143. John E. Walsh, "The University and the Church," in *Academic Freedom and the Catholic University*, ed. Edward Manier and John W. Houck (Notre Dame, Ind.: Fides Publishers, 1967), p. 109. Walsh writes from the perspective of the philosophy of education.

144. Ibid., p. 105.

145. Ibid., pp. 106–7.

146. Ibid., p. 107.

147. Ibid., p. 108.

148. Ibid., p. 109.

149. Ibid., p. 114.

150. Ibid., p. 111. For brief criticisms of Walsh, see Curran, "Academic Freedom," p. 20; and Rock, "The Catholic and Academic Freedom," p. 256.

151. Ladislas M. Orsy, "Academic Freedom and the Teaching Church," *Thought* 43 (Winter 1968): 486.

152. Ibid., pp. 490–91.

153. Ibid., p. 488.

154. Ibid.

155. Ibid.

156. Ibid., p. 492.

157. Ibid., p. 494.

158. Ibid., p. 495.

159. Ibid.

160. Ibid., p. 496.

161. See Robert E. Hunt, "Academic Freedom and the Theologian," *Proceedings of the Catholic Theological Society of America* 23 (1968): 261–67; Gunti, "Academic Freedom as an Operative Principle," chap. 9; Curran, "Academic Freedom," pp. 748–53.

162. Hunt, "Academic Freedom and the Theologian," p. 265.

163. Gunti, "Academic Freedom as an Operative Principle," p. 188.

164. Curran, "Academic Freedom," pp. 740, 750–53.

165. Gunti, "Academic Freedom as an Operative Principle," p. 183.

166. Ibid.

167. Hunt, "Academic Freedom and the Theologian," p. 263. For Hunt, "theology is clearly *in* and *for* the Church" (p. 264).

168. Ibid., p. 265.

169. Curran, "Academic Freedom," p. 750.

170. Ibid.

171. Ibid.

172. Ibid., p. 750.

173. Ibid., p. 751.

174. See Gunti, "Academic Freedom as an Operative Principle," p. 267; Curran, "Academic Freedom," p. 751–52; and Hunt, "Academic Freedom and the Theologian," pp. 264–66.

175. Curran, "Academic Freedom," pp. 751–52.

176. Gunti, "Academic Freedom as an Operative Principle," pp. 262–63.

177. Hunt, "Academic Freedom and the Theologian," p. 266.

178. Curran, "Academic Freedom," p. 752.

179. Telephone interview with Charles E. Curran, Washington, D.C., 16 June 1984. There also remains some ambiguity concerning the place of personal faith-commitment in Curran's notion of competence. In a book co-authored with Hunt a number of years ago, Curran affirmed that "theologians must always function within the context and according to the claims of the Roman Catholic faith-commitment." However, in the article quoted above, no mention of faith is found in Curran's description of competence, although the author does state that theology is a discipline that presupposes faith. See Curran and Hunt, *Dissent*, p. 107, and Curran, "Academic Freedom," p. 750. It is being assumed that when Curran speaks of theology presupposing faith he is referring to the fact that the faith of the Church is the object of theology.

180. Curran, "Academic Freedom," p. 752.

181. Donahue, "Catholicism and Academic Freedom," pp. 555–75.

182. Ibid., pp. 565–66.

183. Reprinted in *America* 117 (August 12, 1967): 154–56. This meeting was focused principally upon the problems of the Catholic university, rather than those of the small liberal arts college. See Neil G. McCluskey's "Introduction: This Is How It Happened," in *The Catholic University: A Modern Appraisal*, ed. Neil G. McCluskey (Notre Dame, Ind.: University of Notre Dame Press, 1970), p. 5.

184. McCluskey, "Introduction," pp. 3–4.

185. "Land O'Lakes Statement," p. 154.

186. Ibid., pp. 155–56.

187. McCluskey, "Introduction," p. 9.

188. Ibid.

189. The "1968 Kinshasa Statement" is reprinted in *The Catholic University: A Modern Appraisal*, ed. Neil G. McCluskey (Notre Dame, Ind.: University of Notre Dame Press, 1970), pp. 342–45. See McCluskey, "Introduction," pp. 9–12.

190. McCluskey, "Introduction," pp. 13–14.

191. Ibid., p. 15.

192. Reprinted in *The Catholic University: A Modern Appraisal*, ed. Neil G. McCluskey (Notre Dame, Ind.: University of Notre Dame Press, 1970), pp. 346–65.

193. Ibid., p. 348.

194. Ibid., p. 349.

195. Ibid.

196. Ibid., p. 350.

197. Ibid.

198. Ibid., p. 349.

199. Ibid., p. 350.

200. Ibid.

201. McCluskey, "Introduction," pp. 22–23.

202. "The Results of the Plenary Session of the Sacred Congregation for Catholic Education," October 1969, quoted in McCluskey, "Introduction," p. 23. See also Neil G. McCluskey, "Rome Replies (Act II)," *America* 122 (March 28, 1970): 330–34.

203. McCluskey, "Introduction," p. 23.

204. Ibid., p. 25.

205. "The Catholic University in the Modern World: Explanatory Note on the History and Nature of This Document," in *Why Should the Catholic University Survive?* ed. George A. Kelly (New York: St. John's University Press, 1973), p. 109.

206. IFCU North American Region, "Freedom, Autonomy, and the University," *IDOC International* 39 (January 1972): 79–88.

207. Ibid., p. 86.

208. "Explanatory Note," p. 109.

209. Ibid.

210. Ibid.

211. Reprinted in *The Notre Dame Journal of Education* 4 (1973): 197–216.

212. Ibid., p. 213.

213. Ibid., pp. 213–14.

214. Ibid., p. 214.

215. Ibid., p. 215.

216. Ibid., p. 214.

217. Ibid., p. 215.

218. Ibid.

219. Ibid.

220. Gabriel-Marie Cardinal Garrone, "To the Presidents of Catholic Universities and the Directors of Catholic Institutions of Higher Learning," 25 April 1973, in *Why Should the Catholic University Survive?* ed. George A. Kelly (New York: St. John's University Press, 1973), p. 104.

221. Ibid.

222. Ibid., p. 105.

223. Ibid.

224. Ibid.

225. See, for example, Vatican II, "Church in the Modern World," no. 59, p. 265.

226. First Vatican Council, "Constitution on the Catholic Faith," chap. 4; and Norbert A. Luyten, "Why a Catholic University?" in *The Catholic University: A Modern Appraisal*, ed. Neil G. McCluskey (Notre Dame, Ind.: University of Notre Dame Press, 1970), p. 47.

4.

The Secular Model of Academic Freedom in the United States: A Descriptive Overview

The secular model of academic freedom commonly accepted in the United States is composed of those definitions and principles that are outlined and developed in the literature of the AAUP.[1] Hence, the major part of this chapter will consist of a descriptive survey of the principal statements of this organization. Such an overview will aid in the delineation of the secular notion of academic freedom particularly as it applies to the professor.

Despite widespread agreement on the principles that constitute the secular model of academic freedom, there is no unanimity among scholars concerning the theoretical justification of such freedom.[2] Clearly, the effective practical application of the principles of academic freedom does not require theoretical agreement on the justification of these principles.[3] Nevertheless, any scholarly investigation of the secular model must take note of the absence of such agreement. Therefore, this chapter will also include a categorization and brief examination of the various justifications of academic freedom proposed by contemporary scholars.

THE SECULAR MODEL OF ACADEMIC FREEDOM: AN OVERVIEW OF THE MAJOR DOCUMENTS OF THE AAUP

As Howard Mumford Jones has observed, the term *academic freedom*, in its American usage, is characterized by a certain ambiguity.[4] In theory, Americans acknowledge the two complementary elements of academic freedom that were first elaborated upon in nineteenth-century Germany, *Lernfreiheit* and *Lehrfreiheit*—freedom to learn and freedom to teach. In reality, however, the idea of *Lernfreiheit* has neither been fully developed nor wholeheartedly accepted in the United States.[5] In American academic circles, the term *academic freedom* more often denotes the freedom of the professor than the freedom of the student to learn.

In the admittedly limited study that follows, the American notion of academic freedom will be examined in its broader meaning as the freedom to learn, as well as the freedom to teach. Although the two elements are closely related, (one might convincingly argue interdependent), in the interest of clarity they will be treated separately, commencing with *Lehrfreiheit*—the freedom of the professor.

Lehrfreiheit: The Academic Freedom of the Professor

Perhaps the best place to begin the study of any concept is with an accepted definition of that concept. In the case of the academic freedom of the professor, the "formal definition of it in American terms is that of the American Association of University Professors, to which even the courts now turn when the issue becomes moot."[6] It is to the major statements of the AAUP that we now turn our attention.

1915 Declaration of Principles

Concern over dismissals, coupled with the desire of many professors to form a national organization, prompted the establishment in 1915 of the AAUP with John Dewey as its first president.[7] Not insignificantly, one of the earliest pronouncements of the Association was the "1915 Declaration of Principles" issued by the Committee on Academic Freedom and Tenure. Within this statement, academic freedom is defined as comprising three elements: "freedom of inquiry and research; freedom of teaching within the university or college; and freedom of extramural utterance and action."[8]

According to the authors of the "Declaration," the right to academic freedom arises out of the function of the scholar and the purposes of the university. It is argued that if education is the cornerstone of society, and if the advancement of knowledge is essential to civilization, then the scholar's role is vital to society.[9] The scholar's function "is to deal at first hand, after prolonged and specialized technical training, with sources of knowledge; and to impart the results of their own and of their fellow-specialists' investigation and reflection, both to students and to the general public, without fear or favor."[10] The exercise of this function requires that professors (as well as their institutions) be protected from external pressures—political or financial—that would adulterate the integrity of their work. As the "Declaration" states, "Universities shall be so free that no fair-minded person shall find any excuse for even a suspicion that the utterances of university teachers are shaped or restricted by the judgment, not of professional scholars, but of inexpert and possibly not wholly disinterested persons outside their ranks."[11]

The fulfillment of the purposes of the university also requires an atmosphere of freedom. These purposes, outlined in the "Declaration," are three in number:

(a) To promote inquiry and advance the sum of human knowledge.
(b) To provide general instruction to the students.
(c) To develop experts for various branches of the public service.[12]

It is argued that freedom is essential to the scholar in his or her pursuit of knowledge. Moreover, the transmission of this knowledge to students requires freedom, for as the authors point out, students will lose respect for and confidence in a teacher if they suspect that the teacher is timid in expressing himself or herself honestly, fully, and with complete intellectual integrity.[13] Ultimately, it is not the university alone that is injured by the restriction of academic freedom; society too suffers when the university is prevented from functioning fully and fruitfully.[14]

The "1915 Declaration of Principles" expands upon each of the three aspects of academic freedom and their correlative obligations and limitations. First, it is asserted that scholars must be free to pursue their investigations wherever they may lead, and to publish the results of their research.[15] In regard to conclusions reached and expressed, scholars are not responsible to the trustees of the university who "have neither competency nor moral right to intervene."[16] The scholar is bound, however, to the norm of competence, which requires that the scholar carry out his or her work "in the temper of the scientific inquirer" according to sound scientific methodologies.[17]

Second, scholars should enjoy freedom in instructing their students. The professor must be fair and comprehensive in his or her teaching, introducing the student to the major published investigations of the issues at hand.[18] Although under no obligation to hide his or her own opinions, the "Declaration" does urge discretion when dealing with impressionable, immature students.[19]

The "Declaration" places the prerogative of judging the fitness of the professor within the domain of his or her scholarly peers. This notion of juridical competence is rooted in the notion of scholarly competence: the rules and methods of an expert are known only by other experts. As Walter P. Metzger puts it, "The professional standing of a professor can only be established by experts, and these experts must be chosen from among his professional peers."[20]

Third, as developed in the "Declaration," academic freedom allows free extramural utterances and activities by the professor. In the extramural arena, the scholar is bound neither by a norm of neutrality, nor by a norm of competence. The freedom of the scholar to express his or her opinions on controversial questions and issues—even those that fall-outside his or her area of specialty—must not be restricted. However, scholars are obligated "to avoid hasty or unverified or exaggerated statements, and to refrain from intemperate or sensational modes of expression."[21]

The 1915 AAUP statement also outlines a number of practical principles. It is affirmed that in matters of faculty reappointments (or the denial thereof), the advice and consent of the faculty members should be secured. Moreover, the "Declaration" states that the protection of permanent tenure should be given to all faculty members above the grade of instructor after ten years of service. Grounds for dismissal must be formulated with reasonable definiteness, and those accused of misconduct should have a fair trial before a committee chosen by the faculty.[22]

The 1940 Statement of Principles on Academic Freedom and Tenure

In 1940, the AAUP, together with the Association of American Colleges, issued a report entitled "Statement of Principles on Academic Freedom and Tenure."[23] Endorsed by numerous learned societies and professional associations, this statement remains, in the opinion of most, the prototypical American formulation of the notion of academic freedom.

The "1940 Statement of Principles" begins by affirming that the institution of higher learning exists for the common good. "The common good," the statement continues, "depends upon the free search for truth and its free exposition."[24] Here is given, in brief form, the basis and justification of academic freedom: indirectly, academic freedom promotes the common good. As in past statements, academic freedom is presented as a threefold reality: it includes freedom of research, teaching, and extramural utterances. "The teacher is entitled to full freedom in research and in the publication of the results, subject to the adequate performance of his other academic duties."[25] Moreover, within the classroom the teacher is entitled to freedom in discussing his subject, although the professor is warned against introducing into his teaching any controversial matter that has no relevance to the subject being explored. Any limits on intramural utterances "because of religious or other aims of the institution should be clearly stated in writing at the time of the appointment."[26]

In keeping with the position of the "1915 Declaration of Principles," the 1940 statement affirms the professor's extramural freedom of speech. When expressing himself or herself as a citizen, the professor should be free from institutional censorship and institutional penalty. However, as in the 1915 document, the professor is reminded of his or her responsibilities and obligations in the extramural arena. He or she "should at all times be accurate, should exercise appropriate restraint, should show respect for the opinions of others, and should make every effort to indicate that he is not an institutional spokesman."[27] In both the 1915 and 1940 statements, the professor, although not bound by the principles of neutrality or competence in extramural speech, is nonetheless bound to certain "obligations" to which other citizens are not.

As a clarification of the section dealing with extramural elements in the "1940 Statement of Principles," the AAUP Committee A on Academic Freedom and Tenure released a report in 1964. This report, entitled "Committee A Statement on Extramural Utterances," affirms that "a faculty member's expression of opinion as a citizen cannot constitute grounds for dismissal unless it clearly demonstrates the faculty member's unfitness for his position." In the opinion of the committee, "extramural utterances rarely bear upon the faculty member's fitness for his position."[28] The question that arises is whether this clarification will be effective in guarding against abuses by enemies of academic freedom. There is, however, underlying the entire problem of faculty extramural utterances, a much deeper question. Do extramural utterances have any relation to academic freedom at all, or are they the proper domain of civil freedoms? This question will be addressed in a later section of this chapter.

The "1940 Statement of Principles" presents tenure as "a means to certain ends; specifically: (1) Freedom of teaching and research and of extramural activities and (2) a sufficient degree of economic security to make the profession attractive to men and women of ability."[29] The achievement of these proximate ends is necessary for the fulfillment of the goals of the university. The system of tenure outlined in the 1940 document is based upon the principle that after a probationary period, not to exceed seven years following appointment to the rank of full-time instructor or higher, teachers and researchers should have permanent tenure. During the probationary period, a teacher should enjoy the same academic freedom as all other faculty members.

Once permanent or continuous tenure has been granted, the professor should be terminated only for adequate cause. What constitutes adequate cause is not made explicit in the statement. However, references are made to moral turpitude and incompetence as possible grounds for dismissal.[30] If termination of a tenured faculty member is sought, the matter should "be considered by both a faculty committee and the governing board of the institution."[31] The accused faculty member should be informed, in writing, of the charges against him or her prior to a hearing. At such a hearing, the accused is entitled to testify in his or her own defense and should be permitted the benefit of an advisor of his or her own choosing. The hearing should include the testimony "of teachers and other scholars, either from his own or from other institutions."[32] Professional competence is best judged by a professor's scholarly peers.

The Church-Related College and University

The problem of academic freedom in the church-related institution is addressed in both the 1915 and 1940 documents of the AAUP. In the "1915 Declaration of Principles," the issue is indirectly treated in the context of a discussion of the responsibilities of boards of trustees. When an institution of higher learning is founded by a denomination for the propagation of specific religious doctrines, the authors of the "1915 Declaration" recognize the right of its board to govern the institution in light of this end. However, such institutions "should not be permitted to sail under false colors."[33] Insofar as such an institution restricts intellectual freedom in order to propagate certain doctrines, it remains in a moral sense a "private proprietorship" rather than a "public trust," and has no claim to general support.[34]

The authors' insistence that proprietary institutions not be allowed "to sail under false colors" indicates that such institutions are not considered colleges or universities in the American sense of the term. What is implied is that academic freedom defines the true university, and any abridgment of this freedom undermines the nature of the university while raising ethical questions in the area of "truth in packaging."

The "1940 Statement of Principles" insists that "limitations of academic freedom because of religious or other aims of the institution should be clearly stated in writing at the time of the appointment."[35] It should be noted that this special limitation clause is included within the section of the statement dealing with freedom *in the classroom*. Hence, it is not considered applicable to extramural expression.[36]

During the 1965 Annual Meeting of the AAUP, a motion was passed establishing a committee "to study and make more explicit" the application of the "1940 Statement of Principles" to the denominational context.[37] There arose from this committee a draft statement entitled "Statement on Academic Freedom in Church-Related Colleges and Universities."[38] In the report of the committee issued with the statement, committee chairman William J. Kilgore states that "the Association from its beginning has insisted that any restrictions on the academic freedom of faculties in church-related or proprietary institutions be directly related to institutional aims, and that they be published. And it has noted that each restriction might diminish the institution's academic effectiveness and standing."[39] Quoting a 1964 report, Kilgore pointed out that there comes a point under such restrictions, that a college or university may "cease to be an institution of higher education according to the prevailing conception."[40]

The "Statement on Academic Freedom in Church-Related Colleges and Universities" affirms that faculty members of church-related institutions must be fully protected under the principles of the "1958 Statement on Procedural Standards in Faculty Dismissal Proceedings" and the "1964 Statement on Extramural Utterances."[41] Moreover, the "Statement" makes the following recommendations:

1. Any limitation on academic freedom should be essential to the religious aims of the institution, and should be imposed only after consultation among faculty, administration, and governing body. Student opinion on such limitation also would be helpful.
2. Such limitation, with its supporting rationale and relevance to the institution's educational objectives, should be clearly stated in writing with reasonable particularity and made a matter of public knowledge.
3. The faculty member should respect the stated aims of an institution to which he accepts an appointment, but academic freedom protects his right to express, clarify, and interpret positions—including those identified as his own—which are divergent from those of the institution and of the church which supports it.
4. The faculty member, lay or clerical, should not be subject to discriminatory or preferential treatment based on religious grounds with respect to professional privileges, opportunities, and advancements.[42]

It should be pointed out that the committee did not perceive as its task the judgment of whether the limitation clause of the "1940 Statement" should be eliminated. Hence, it devoted its attention to the clarification of the clause, leaving aside the question of its retention or abandonment.

Questions concerning the limitation clause in the "1940 Statement of Principles" were in theory resolved following the publication, in 1970, of "Interpretive Comments" on that statement. These interpretations—approved by the Council of the AAUP and endorsed as Association policy in April 1970—include the declaration that "Most church-related institutions no longer need or desire the departure from the principle of academic freedom implied in the 1940 Statement, and we do not now endorse such a departure."[43] It would appear that the AAUP will no longer allow limitations of academic freedom on church-related campuses to be legitimated on the basis of the special limitation clause of the "1940 Statement of Principles."

Lernfreiheit: The Freedom to Learn

As we have seen, the nineteenth-century German notion of academic freedom was composed of two inseparable ideas: *Lehrfreiheit* and *Lernfreiheit*.[44] The student in Germany did not merely enjoy the fruits of his professor's freedom, but also possessed the privilege of academic freedom.[45] When the German concept of academic freedom reached the shores of the United States, it underwent a transformation. One aspect of this transformation was the abandonment of a strong notion of *Lern-freiheit*, especially as applied to the undergraduate. For instance, after defining academic freedom as including the idea of *Lernfreiheit*, as well as *Lehrfreiheit*, the authors of the "1915 Declaration of Principles" state that it "need scarcely be pointed out that the freedom which is the subject of this report is that of the teacher."[46] This phrase would set the tone of the next fifty years—the amount of time before the AAUP would release a comprehensive statement on academic freedom as it applies to the student.

To what can the de-emphasizing of *Lernfreiheit* be attributed? Metzger speculates that the advances made in the area of student rights in the late nineteenth century (e.g., the elective system), together with the frequency of friction between professors and administrations, tended to shift attention almost exclusively to *Lehrfreiheit*.[47] Although this elucidates the context in which the "1915 Declaration of Principles" arose, it cannot explain the continuing lack of emphasis upon *Lernfreiheit* in the United States.

Jones offers an explanation for this ongoing neglect of the idea of *Lernfreiheit*. He points out that "American institutions have had to accept a quality of responsibility for student learning that differs significantly from the old German theory."[48] There have been four reasons for this. First, the college *had* traditionally been viewed as standing *in loco parentis* with reference to its students.[49] Thus, colleges were required to accept a responsibility for student welfare unknown to the Germans. A second, and related reason is that the American college has attempted to be home away from home, offering a variety of services (residential, social, religious, medical) that have necessitated the creation of innumerable college regulations.[50]

The attitude of the student is the third reason. Jones claims that the American inability to accept the total concept of *Lernfreiheit* is partially the fault of students themselves who want freedom, but not the accompanying responsibility. American students want a structured course of studies. They "want a pattern to adhere to so that they will know when they are done; they want, having paid out their money or their parents' money, to receive tangible wares in return."[51] Although this attitude is very often found among undergraduates, it is not unknown among graduate students.

Finally, the structure of the American university has not been conducive to the development of a strong idea of *Lernfreiheit*. The Continental university often confers only the Ph.D. Thus, a German university student is, what would be considered in the United States, a graduate student. The first two years of American undergraduate instruction are more akin to secondary school than to university study in the Continental sense. Hence, the American professor must deal with immaturities not faced by his German counterparts.

In order to have risen above these factors and survived, a strong concept of *Lernfreiheit* would have needed many professorial defenders. Generally speaking, few came forth. However, the place of the idea of *Lernfreiheit* has improved in recent years. Support for the student's right to due process of law first came from the case of *Dixon v. Alabama State Board of Education*, 294 F.2d 150 (1961). Students, in good standing, were expelled from Alabama State College for participating in a civil rights demonstration. They were expelled without notice, hearing, or appeal, and thus claimed that they were deprived of due process of law. The court ruled in the students' favor.[52] The student's right to due process of law within the university would later be reaffirmed by the AAUP "1964 Statement on the Academic Freedom of Students," to which we now turn.

The "Statement on the Academic Freedom of Students" represents the first comprehensive report on the subject issued by the AAUP and virtually the first statement of its kind to arise out of the American academic community.[53] This document was passed as a tentative statement of Association policy with the hope that a joint statement issued with other national organizations would follow. A statement was formulated in 1967 by a committee composed of representatives of the AAUP, the National Student Association, the Association of American Colleges, the National Association of Student Personnel Administrators, and the National Association of Women Deans and Counselors. This document—"The Joint Statement on Rights and Freedoms of Students"—is similar in tone and content to the earlier AAUP statement.[54]

The 1967 statement elaborates upon the notion of student academic freedom as it applies to six areas: access to higher education, the classroom, student records, student affairs, off-campus activities, and disciplinary proceedings. It is affirmed that admission policies are a matter of institutional choice, though no student should be denied admission to an institution because of race. While a church-related institution may give preference to applicants who are members of its sponsoring church, this preference must be stated clearly and publicly.

In the classroom, students should be allowed freedom of expression. They "should be free to take reasoned exception to the data or views offered . . . and to reserve judgment about matters of opinion."[55] The evaluation of students should be based solely on academic criteria, and students should be protected from the improper disclosure of their views, beliefs, and political associations as expressed to their professors. The method of keeping student records must respect the freedom of the student.[56] Under no circumstance should records of the political activities or beliefs of students be kept.

In its section on student affairs, the statement affirms that on the college campus, students should enjoy freedom of association. "Students and student organizations should be free to examine and to discuss all questions of interest to them, and to express opinions publicly and privately."[57] They should be entitled to invite and hear guest speakers of their choice. In this regard, institutional control of facilities should never be used as a method of censorship. Students should be free to express their views on institutional policy, and student publications should be immune from censorship.

Off campus, the student enjoys the same rights and freedoms as every other citizen. If off-campus activities result in the violation of a civil law, institutional authority should not be used to duplicate the penalties imposed by civil authority. "Only where the institution's interests as an academic community are distinct and clearly involved should the special authority of the institution be asserted."[58]

The final section of the statement deals with disciplinary procedures. Students should be held accountable only for standards of conduct that have been formulated with student participation and published in advance. A student accused of serious misconduct should have the right to a hearing before a regularly constituted committee that may be composed of both faculty and student members. The accused should be entitled to choose an advisor for the hearing, to present evidence and witnesses, and to testify on his or her own behalf.

The "1967 Joint Statement on Rights and Freedoms of Students" outlined above is a significant step toward salvaging the notion of *Lernfreiheit* in the United States. It goes well beyond those theories that consider *Lernfreiheit* as merely the advantages of *Lehrfreiheit* as they affect the student.[59] It might be pointed out, however, that this statement, like the 1964 AAUP statement, pays relatively little attention to freedom as applied to strictly academic matters, and emphasizes those issues that might be considered "campus civil rights."

The limits of the academic freedom of undergraduate students remain disputed. Although most theorists would accept the validity of an elective system, few would be willing to give students actual power over the curriculum. Most would reject such an extension of student freedom on the grounds outlined by John S. Brubacher. He points out that the choice of lecture subjects and the selection of problems for research are the proper domain of *Lehrfreiheit*, which "is the privilege of those disciplined in the techniques of handling the higher learning. Since students are only beginners, they are not mature enough scholars for full academic freedom."[60] Hence, in Brubacher's view, the notion of competence would argue against extreme extensions of student power into strictly academic areas. It is a view that is difficult to dispute. In accepting it, however, one need not deny the importance of student input into all areas of university governance, especially those having a direct relation to the curriculum.

JUSTIFICATIONS OF THE ACADEMIC FREEDOM OF THE PROFESSOR

According to Sidney Hook, the academic freedom of the professor can be defined as "the freedom of professionally qualified persons to inquire, discover, publish and teach the truth as they see it in the field of their competence, without any control or authority except the control or authority of the rational methods by which truth is established."[61] On what basis is this freedom justified? Educational theorists have offered various arguments in support of the right to academic freedom. These are usually wedded—implicitly or explicitly—to a particular view of the nature and purpose of higher learning, or what might be called a philosophy of higher education.

Prior to presenting an overview of the justifications of academic freedom developed by educational theorists, the philosophies of higher education to which these various justifications are implicitly or explicitly related will be examined briefly. The twofold typology of philosophies of higher learning that will be developed can then serve as the basis of a categorization that, despite its limitations, will be helpful in the examination of current justifications of academic freedom.

Philosophies Legitimating Higher Education

Knowledge can be regarded as an end in itself or as a means to another end. To those for whom knowledge is capable of being its own end, the pursuit of knowledge is an intrinsically worthwhile undertaking that requires no legitimation beyond that which arises from the recognition of the eminently human and intellect-perfecting character of such pursuit. However, knowledge or the pursuit thereof is valued by some principally because it is a means to an important end, be it action, production, or application. Knowledge from this perspective is considered significant for its contribution to the common good or to the body politic. Adopting Aristotelian terminology, the former approach to knowledge and higher learning will be labeled *theoretical*, the latter *practical*.[62]

It may be recalled that Aristotle distinguishes between theoretical sciences, the end of which is knowledge (or the perfection of the intellect), and practical sciences, the end of which is action.[63] Theoretical knowledge is pursued for its own sake, while practical knowledge is pursued for the sake of action.[64] It should be noted:

> Aristotle sometimes isolates the practical sciences in general by this contrast to the theoretical sciences, and sometimes when his attention is turned to the differences among the ends of human purposes and operations, he differentiates the processes of making, which depend on an external matter, from those of doing, and thereby separates the arts from the virtues or the productive sciences from the practical sciences in the strict or narrow sense.[65]

Thus in *Topics*, Aristotle presents a threefold division of knowledge: theoretical, practical, and productive.[66] However, in adapting Aristotle's terminology to the purposes of the present work, only the two general classifications of theoretical and practical knowledge will be utilized.

The two categories to be employed are organizational tools that constitute "ideal types" in the sense described by Max Weber.[67] Hence, they will not be found in reality in a "pure" form; nor will the theorists subsumed under each category "fit" unambiguously. Moreover, in contradistinction to Aristotle's usage of the terms theoretical and practical, within the present work they do not represent divisions of the sciences or of academic disciplines, but rather describe broad approaches to knowledge that have undergirded legitimations of higher education in general and justifications of academic freedom in particular.

Theoretical Philosophy of Higher Learning

Within the ideal type, which has been termed the theoretical approach to higher learning, the university is conceived of as the place wherein the *self-legitimating* search for truth is carried out.[68] This quest for truth is valued not for its social utility or as a means to other ends, but as an intrinsically worthwhile undertaking. Robert Nisbet writes that the "dogma" upon which the university is built is simply: "Knowledge is important. Not 'relevant' knowledge; not 'practical' knowledge; not the kind of knowledge that enables one to wield power, achieve success, or influence others. Knowledge!"[69] From this perspective then, "knowledge is capable of being its own end."[70]

Accompanying the theoretical philosophy of higher education is a particular conception of the nature of the scholar's task. It is unequivocally affirmed that the scholar's first responsibility is to the truth. Kenneth Minogue has remarked that while in the world of practice the relevant criterion is effectiveness—that which "works," in the academic world the only relevant criterion is that of truth or falsity.[71]

Hence, scholars whose thought approximates the theoretical philosophy of higher education tend to separate, to varying degrees, the academic and the practical worlds. Although not necessarily viewing the university as an isolated ivory tower, these thinkers insist that the university's central functions be made clear. The identification of these functions vary somewhat from writer to writer. Abraham Flexner, for example, defines the university as "an institution consciously devoted to the pursuit of knowledge, the solution of problems, the critical appreciation of achievement, and the training of men at a really high level."[72] Nisbet, whose formulation of the "academic dogma" was presented earlier, conceives of the university as an institution devoted to "the discovery and the teaching of knowledge as this was made manifest by cumulative scholarship."[73]

As early as 1930, Abraham Flexner was lamenting the fact that American universities had "needlessly cheapened, vulgarized, and mechanized themselves."[74] They had, in his estimation, lost sight of their purposes, having become "secondary schools, vocational schools, teacher-training schools, research centers, 'uplift' agencies, businesses—these and other things simultaneously."[75]

Nisbet has more recently voiced a similar indictment of American colleges and universities. While recognizing that from earliest times the university was "predicated upon a powerful sense of service to society," he argues that the service offered by the university was always *indirect*.[76] This indirect service function is exercised through the preparation of students who "go forth and serve the more important, the widely recognized needs of the social order."[77] However, in recent decades, universities have become clearinghouses for direct service to agriculture, business, government, and society in general. The principal purposes of the university—the self-legitimating accumulation and transmission of knowledge—have been obscured by its preoccupation with practical pursuits.[78]

The practical approach to knowledge is, according to Minogue, incongruous with what should be the activity of university scholars. "Academic inquiry is a manner of seeking to understand anything at all, . . . distinguished above all by a quite different logic from that of practice."[79] The logic of practice is based upon application, while the university deals primarily with pure theory.[80] How theory is applied "depends upon ends generated by human desires, which it is no business of the universities to inquire into."[81]

Related to this view are the very different criteria under which the practical and academic worlds operate. Minogue writes that "in the academic world the only relevant criterion is that of truth or falsity; in practice, on the other hand, the criterion may be summed up in portmanteau fashion as effectiveness. Truth is very frequently a part of effectiveness, but by no means the only part (or indeed, in many cases, the main part)."[82]

From this perspective then, the injection of practical pursuits and responsibilities into the university imposes foreign criteria and, indeed, a foreign "logic" upon it. Moreover, the "practical" distracts the university scholar from the central task of the university—the self-legitimating pursuit of truth and the transmission of knowledge.

Practical Philosophy of Higher Education

Within the practical approach to higher learning, knowledge is not merely valued for its own sake, but also as a means toward political or social ends.[83] From this perspective, service to society is included among the goals and functions of the university.

The practical legitimation of higher education has come to ascendance as universities have been increasingly called upon to address the problems of government, industry, agriculture, and social welfare.[84] In the United States, this tendency toward social service began with the "land grant movement." The Morrill Act of 1862 was enacted in response to rapid industrial and agricultural development.[85] The universities founded under the provisions of this act were to assist national development through training and research related to farming and manufacturing.[86]

The movement toward a service role for the American university was greatly accelerated by the federal support of scientific research that began on a large scale during World War II.[87] By 1960, seventy-five percent of all university research was funded by the federal government, most of it in scientific areas.[88] Moreover, in recent decades there has also developed a close relationship between industry and the major universities.[89]

What has been termed the practical philosophy of higher learning encompasses a number of diverse approaches to higher education including some that are quite radical. A moderate representation of the practical philosophy can be found in the work of Clark Kerr. In his brief book *The Uses of the University*, Kerr not only describes, but also seems to celebrate the modern university—the "multiversity"—in service to government and industry.[90] Addressing the concerns of those who believe that such social service is an adulteration of the mission of the university, Kerr writes:

There are those who fear the further involvement of the university in the life of society. . . .There are those who fear that the university will be drawn too far from basic to applied research and from applied research to application itself. But the lines dividing these never have been entirely clear and much new knowledge has been generated at the borders of basic and applied research and even of applied knowledge and its application.[91]

Apparently, Kerr rejects a narrowly conceived theoretical approach to higher education and the strict differentiation of the academic and practical worlds.

In a more radical vein, William Arrowsmith argues that what the contemporary world needs is a new kind of higher educational institution—"a college or university of the public interest "[92] He believes that current world problems must be addressed not in a fragmentary way by specialists concerned with particular aspects of such problems, but holistically so that specialized skill can be exercised in the context of larger concerns.[93] Arrowsmith would plunge the university deeply into the waters of social service. This would, in his view, necessitate the abandonment of many conventional educational notions. He writes:

Do away with "disinterestedness," and the old invidious distinctions between "research" and "application," between "scholarship" and "popularization," between "pure" and "applied" knowledge, immediately vanish, as they should. We can no longer indulge in the old classical contempt for the practical, by which "pure" scientists talk of technology and engineeers with the contempt reserved by the humanists for the mass media and the popularizer. We should also radically modify the assumption that the university's function is to produce knowledge or pursue truth, and that the public applications of knowledge can safely be left to others.[94]

Arrowsmith would have the university not only engaged in social service, but also performing an active leadership role in the solving of world problems.[95]

Despite a diversity of perspectives within the practical approach, an emphasis on the uses of knowledge—particularly its contribution to the common good—remains the unifying factor in this approach. Therefore, for those who accept a practical legitimation of higher education, the ends of the university could be identified as "the preservation of the eternal truths, the creation of new knowledge," *and* "the improvement of service wherever truth and knowledge of high order may serve the needs of man."[96]

Theoretical Justifications of Academic Freedom

Theoretical justifications of academic freedom are related—implicitly or explicitly—to the theoretical philosophy of higher learning examined briefly above. The basic foundation of these justifications is the view that the pursuit of knowledge is a value in itself, a self-legitimating activity. As such, those who have dedicated their lives to this activity are said to have a right to the freedom necessary to its performance.

This view arises out of particular conceptions of the nature of the human being, and of the nature and dynamics of the pursuit of knowledge (or of the intellectual task). For example, from this perspective it can be argued that the pursuit of knowledge is an eminently human undertaking, an undertaking that perfects the intellect, humanizes and liberates the human being, and expresses the transcendence of the human spirit. As such, one frustrates such an activity only at the risk of violating a basic human right or compromising human dignity. It is claimed, therefore, that academic freedom—an atmosphere necessary to the pursuit of knowledge—must be protected.

Russell Kirk clearly adopts a theoretical justification for the right to academic freedom. Rejecting the practical social-utilitarian argument in support of such a right, Kirk states:

I do not think that academic freedom deserves preservation chiefly because it "serves the community," though this incidental function is important. I think, rather that the principal importance of academic freedom is the opportunity it affords for the highest development of private reason and imagination, the improvement of mind and heart by the apprehension of Truth, whether or not that development is of any immediate use to "democratic society."[97]

In Kirk's estimation, to justify academic freedom on the basis of its direct or indirect contribution to the well-being of a particular society, is to place a scholar's responsibility to that community before his or her responsibility to truth, and ultimately to leave the scholar vulnerable to the whims and prejudices of the multitude.[98]

Kirk constructs his own justification of academic freedom on the basis of a conception of natural law, arguing that academic freedom is a natural right arising out of this law.[99] He does make it clear, however, that the right to academic freedom is not to be identified with the general "human" or "civil" right to free speech, for academic freedom is a privilege enjoyed only by members of the academy.[100] Drawing upon historical evidence, Kirk argues that

in the Middle Ages, as in classical times, the academy possessed freedom unknown to other bodies and persons because the philosopher, the scholar, and the student were looked upon as men consecrated to the service of Truth; and that Truth was not simply a purposeless groping after miscellaneous information, but a wisdom to be obtained, however imperfectly, from a teleological search.[101]

Academic freedom, then, is a natural right of those who are what Kirk terms "Bearers of the Word"—those whose lives are dedicated to the service of the Truth.[102] It should be noted, however, that Kirk's conception of abiding Truth has religious dimensions which remain non-specific or unthematic. Ultimately, his justification of academic freedom as a natural right of scholars is based upon the existence of a First Truth or an Author of Being. Indeed, Kirk argues that scholars who "will not acknowledge the Author of their being have no sanction for truth," or at least no unalterable sanction.[103] "Dedication to an abiding Truth and to the spiritual aspirations of humanity excised, we would be left with no reason for learning, or for freedom, except service to 'the people'.

And what is man, that we should serve him, except that man is made, however imperfectly, in the image of Another?"[104] Academic freedom—indeed the entire scholarly endeavor—is, for Kirk, integrally related to the Transcendent.

Although Nisbet does not offer his readers a developed justification of academic freedom, his brief discussion of the basis of this freedom in *The Degradation of the Academic Dogma* indicates that he approaches the subject from the perspective of the theoretical. Nisbet views academic freedom as rooted in the "academic dogma" that has traditionally undergirded the academy: namely, the notion that knowledge—for its own sake—is important.

Nisbet argues that the academic dogma is (and has been) accompanied by certain attendant concepts, among them the concept of honor.[105] It is this concept that is most directly linked to the notion of academic freedom. Nisbet claims that the notion of freedom has traditionally carried a specialized meaning in academic circles.

And this meaning was rooted deeply in the prior notion of the differential honor that inhered in scholarship and science. What this meaning suggested was that along with the ordinary civil and political rights possessed by all citizens in a democracy was the right flowing directly from academic function that made for full autonomy in the performance of one's academic duties.[106]

Academic freedom, then, has traditionally been a privilege that accompanies the honor inherent in dedication to the pursuit of knowledge, a pursuit that is an intrinsically worthwhile undertaking.

Prior to bringing this section to a close, it should be pointed out that some justifications of academic freedom have been offered that purportedly avoid a practical social-utilitarian argument by basing such freedom on "moral" grounds. Hardy E. Jones, for example, affirms that academic freedom is a moral right that arises out of the respective obligations of the university and the scholar.[107] Educational institutions expect (or should expect) the scholar to seek the truth. Therefore, academics have the obligation to teach and publish that which they believe to be true. The university, on the other hand, has the obligation to allow the scholar to carry out that which the university expects of him. Hence, it has the obligation to allow and to protect the academic freedom of the faculty member.[108]

A question arises, however. Why ought a university expect (and allow) the scholar to seek the truth? Jones addresses this question as follows:

The moral obligation to seek the truth, and thus the right of academic freedom to teach and publish, can be based on the significant fact that the circumstances and consequences of human actions are morally relevant and crucially important in deciding what ought to be done. One of the main sources of moral perplexity is that we do not know enough of what are commonly called "the facts." By seeking the truth and by giving professors the security and freedom to do so as a vocation, agents are put in a better position for knowing what to do.[109]

Academic freedom indirectly advances the human ability to make responsible ethical decisions and is, therefore, justified. Ultimately this "moral argument" defends academic freedom on the basis of its social usefulness, or on the relevance of the knowledge whose discovery such freedom facilitates.[110] It is to such practical justifications that attention will now be directed.

Practical Justifications of Academic Freedom

Generally speaking, practical justifications of academic freedom defend such freedom as necessary for the generation of socially useful or relevant knowledge. A practical justification might, therefore, take the following form:

(1) the aim of the university is to advance well-being or at least to minimize misery; (2) a necessary condition of the advancement of either of these ends is the discovery, publication, and teaching of the truth; (3) the discovery, publication, and teaching of the truth can only take place in the presence of academic freedom; and (4) therefore academic freedom should be allowed to each academic.[111]

This argument is similar to those advanced in the "1915 Declaration of Principles" and the "1940 Statement of Principles." As we have seen, within the "1915 Declaration," it is argued that the need for academic freedom is intrinsically related to the nature of the university and of the scholar's task, which is the disinterested pursuit and transmission of knowledge. Yet the authors of the document ultimately fall back upon a practical justification of academic freedom, pointing out that "any restriction upon the freedom of the instructor is bound to react injuriously upon the efficiency and the *morale* of the institution, and therefore utlimately upon the interests of the community."[112] The "1940 Statement" is more directly practical in its justification of academic freedom as is evidenced by its clear affirmation that the "common good depends upon the free search for truth and its free exposition."[113]

Most educational theorists tend to justify academic freedom on a practical basis.[114] Sidney Hook, for example, claims that the justification of academic freedom lies in its "fruits."[115] He argues that there are at least five reasons why a community should recognize the validity of the claim to such freedom. First, academic freedom allows truth and new knowledge to be more easily pursued. Second, "academic freedom, by enabling alternative policies to be stated, and by permitting inquiry into facts which are relevant to decisions of policy, contributes to the development of human wisdom."[116] Third, freedom of inquiry aids in the discovery of solutions to the problems of society. Fourth, academic freedom is necessary for the development of a critical temper among students. "Finally, limitations today upon academic freedom tend to weaken the vitality of intellectual and cultural freedom in the community at large."[117]

In Hook's view, his partial list of justifications of academic freedom shows that they have one thing in common: "they point to the fact that academic freedom exists not merely for the sake of the professor but for the sake of the community also, and that its ultimate fruits are to be found not in the private, professional delight of the connoisseur of ideas, . . . but in the public good."[118] Hook does recognize that justifications of academic freedom are not absolute, and he offers two conditions under which a society may legitimately limit the academic freedom of a university: if an institution were unable to achieve its educational goals (transmission of knowledge, etc.), or if the university violated moral values more fundamental than the university's right to seek the truth (e.g., cruel human experimentation).

Robert M. MacIver also justifies academic freedom on the basis of its social usefulness. In *Academic Freedom in Our Time*, he writes that "the open search for truth has rendered great services to mankind. . . . From this function the claim to academic freedom derives."[119]

Similarly, in the landmark Supreme Court decision of *Sweezy v. New Hampshire*, Justice Felix Frankfurter advances a practical argument on behalf of academic freedom. With reference to the social sciences, he states:

For society's good—if understanding be an essential need of society—inquiries into these problems, speculations about them, stimulation in others of reflection upon them must be left as unfettered as possible. Political power must abstain from intrusion into this activity of freedom pursued in the interest of wise government and the people's well-being, except for reasons that are exigent and obviously compelling.[120]

Hence, knowledge or "understanding" is assumed to be an "essential need" of society, while academic freedom is assumed to be a necessary prerequisite for the advancement of such knowledge.

Elements of both theoretical and practical approaches to the justification of academic freedom can be perceived in the work of those Catholic theorists who would support the extension of such freedom to the Catholic university. Adopting a largely theoretical justification of academic freedom, Frederick W. Gunti argues that academic freedom is a basic human right that flows from human dignity and, in the case of theology, from the responsibilities that accompany the exercise of the "theological ministry."[121] John E. Walsh also justifies academic freedom principally on theoretical grounds. In his view, such freedom is based on the nature of teaching (and of learning) and the accompanying obligation of intellectual honesty.[122]

Charles E. Curran justifies academic freedom on practical and theoretical grounds. In general terms, he argues that academic freedom fosters and is, therefore, based upon the common good because society is best served by institutions of higher education (Catholic and non-Catholic) wherein truth is freely pursued and disseminated.[123] When he deals with the specific issue of the academic freedom of the theologian in the Catholic university, his justification of such freedom becomes twofold. From a theological perspective, the right to academic freedom flows from the nature of the discipline of theology and from the interpretive function of the theologian vis-à-vis the sources of revelation and the teaching of the hierarchical *Magisterium*.[124] However, adopting a practical line of argumentation, he adds that academic freedom is not only good for theology and the university, but also for the Church.[125] The church is best served when theologians are able to pursue their endeavors freely.

Academic Freedom and Civil Liberty

Most scholars distinguish between academic freedom and the freedom of speech regarded in many societies as a civil right. For example, Hook writes that "the right of academic freedom is not a civil right or a human right despite widespread opinion to the contrary."[126] Machlup points out that "academic freedom requires special safeguards quite different from those provided by the freedom of speech guaranteed in the Constitution."[127] Finally, Kirk, while defining academic freedom as a natural right, limits its applicability to academics alone. He asserts that academic freedom "is the right, or group of rights, intended to make it possible for certain persons (always few in number, in any society, when compared with the bulk of the population) to teach truthfully and to employ their reason to the full extent of their intellectual powers."[128]

William Van Alstyne points out that the difference between academic freedom and the civil right to free speech has been obscured, with negative results. Among the more important is the identification of violations of the professor's right to speak politically outside the university with violations of his or her academic freedom. Such an identification invites an inappropriate review—in light of a professional standard—of the professor's extramural utterances.[129] This is precisely the trap into which the 1915 and 1940 AAUP statements have fallen.

For Van Alstyne, academic freedom specifically applies to the research, teaching, and publication of any subject of professional interest. In these pursuits, the scholar should be free from vocational jeopardy except in cases involving a breach of professional integrity. When no claim of professional academic endeavor is present (e.g., in the case of professors' political activities), the claim of academic freedom cannot be invoked. Non-professional activity is neither covered by academic freedom nor bound by the special accountability that accompanies this freedom. Thus, all institutional penalties that result from the non-professional activity of a scholar are a violation of that scholar's civil rights, not of his or her academic freedom.[130]

John R. Searle takes a much different view of the relation between academic freedom and civil liberties. In polar opposition to Van Alstyne, Searle states that the "special" or limited definition of academic freedom is inadequate. By special theory, he means "the right to pursue knowledge enjoying freedom of inquiry and ... the right to disseminate that knowledge in the classroom and through publication."[131] Such a theory, he states, fails to cover the plight of the physics professor who, because of extramural political activities, is fired. In its place he offers a new "general" theory of academic freedom: "Professors and students have the same rights of free expression, freedom of inquiry, freedom of association, and freedom of publication in their roles as professors and students that they have as citizens in a free society, except insofar as the mode of exercise of these freedoms needs to be restricted to preserve the academic and subsidiary functions of the university."[132]

Searle does not advocate the abandonment of the special theory. Doing so would compromise the position of universities situated in those countries where civil rights are not well protected. Moreover, he argues that even in the context of a free society, both theories are necessary. Since most academic freedom cases in the past have involved extramural activities or utterances, the general theory is a necessary supplement to the special theory.

Searle is attempting to extend the notion of academic freedom to the same area from which Van Alstyne wishes to remove it. In doing so, he has identified academic freedom as one application of general civil liberty. Aside from his somewhat ambiguous retention of the special theory, one can rightfully question whether Searle, in outlining the general theory, is sketching a theory of academic freedom at all.[133]

In recent years, American courts have come to see "academic freedom as an indispensable dimension of First Amendment rights."[134] The AAUP "Interpretive Comments" on the "1940 Statement of Principles," reflect a recognition of this fact.[135] Yet, Van Alstyne has pointed out that "it is clear that closure between the First Amendment and a distinct right of academic freedom has not yet been made."[136] Part of the reason for this, according to Van Alstyne, is the tendency to blur the difference between academic freedom and the freedom of speech. Hence, the identification of academic freedom (narrowly construed as freedom of research, teaching and publication) as a subset of First Amendment rights has been postponed because of the tendency within the academic community to consider reprisals for the non-professional activities of a scholar a violation of his or her academic freedom, rather than a violation of the scholar's civil right to freedom of speech.[137]

CONCLUSION

In this chapter, the principles and rubrics that constitute the American secular model of academic freedom have been described through an examination of the major documents of the AAUP. In an effort to set these principles into a broader context, an overview of the principal justifications of academic freedom has been offered.

Thus far, our approach to the various models of academic freedom—Catholic and secular—has been generally descriptive. No critique of these models has been offered; nor has the applicability of the American model of academic freedom to the Catholic context been discussed. It is these tasks that will occupy our attention in the chapters that follow.

NOTES

1. See Howard Mumford Jones, "The American Concept of Academic Freedom," *The American Scholar* 29 (1960): 98.

2. Edmund L. Pincoffs, "Introduction," in *The Concept of Academic Freedom*, ed. Edmund L. Pincoffs (Austin: University of Texas Press, 1974).

3. Edward Manier, "Introduction," in *Academic Freedom and the Catholic University*, ed. Edward Manier and John W. Houck (Notre Dame, Ind.: Fides Publishers, 1967), p.2.

4. Jones, "American Concept of Academic Freedom," pp. 94–95.

5. Ibid.

6. Ibid., p. 98.

7. See Hofstadter and Metzger, *Development of Academic Freedom*, pp. 468–77.

8. AAUP, "1915 Declaration of Principles," p. 93.

9. Ibid., p. 97.

10. Ibid.

11. Ibid., p. 98.

12. Ibid., p. 99.

13. Ibid., p. 100.

14. Ibid., p. 101.

15. Ibid., p. 100.

16. Ibid., p. 98.

17. Ibid., p. 104.

18. Ibid., p. 105.

19. Ibid., p. 106.

20. Hofstadter and Metzger, *Development of Academic Freedom*, p. 365. See AAUP, "1915 Declaration of Principles," pp. 105–6. In the "1915 Declaration"

it is acknowledged that trustees are competent to judge cases of habitual neglect of duty and grave moral delinquency (p. 109).

21. AAUP, "1915 Declaration of Principles," p. 108.

22. Ibid , pp. 110–11.

23. The 1940 document superseded the brief "1925 Conference Statement," *AAUP Bulletin* 45 (March 1959): 110–111.

24. AAUP, "1940 Statement of Principles," p. 108.

25. Ibid.

26. Ibid.

27. Ibid.

28. AAUP, "Committee A Statement on Extramural Utterances," *AAUP Bulletin* 51 (Spring 1965): 29.

29. AAUP, "1940 Statement of Principles," p. 108. See Fritz Machlup, "In Defense of Academic Tenure," *AAUP Bulletin* 50 (1964): 112–24; and *The Concept of Academic Freedom*, ed. Edmund L. Pincoffs (Austin: University of Texas Press, 1975).

30. See note 8 in *Academic Freedom and Tenure*, ed. Louis Joughin (Madison, Wis.: University of Wisconsin Press, 1967), p. 37. On the meaning of "moral turpitude," see the AAUP, "Academic Freedom and Tenure: 1940 Statement of Principles and Interpretive Comments," *AAUP Bulletin* 56 (Fall 1970): 325–26. Academic freedom is not synonymous with academic license; hence, the rights associated with academic freedom carry with them correlative duties and obligations. See AAUP, "1966 Statement on Professional Ethics," in *Academic Freedom and Tenure*, ed. Louis Joughin (Madison, Wis.: University of Wisconsin Press, 1967), pp. 87–89.

31. AAUP, "1940 Statement of Principles," p. 109.

32. Ibid. See the AAUP, "1958 Statement on Procedural Standards in Faculty Dismissal Proceedings," in *Academic Freedom and Tenure*, ed. Louis Joughin (Madison, Wis.: University of Wisconsin Press, 1967), pp. 40–45.

33. AAUP, "1915 Declaration of Principles," p. 95.

34. Ibid., pp. 95–96.

35. AAUP, "1940 Statement of Principles," p. 108.

36. Hunt, et al., *Responsibility of Dissent*, pp. 87–88

37. "Report of the Special Committee on Academic Freedom in Church-Related Colleges and Universities," by W. J. Kilgore, Chairman, *AAUP Bulletin* 53 (Winter 1967): 369.

38. *AAUP Bulletin* 53 (Winter 1967): 370–71.

39. Kilgore, "Report of the Special Committee," p. 369.

40. Ibid.

41. AAUP, "Statement on Academic Freedom in Church-Related Colleges and Universities," p. 370.

42. Ibid., pp. 370–71.

43. AAUP, "Interpretive Comments," p. 325. While affirming the basic principles and procedures of academic freedom commonly accepted in the United States, a 1960 statement of the American Association of Theological Schools interprets these principles in light of the confessional commitment of the institution. Hence, it is stated that "*so long as the teacher remains within the accepted constitutional and confessional basis* of his school he should be free to teach, carry

on research, and to publish. . . ." The authors argue that "a concept of freedom appropriate to theological schools will respect this confessional loyalty, both in institutions and their individual members." See "Academic Freedom and Tenure in the Theological School," *AATS Bulletin* 24 (June 1960): 35. The 1976 revision of this statement abandons the "so long as" qualification, though retains the notion that an appropriate concept of academic freedom will respect the confessional loyalty of the institution. The revised statement is reprinted in *Theological Education* 12 (Winter 1976): 85–105.

44. Hofstadter and Metzger, *Development of Academic Freedom*, p. 389.

45. Ibid., p. 386.

46. AAUP, "1915 Declaration of Principles," p. 93.

47. Hofstadter and Metzger, *Development of Academic Freedom*, pp. 397–98.

48. Jones, "American Concept of Academic Freedom," p. 95.

49. This is no longer so. For example, in *Moore v. Student Affairs Committee of Troy State University*, 284 Fed. Supp. 725 (1968), the court declared: "The college does not stand, strictly speaking, *in loco parentis* to its students."

50. Jones, "American Concept of Academic Freedom," p. 95.

51. Ibid.

52. John S. Brubacher, *The Courts and Higher Education* (San Francisco: Jossey-Bass Publishers, 1971), p. 24.

53. AAUP, "1964 Statement on the Academic Freedom of Students," in *Academic Freedom and Tenure*, ed. Louis Joughin (Madison, Wis.: University of Wisconsin Press, 1967), pp. 66–72. The American Civil Liberties Union released a similar statement in September, 1966. It is reprinted in *Freedom and Order in the University*, ed. Samuel Gorovitz (Cleveland: The Press of Western Reserve University, 1967), pp. 191–205.

54. *AAUP Bulletin* 54 (Summer 1968): 258–61.

55. Ibid., p. 259.

56. Ibid.

57. Ibid.

58. Ibid., p. 260.

59. Fritz Machlup has written: "In the present-day United States, the only important issue regarding the freedom to learn is linked with possible restrictions of the freedom to teach." See "Concerning Academic Freedom," p. 754.

60. John S. Brubacher, *On the Philosophy of Higher Education* (San Francisco: Jossey-Bass Publishers, 1977), p. 50.

61. Sidney Hook, *Heresy Yes Conspiracy No* (New York: John Day Co., 1953), p. 154. Cf. Hook, *Academic Freedom*, p. 34.

62. John S. Brubacher also utilizes a twofold categorization: epistemological philosophies emphasizing knowledge for its own sake, and political philosophies within which knowledge is valued for its significance for the body politic. See *Philosophy*, pp. 12–21. See also the threefold categorization found in the 1973 Carnegie Commission Report *The Purposes and the Performance of Higher Education in the United States* (New York: McGraw-Hill Book Company, 1973), pp. 81–94; and the general discussion found in Ernest L. Boyer and Fred M. Hechinger, *Higher Learning in the Nation's Service*, Carnegie Foundation Essay (Washington, D.C.: Carnegie Foundation for the Advancement of Teaching, 1981).

63. Aristotle, *Topics*, bk. 6, chap. 6, in *Great Books of the Western World*, ed.

Robert Maynard Hutchins, trans. W. A. Picard-Cambridge, vol. 8: *Aristotle I* (Chicago: Encyclopedia Britannica, Inc., 1952), p. 198. See the discussion in Richard McKeon, "General Introduction," in *Introduction to Aristotle*, ed. Richard McKeon (New York: Modern Library/Random House, 1947), p. xxi.

64. *Encyclopedia of Philosophy*, 19th ed., s.v. "Aristotle."

65. McKeon, "Introduction," p. xxi.

66. Aristotle, *Topics*, bk. 5, chap. 6, p. 198.

67. H. H. Gerth and C. Wright Mills define the Weberian notion of ideal type as a "construction of certain elements of reality into a logically precise conception." See *From Max Weber: Essays in Sociology*, ed. H. H. Gerth and C. Wright Mills (New York: Oxford University Press, 1946), p. 59.

68. The theoretical philosophy has close affinities to what Brubacher terms the epistemological philosophy.

69. Robert Nisbet, *The Degradation of the Academic Dogma* (New York: Basic Books, 1971), pp. 23–24. In this context, Nisbet defines knowledge as the cumulative, corporate knowledge of scholarship. See pp. 30–33.

70. John Henry Newman, *The Idea of a University* (London: Longmans, Green, and Co., 1902), p. 103.

71. Kenneth R. Minogue, *The Concept of a University* (Berkeley: University of California Press, 1973), p. 83.

72. Abraham Flexner, *Universities: English, German, and American* (New York: Oxford University Press, 1930), p. 42.

73. Nisbet, *Academic Dogma*, p. 47.

74. Flexner, *Universities*, p. 44.

75. Ibid., p. 179.

76. Nisbet, *Academic Dogma*, p. 34.

77. Ibid., p. 128. Flexner argues similarly. See his *Universities*, pp. 130–33.

78. Nisbet, Academic Dogma, pp. 129, 134–36.

79. Minogue, *Concept of a University*, p. 76.

80. Ibid., p. 78.

81. Ibid. Minogue notes that the distinction between the practical and the academic is not equivalent to the distinction between value and fact.

82. Ibid., p. 83.

83. Within what Brubacher calls the political philosophy of higher learning, knowledge is valued for "its far-reaching significance for the body politic." *Philosophy*, p. 13.

84. Ibid., pp. 13–15.

85. Clark Kerr, *The Uses of the University* (Cambridge: Harvard University Press, 1963), p. 10.

86. Ibid., p. 47.

87. Ibid., p. 48.

88. For further discussion of this, see Wilbur Cohen, "Higher Education and the Federal Government," in *Higher Education: From Autonomy to Systems*, ed. James A. Perkins (New York: International Council for Educational Development, 1972); and Kerr, *Uses of the University*, pp. 46–84.

89. Kerr, *Uses of the University*, pp. 88–94. See also the AAUP, "Committee A Report: Corporate Funding of Academic Research," *Academe* 69 (November-December 1983): 18a–21a.

90. See Kerr, *Uses of the University*, especially chaps. 2–3.

91. Ibid., pp. 116–17.

92. William Arrowsmith, "Idea of a New University," *Center Magazine* 3 (1970): 51.

93. Ibid., pp. 48–49.

94. Ibid., p. 49.

95. See Ibid., pp. 53–60.

96. Kerr, *Uses of the University*, p. 38.

97. Kirk, *Academic Freedom*, p. 27. See also his *Decadence and Renewal in the Higher Learning* (South Bend, Ind.: Gateway Editions, 1978), p. 16.

98. Kirk, *Academic Freedom*, p. 12.

99. Ibid., p. 5.

100. Ibid., pp. 3–5, 7–9.

101. Ibid., p. 17.

102. Kirk's assumption is that there exists an "abiding Truth."

103. Kirk, *Academic Freedom*, p. 91.

104. Ibid.

105. Nisbet, *Academic Dogma*, pp. 52–55.

106. Ibid., p. 64.

107. Hardy E. Jones, "Academic Freedom as a Moral Right," in *The Concept of Academic Freedom*, ed. Edmund L. Pincoffs (Austin: University of Texas Press, 1975), pp. 37–51.

108. Ibid., pp. 46–49.

109. Ibid., pp. 49–50.

110. See Pincoffs, "Introduction," p. xiv.

111. Ibid., pp. xiii–xiv.

112. AAUP, "1915 Declaration of Principles," p. 101.

113. AAUP, "1940 Statement of Principles," p. 108.

114. David Fellman, "Academic Freedom and the American Political Ethos," in *Academic Freedom and the Catholic University*, ed. Edward Manier and John W. Houck (Notre Dame, Ind.: Fides Publishers, 1967), pp. 65–69.

115. Hook, *Heresy Yes Conspiracy No*, p. 154.

116. Ibid., p. 156.

117. Ibid.

118. Ibid., p. 157.

119. MacIver, *Academic Freedom in Our Time*, p. 11.

120. 354 U.S. 234 (1957), quoted in Brubacher, *Courts and Higher Education*, p. 59.

121. Gunti, "Academic Freedom as an Operative Principle," p. 188.

122. Walsh, "University and the Church," pp. 105–7.

123. Curran, "Academic Freedom," pp. 739–40. See also "The Catholic University in the Modern World," p. 204.

124. Curran, "Academic Freedom," pp. 750–51.

125. Ibid., p. 753.

126. Hook, *Academic Freedom*, p. 35.

127. Machlup, "Concerning Academic Freedom," p. 755.

128. Kirk, *Academic Freedom*, p. 3.

129. William Van Alstyne, "The Specific Theory of Academic Freedom and

the General Issue of Civil Liberty," in *The Concept of Academic Freedom*, ed. Edmund L. Pincoffs (Austin: University of Texas Press, 1975), p. 69.

130. This has been upheld by the Supreme Court in *Perry v. Sinderman* 408 U.S. 593,596 (1972). See Ibid., pp. 68–69.

131. John R. Searle, "Two Concepts of Academic Freedom," in *The Concept of Academic Freedom*, ed. Edmund L. Pincoffs (Austin: University of Texas Press, 1975), p. 89.

132. Ibid., p. 92.

133. Pincoffs, "Introduction," p. xviii.

134. Brubacher, *Courts and Higher Education*, p. 57. *Sweezy v. New Hampshire* is considered a landmark case in this regard.

135. See the AAUP, "Interpretive Comments," p. 325.

136. Van Alstyne, "Specific Theory of Academic Freedom," p. 67.

137. Ibid., pp. 67–68.

5

A Critical Examination of Existing Catholic Approaches to Academic Freedom

From the preceding overview of the current Catholic and secular models of academic freedom, four major aspects of the problem of academic freedom in the American Roman Catholic university emerge. These are first, the issue of the general nature and basis of academic freedom; second, the question of the approach to knowledge that should undergird a model of academic freedom applicable to the Catholic college and university; third, the problem of the nature of institutional religious commitment; and fourth, the problem of reconciling Catholic university theology and academic freedom.

Although not an exhaustive summary of the issues raised by an examination of the problems of academic freedom in the Catholic college or university, the foregoing can provide the basis upon which to develop a critique of current Catholic approaches. It is hoped that critical reflection upon these approaches will not only extend the parameters of the discussion of this issue, but also aid in the development of a new, more adequate, interpretation of academic freedom applicable to the Catholic college and university.

DEVELOPING THE CRITIQUE

It would seem that in order for an American Catholic college or university to be both Catholic and a college or university (as these institutions are generally understood in American society), it must possess certain characteristics. As a *university*, it should be characterized by the academic freedom necessary to the fulfillment of the purposes of a university. As a *Catholic* university, it should be holistic in its approach to education, be creative in the actualization of its distinctive commitments, and be a locus for appropriate theological scholarship.

A model of academic freedom that is truly applicable to the Catholic institution must be able to provide an adequate rationale for these characteristics, or at least not be incongruous with them. In the section to follow, these characteristics will be explored, defended, and translated into critical questions that will be addressed to current Catholic approaches to academic freedom.

Freedom and the University

Thesis One

> *The American Roman Catholic college or university should be characterized by the academic freedom necessary to the fulfillment of its purposes as a university.*

Despite its distinctive commitments,[1] the contemporary American Roman Catholic college or university is a college or university in the American understanding of these terms, and shares with all colleges and universities the same basic purposes. These purposes include the pursuit of truth through research, the dissemination of knowledge through teaching and publication, and the preparation of experts for society.[2] As discussed in the historical overview presented in Chapter 2, the scholarly purposes of the Catholic college into the twentieth century were qualified by overriding religious aims and by an educational philosophy based upon the view that education consisted of "passing on" a preestablished body of truths. It might be recalled, however, that over the course of recent decades a shift has occurred. "Now . . . the leading Catholic institutions are dedicated to the *discovery* of truth, and Catholic educators have lost the old assurance in their grip on truth."[3] Moreover, the religious commitment of a Catholic university can now be viewed not as something that detracts from its purposes as a university, but rather something that adds a distinctive dimension to them.

It can be argued, for example, that as a Catholic institution the Catholic college or university has a unique motivation for the pursuit of truth in that this pursuit can be viewed as a quest with quasi-religious dimensions. In the Catholic perspective, truth resides in God, and God is the highest and First Truth.[4] The search for truth is—albeit in a veiled manner—a search for God. The pursuit of truth is directed toward knowledge of the real—of being—and, thus, necessarily brings one into confrontation with questions concerning the ultimate ground of the intelligible world. Gerhart Niemeyer has written that "raising questions about finite things propels the mind toward raising questions about transcendence which intrudes on all knowledge as the dimension of 'the beginning,' and on all human experience as the realm of 'the beyond.' " In short, "wonderment about being must include the ground of being."[5]

In a similar vein, David Tracy, following the work of Bernard Lonergan, speaks of the religious dimension of scientific inquiry. He writes that "unless he wishes to abandon the search for authentic self-transcendence the scientist cannot silence the question of the final horizon of scientific inquiry."[6] Seen in this context, human inquiry takes on religious import, and one would expect a Catholic university to be tireless in the encouragement of such inquiry.

The notion that the Catholic university is indeed a true university (as understood in the American context) is supported by the opinions of Catholic educational theorists, by the claims of Catholic institutions themselves, and by the legal status accorded Catholic institutions. Most Catholic educational theorists have come to acknowledge that the Catholic university shares in the basic purposes of all universities. Hence, the group of leaders of Catholic higher education that assembled for the 1967 Land O'Lakes Conference wrote that "the Catholic university participates in the total university life of our time, has the same functions as all other true universities and, in general, offers the same services to society."[7]

Even as conservative a theorist as S. Thomas Greenburg admits that the secular university and the Catholic university share the same abstract nature.[8] They both constitute academic communities that pursue truth through instruction and research.[9] He does, however, argue that the sources of the actual existence of each type of university differ (the state or a private group, on one hand, the Church on the other), giving rise to differing commitments and differing conceptions of academic freedom. It appears that his view does not represent the mainstream of Catholic thought, nor does the view of those who continue to define Catholic purpose in higher education in terms of the student's " 'acquisition of and conformity to the cognitive, catechetic, and normative definitions' of Catholic Christian teaching."[10]

Most Catholic institutions view themselves as full American colleges and universities, although some, perhaps, do not recognize the full ramifications of such a self-perception. Yet the self-perception remains and is reflected in declarations found in the catalogues of most Catholic colleges and universities: "The Catholic University of America is a community of scholars, both faculty and students, set apart to discover, preserve, and impart the truth in all its forms. . . ." "Nazareth is, first of all, a place of study and scholarship. . . ." "The purpose of graduate study at Assumption College is the development of the scholar, one knowledgeable of methods, of research, of original thinking in a professional career, and of creative achievement in the advancement and extension of knowledge."[11]

Legally, that is, in the view of the state that grants the university's charter, the Catholic college or university shares the basic function of all other colleges and universities. Michael P. Walsh, who served as president of Boston College and Fordham University, comments:

At the founding of any Catholic university a group of persons made a contract with the state to set up a kind of public trust for the betterment of the commonweal. Trustees were appointed with the serious civil and moral obligation of seeing that the trust was carried out. What goes on in the Catholic university then, is not an exclusively intramural affair. The state has understood that the institution is to be a real university, and the bishop or religious congregation has publicly agreed to this. Undoubtedly much leeway has been given here, and restrictions for purely religious purposes have been accepted before the law. Yet in the minds of the public the term "university" means at the least that the institution be academically respectable and that it strive to some degree toward academic excellence.[12]

Catholic universities, then, are both legally and morally bound to those purposes that all universities share: legally by state contract, and morally in order to avoid misrepresenting themselves to the public. The terms *college* and *university*—despite the relativity of the realities they represent—have a specific meaning in the American context. Beneath the pluralism of approaches and commitments found in American colleges and universities, there should exist a commitment shared by all institutions that label themselves colleges and universities: the commitment to the pursuit of knowledge and its dissemination through teaching.[13]

In order to fulfill its purposes, the college or university must first of all be autonomous.[14] A university cannot carry on its work properly if certain issues (e.g., political issues) are precluded as areas of study, or if the results of research and the content of teaching are preordained by non-scholarly authorities external to the university.[15] Furthermore, each scholar in every discipline must be accorded freedom to carry out his or her tasks. As the AAUP in its "1940 Statement of Principles" insists, freedom is required by the nature of truth-seeking and for effective teaching and learning.[16]

It is not necessary to argue at length on behalf of the close relation that exists between the fulfillment of the basic purposes of the American university and academic freedom. This relation has been discussed at length in Chapter 4. It suffices to say that in the American context, academic freedom has come to define the true university.[17]

Therefore, insofar as the American Catholic college or university is a type of American university, it shares in its purposes and functions. And the effective performance of these functions requires an atmosphere of academic freedom and a true autonomy.[18] This assertion leads to the formulation of the first critical question to be applied to current Catholic models of academic freedom: Does this model provide an adequate rationale for the freedom necessary for the fulfillment of the Catholic university's purposes as a university?

Approach to Knowledge

Thesis Two

> *In light of the Catholic perspective on the nature of reality, the Catholic university should be holistic in its approach to knowledge, eschewing both the narrow positivism once characteristic of some sectors of secular academia and a dualism that would radically separate the theological and secular disciplines.*

In the early part of this century, certain sectors of secular academia implicitly or explicitly adhered to an epistemology that tended to limit what was considered knowledge to the products of empirical scientific investigation.[19] Contemporary higher education has, in general, abandoned such a narrow approach to knowledge, though perhaps some remnants of it remain. For example, Protestant theologian Julian Hartt has observed that there is within the university "an unresolved argument over the place of everything but science in the cognitive enterprise."[20] Hence, the humanities, arts and theological disciplines have been sometimes looked upon as stepchildren in the academic family. James T. Burtchaell, a Catholic scholar, argues that a single model of scholarship has been dominant in higher education. This model—the model of empirical scientific verification—was first developed in the physical sciences and later adopted by the social sciences and to some degree by the humanities. "Many practitioners of the scientific method who know no other forms of scholarly inquiry or discourse are drawn to regard these other activities as matters of guesswork, whim or emotion."[21]

Irrespective of the extent to which such attitudes survive in contemporary academia, it seems clear that a narrow empiricism is incongruous with the Catholic conception of reality and has no place in the Catholic college or university. In the Catholic perspective, human experience and knowledge transcend the narrowly scientific. The Christian realizes that "science does not lead us directly into the heart of reality, as is popularly assumed; rather, it creates highly artificial situations and permits attention only to highly specialized phenomena, *while leaving other ranges of experience wholly and deliberately out of account.*"[22] Left out of account are the humanistic, aesthetic, valuational, and religious dimensions of experience.

Of central importance in the Catholic view is precisely the religious dimension of human existence. The religious element is not considered something set apart from human life, or a foreign dimension added to it.[23] Indeed, contemporary theologians—notably Karl Rahner—have attempted to avoid such extrinsic or dualistic conceptions of the relation of nature and grace.[24] Such a dualism recognizes a transcendent realm, but sharply separates it from other aspects of human life. Applied to the university context, this dualism would lead to a strict division between the theological and the human sciences.

In contrast to the dualistic approach, Rahner and others have affirmed that "human existence in its actual condition is radically oriented toward God."[25] Moreover, through God's creative self-expression in Christ, there is an

inner openness of the natural creation toward the divine self-communication in grace. . . . We can speak of it, beyond this, in the sense that in the concrete order of supernatural divine self-communication as in fact willed by God, every natural created entity is ordered to this grace in such a way that it cannot remain really whole and healthy in itself, nor achieve the completion required by its own nature, except as integrated into the supernatural order of grace. . . . The "relative autonomy" of the natural physical and cultural spheres never extends, in Catholic teaching, to the implication that they can achieve even the significance which is their own and immanent to them, except through the grace of God in Jesus Christ.[26]

Any extensive consideration of the relation between nature and grace or between creation and redemption is certainly beyond the scope of the present work. The point relevant to our discussion is that there is within Catholic theology, a conscious attempt to reach a more holistic, and less dualistic understanding of the relation of these realms. Such a holistic perspective in Catholic theology could (and should) become the foundation for a more holistic view of the university curriculum in general, and of the relation of theology to other disciplines in particular. Needless to say, the integration of theology with other disciplines must not involve any type of theological imperialism.

Not only does the Catholic perspective necessitate a broader approach to knowledge as reflective of human experience beyond the scientific, but it also affirms what can be recognized by all who eschew an anti-metaphysical stance: that questions of meaning and value are implicit in scientific inquiry itself. As was discussed earlier in this chapter, "Scientific questioning impels one past an experienced world of sensitive immediacy to an intelligently mediated and deliberately constituted world of meaning."[27] In short, scientific inquiry leads one into confrontation with questions properly called religious: Is fruitful inquiry possible if the world is not intelligible? Upon what is the intelligibility of the world grounded? Are the values upon which findings are evaluated worthwhile? "Is it worthwhile to ask whether our goals, purposes, and ideals are themselves worthwhile? Can we understand and affirm such a demand for worth-whileness without affirming an intelligent, rational, responsible source and ground for them?"[28] The adoption of a narrow notion of truth not only leads to the neglect of important areas of human experience—the experience of the spiritual—but also to the disregarding of those deeper (religious) questions of meaning and value implicit in scientific inquiry itself.

Because of the theological perspective to which it is related, the Catholic university is particularly suited to lead the way toward a broader approach to knowledge and scholarship. Gerhart Niemeyer's thoughts on this point are worth quoting at length. He writes:

Western civilization finds itself in a crisis stemming from the ban of transcendence that originated in natural philosophy and natural science. In this situation, a university in which the pursuit of truth and the transmission of knowledge are systematically kept open to the presupposition of a divine salvation has something to give that is now lacking at secular universities. . . . Unless the Catholic faith makes a difference in its *approach to knowledge,* no other features of personnel or atmosphere could constitute a Catholic university. Today the Catholic university stands out among other universities not as an institution where learning is kept on a leash, but on the contrary, as one with the capacity and equipment to liberate science from the positivist "taboo on theory. . . ."[29]

Niemeyer's summary leads to the formulation of the second critical question to be applied to current Catholic approaches to academic freedom: Does this model of academic freedom contain (implicitly or explicitly) a rationale for intellectual openness to the full range of human experience, thus avoiding both a narrow empiricism and a dualism that would radically separate the theological and the secular disciplines?

Institutional Commitment

Thesis Three

> *If it is to constitute a Catholic presence in the academic world, yet be a university or college as these terms are understood in the American context, the Catholic college or university must creatively actualize its distinctive commitments in a manner consonant with the basic principles of academic freedom and scholarly autonomy that are fundamental to the purposes of the university.*

The Catholic experience demonstrates that it can be quite difficult to reconcile Catholic institutional commitment with the basic commitment of the American university to the free pursuit of truth and the dissemination of knowledge. As Walsh observes, a great part of the difficulty can be traced to the narrow interpretation that has been given to the notion of Catholic commitment.[30] Until recent times, Catholic institutional commitment has been interpreted chiefly as an adherence to doctrinal orthodoxy and an acceptance of the subordination of the university to the hierarchical *Magisterium*. This is undoubtedly the present interpretation of Catholic commitment found in those colleges and universities that fall in or near the category referred to as the "Model of Catholic Exclusivity."[31] Moreover, the Code of Canon Law would appear to be based upon this traditional conception of Catholic commitment.[32] Such interpretations of Catholic commitment or "church-relatedness" violate accepted principles of academic autonomy.[33] Furthermore, any interpretation that would require the imposition of a doctrinal orthodoxy upon Catholic university scholars—irrespective of whether that imposition is by authorities external to or within the university—would raise serious questions concerning the status of the scholarly work performed under such conditions and the status of the institution itself.

Another interpretation of Catholic commitment includes the acknowledgment that "fidelity to the Christian message as it comes . . . through the Church" is an essential characteristic of the Catholic university, though it rejects hierarchical intervention into the affairs of the university as a means of insuring such fidelity.[34] Here too, important questions concerning academic freedom arise. Does fidelity to the Christian message involve the imposition of an orthodoxy upon all disciplines or upon Catholic theology alone? Does this fidelity preclude what theologians have termed legitimate dissent from noninfallible teaching? Who is juridically competent to judge departures from the Christian message?

The difficulties surrounding the nature and implications of institutional commitment have not been entirely resolved.[35] A few institutions—those that whould fall into the category of the "Catholic Secular Model"—have reached the conclusion that balancing Catholic commitment and the basic commitment of the university is an impossible task.[36] However, if the self-destruction of Catholic higher education is considered an unacceptable option, a creative theoretical and practical reconciliation of the two commitments—perhaps through a broadening of the interpretation of Catholic commitment—is necessary. Hence, the third critical question to be addressed to current Catholic models of academic freedom: Does this model reconcile adequately the scholarly and religious commitments of the Catholic university?

Theological Scholarship

Thesis Four

> *The Catholic college or university should be the locus for theological scholarship that is consonant with and appropriate to its nature as a college or university.*

As an institution devoted to humanistic study, specifically to the intellectual investigation of the *totality* of human experience, the Catholic college or university will direct particular intellectual attention to the realm properly termed the religious. Protestant scholar Clyde Holbrook, in his well-known book *Religion: A Humanistic Field*, writes that "the humanities find their characteristic subject matter in those significant achievements of the human race which illuminate and illustrate the distinctive characteristics of man as a rational and spiritual being."[37] Those characteristics include the human capacity for self-transcendence, imagination, and volition. Hence, in Holbrook's view, religion should occupy an important place among the humanities. "To attempt to understand man without reference to the systems of belief and insight within which he has attempted to understand himself is to reduce and distort his images of himself by which humanistic education at its best tries to direct its steps."[38]

The Catholic university possesses an added motivation for directing intellectual attention to the religious dimension of human experience in that from the Catholic faith perspective, "the person is oriented beyond himself or herself toward God as the source, sustainer, and final perfection of the person's existence."[39] As an institution founded upon a particular view of the religious dimension of human existence, the Catholic university's attention to religion should go beyond including in its curriculum a program in general or comparative religious studies, as necessary as this is. In the Catholic college and university, intellectual reflection upon the Catholic faith perspective in particular has occupied, and should continue to occupy, a central place.

That the Catholic university should be a locus for theological scholarship—especially though not exclusively Catholic theological scholarship—appears to be an undisputed assertion among Church authorities and Catholic educators. The Catholic educators gathered at the 1967 Land O'Lakes Conference argued that the Catholic presence that distinguishes the Catholic university "is effectively achieved first of all and distinctively by the presence of a group of scholars in all branches of theology."[40] Moreover, the university delegates of the 1972 Rome Congress affirmed that "one of the principal tasks of a Catholic university, and one which it alone is able to accomplish adequately, will be to make theology relevant to all human knowledge, and reciprocally all human knowledge relevant to theology."[41]

The important place that theology should occupy in the American Catholic college or university is particularly emphasized by Church authorities. The bishops of the United States write that despite the diversity of programs and degrees in Catholic colleges and universities, "theological education has maintained a role that is central to their mission."[42]

Although one may grant that Catholic theological reflection is a desirable and important aspect of the Catholic university's endeavor, the important issue is the appropriate form theological reflection should take on the Catholic campus. This issue is acknowledged by the American bishops:

Theology is not the same as faith or spirituality or holiness. These, too, are important values of Catholic education, but here we want to emphasize that the distinguishing mark of every Catholic college or university is that, *in an appropriate academic fashion*, it offers its students an introduction to the Catholic theological heritage.[43]

If theological study is to occupy a place in the Catholic university, it must be conceived as a full academic discipline whose methods are *appropriate to the nature of the university*. Such an argument does not preclude the free acceptance, by theologians, of the supernatural sources upon which theology is said to be based. What is precluded is the imposition—by authorities either within or external to the university—of the content of those sources or of a confining dogmatism, whatever the form.[44] Hence, the fourth critical question to be applied to current Catholic models of academic freedom comes to the fore: What conception of theology undergirds this approach to academic freedom, and is this conception consonant with the nature of the college or university as understood in the American context?

Summary

From the presentation and defense of the foregoing four theses, four critical questions have emerged, questions that will form the basis of a critical reflection upon current Catholic conceptions of academic freedom.

1. Does this model of academic freedom provide an adequate rationale for the freedom necessary for the fulfillment of the Catholic university's purposes as a university?
2. Does this model of academic freedom contain—either implicitly or explicitly—a rationale for intellectual openness to the full range of human experience, thus avoiding both a narrow empiricism and a dualism that would radically separate the theological and the "secular" disciplines?
3. Can this model of academic freedom reconcile adequately the scholarly and religious institutional commitments of the Catholic university?
4. What conception of theology undergirds this approach to academic freedom, and is this conception consonant with the nature of the Catholic university as a university?

These questions, based upon four major areas of tension in the juxtaposition of academic freedom and the Catholic institution, serve to focus and organize critical reflection. No claim is being made that they provide a comprehensive critical framework. However, they are fundamental questions, and as such they can provide the foundation for a relatively comprehensive critical reflection.

A CRITICAL EXAMINATION OF CURRENT CATHOLIC MODELS OF ACADEMIC FREEDOM

Utilizing the categorical scheme employed in Chapter 3, current Catholic models of academic freedom will be examined in light of the critical questions developed above.[45] Following this critical examination, a reflection upon selected *Magisterial* statements in view of the same critical questions will be carried out, although it is recognized that insofar as no developed defense of a position on academic freedom is offered in them, the direct applicability of these questions will be limited.

Restrictive Models of Academic Freedom

Do the Restrictive Models of academic freedom provide an adequate rationale for the freedom necessary for the fulfillment of the Catholic university's purposes as a university?

In general, restrictive models do not in theory provide for what has been identified as a necessary academic freedom. The model of S. Thomas Greenburg, for example, is based upon the view that academic freedom, as understood in the United States, is inapplicable to the Catholic university. Greenburg grants that the Catholic university shares with all universities the same abstract nature "as an academic community which pursues truth through the teaching of, and research into, the various academic disciplines."[46] He argues, however, that this nature, in order to be manifested in reality (that is, outside the mind), requires an "existent source," which may be a church, the state, or a group of private sponsors. Such an existent source gives the university its existence, shapes its commitments, and determines "the manner in which the potential of the nature will be developed in the concrete world."[47]

Catholicity, according to Greenburg, is not a part of the nature of the university, nor does it change that nature.[48] Rather Catholicity conditions the manner in which the nature of the university will be fulfilled in the concrete. The Catholic university—a concrete fulfillment of the nature of the university with the Church as its existent source—will have "commitments from its source that *will condition the manner in which the potential of the university nature will be fulfilled*: and, will condition the manner in which the one and the same truth will be pursued."[49] Hence, Catholicity, as a condition of the manifestation of the abstract nature of the univer-

sity, necessitates the redefinition of the concepts of institutional autonomy and academic freedom. "In the Catholic university, academic freedom must recognize 'the fidelity to the Christian message.' "[50]

Greenburg's observation that the particular manifestation of the nature of the university will vary according to context is certainly a valid
one—at least in a general sense. However, serious questions concerning
his overall approach can be raised. Is Greenburg's definition of the
nature of the university adequate? Is the application of this definition
in the context of his argument coherent?

Both questions must be answered negatively. If Greenburg is going
to define the nature of the university as an academic community that
pursues truth through teaching and research and also claim that it is
precisely the manner in which truth is pursued that changes according
to a university's existent source and commitments, then can he legitimately claim that the nature of the university remains the same in the
case of the private, state, and Catholic institution? It is doubtful. For in
light of his definition, to make such a claim requires that the pursuit of
truth through research be defined similarly in each context. In that its
meaning is changed according to the context (Catholic, state, or private
university), the notion of pursuing the truth through research is emptied
of content, and is rendered ineffective as a distinguishing characteristic
common to all universities. What is it about the pursuit of truth through
teaching and research that remains constant in all "existent" universities
and constitutes the natue that they share? Greenburg is far from clear
on this point.

According to most American educational theorists, among those things
considered constant in the nature of the university is that the university's
pursuit of truth through research is a relatively free pursuit. Greenburg's
model does not provide a rationale for the academic freedom necessary
to the Catholic university as a university. Rather, his model attempts—
unsuccessfully—to justify the limitation of such freedom by defining the
nature of the university in such a way that it can be argued that academic
freedom, as understood in the United States, is related not to the nature
of the university, but to a particular concrete manifestation of that nature—the secular state university.[51]

Although Germain Grisez argues that "institutions that preserve their
Catholic identity must allow full scope for *authentic* academic freedom,"
his model neither provides a rationale for, nor would in practice engender, the freedom necessary for the fulfillment of the purposes of the
Catholic university as a university.[52]

His approach to academic freedom, based upon a rejection of the
"liberal faith" inherent in the secular model, precludes what has been
considered a necessary academic autonomy. Grisez states that "procedures must be developed that will reflect in practice the fact that a

Catholic institution owes allegiance to the ecclesiastical magisterium."[53] What form such allegiance might take is never made explicit. It appears, however, that in cases of conflict, this allegiance would take precedence over scholarly freedom and academic autonomy. In Grisez's estimation, "The Catholic character of a college or university is at stake . . . if rejection of the Church's *magisterium* is defended in the name of academic freedom."[54]

Grisez's position is understandable if one bears in mind that he presupposes that freedom in the pursuit of truth is only of secondary importance for believers. Of primary importance for the attainment of truth is humility and the obedience of faith that opens the mind to the First Truth who has revealed Himself. This faith is not merely a personal experience for Grisez, but something concretized in human language. Such presuppositions are not necessarily problematic for the scholar. A scholar may hold religious convictions without these necessarily corrupting scholarship. They can enrich scholarship by fostering a fuller vision of human experience. Problems do arise, however, when Grisez argues for the *necessity* of recognizing *Magisterial* authority *within* the university.[55]

It should be borne in mind that in Grisez's approach, the influence of the *Magisterium* could, at least in theory, be extended to disciplines other than theology. Grisez argues that faculty members in all disciplines should be both committed scholars and committed Catholics.[56] Only thus could an integration of faith and learning take place. He writes that "we need not imagine a discipline such as 'Catholic physics' in competition with ordinary secular physics. But we should not exclude a priori the possibility that the light of faith might make some difference to the development of physics."[57] Although it has been argued above that a holistic approach to knowledge is necessary in the Catholic context, the integration of knowledge that Grisez envisions raises a number of questions concerning academic freedom and academic autonomy. Insofar as one imposes specific authoritative formulations of the Catholic faith upon a discipline, a narrow theological imperialism, rather than a creative integration, results. Moreover, this theological imperialism can potentially become an ecclesiastical imperialism in that these formulations carry with them the authority of the hierarchical *Magisterium* to which the Catholic university—in Grisez's opinion—owes a direct allegiance.

Grisez endorses the AAUP "1940 Statement of Principles" *as a procedural norm.*[58] What he means by this, or more to the point, what possible meaning this could have in light of his conceptions of scholarly freedom and autonomy, is unknown.

The approach to academic freedom outlined by Augustine Rock also fails to provide an adequate rationale for the freedom necessary to the Catholic college or university as a college or university. According to

Rock, academic freedom, as understood in the American context, must be reinterpreted on the Catholic campus (particularly in the theological disciplines) insofar as Catholics "must give full assent to truth formally proclaimed by the Church as revealed."[59]

This position is incongruous with academic freedom as necessary to the Catholic university as a university not because it involves the acceptance of the revealed truth of the Christian message by individual scholars or because it involves the commitment of the institution itself to that truth. Rather, the incongruity lies in the fact that the acceptance of such truth is, in Rock's model, imposed on scholars or made a criterion for their continued employment. Rock claims that full assent to truth formally proclaimed by the church as revealed does not curtail freedom insofar as such assent is a free decision to which one is moved by grace. From the Catholic Christian perspective he is absolutely correct. However, this observation does not address the central problem. Religious commitment becomes incongruous with academic freedom only when enforced by authorities external to or within the university. Hence, the difficulty with Rock's approach. He openly condones intervention into the university by the Holy See or the local ordinary in order to insure orthodoxy in the theological teaching of Catholic colleges, or to protect infallible truths of faith in the full university.[60]

The usual response to questions raised about models such as Rock's is that full assent to revealed truths by the theologian is necessitated by the nature of Catholic theology. Hence, such assent can and must be enforced (whether by the hierarchy, the college administration, or faculty peers) as a criterion of competence of the Catholic university theologian. If this is the case, the question that arises is whether theology so conceived has any place in a university or college as these institutions are understood in the American context. To reiterate, it is not belief (understood as assent to divine truth) on the part of the scholar that is potentially problematic in the college or university setting, but the imposition of belief as a criterion of scholarly competence.

> *Do the Restrictive Models of academic freedom contain—either implicitly or explicitly—a rationale for intellectual openness to the full range of human experience, thus avoiding both a narrow empiricism and a dualism that would radically separate the theological and the "secular" disciplines?*

There is no tendency toward scientific positivism in any of the three models under consideration. Rather, these models represent an effort to reconcile academic freedom with the study of the religious dimension of human experience from the Catholic perspective. However, the extent to which these approaches foster an integration of theology and other disciplines remains subject to dispute for two major reasons. First, it is not entirely certain that the models under consideration are sufficiently clear on this issue to allow any firm judgment to be made. Second, in Grisez's model the *tendencies* that can be perceived are toward what theologians have called "theological positivism," which militates against a truly integrative approach.

A theological positivist is described by Richard P. McBrien as "one who equates theology with the study of a given source or sources. Thus, theology is not . . . the process of giving expression to our experience of God, but rather the study of documents in which the experience of God has been recorded and interpreted (especially the Bible or the official teachings of the Church)."[61]

Grisez reaffirms the Catholic position that the substance of faith is expressed in "definitive articles which are proposed (and disputes concerning which are adjudicated) by the living *magisterium*."[62] Although Grisez argues that theologians "must be creative and capable of developing doctrine within the framework of the authentic tradition" of the Catholic Church, his model does not truly allow for much creativity.[63] In Grisez's approach, one who dissents from the teaching contained in *Humanae Vitae* is not a suitable individual for a faculty position in a Catholic university department of theology.[64] Such positions should be open to committed Catholics only, with the content of commitment being determined by "the actual status of the Church's teaching at a given time."[65]

A positivist theology brings to the task of the integration of disciplines and knowledge definitive formulas as proposed by the *Magisterium*.[66] As discussed above, such an approach can disintegrate into a narrow theological imperialism. It is significant that while Grisez acknowledges "the possibility that the light of faith might make some difference to the development of physics," he fails to mention that the study of physics might aid theological understanding.[67]

Can these restrictive models of academic freedom adequately reconcile the scholarly and religious commitments of the Catholic university?

It seems that Greenburg does not define Catholic commitment in terms of the nature of, and exigencies arising from, the university, but rather he redefines the university in terms of his conception of Catholic institutional commitment. In Greenburg's understanding, the nature of the university takes on a concrete form that reflects the commitments arising out of its source, which in the case of the Catholic university is the Church.[68] In view of its existent source, the Catholic university will be defined in part by its commitments to the Christian message as interpreted by the teaching authority of the Church, and "to fulfill the Church's ministry of evangelization."[69]

Are such commitments irreconcilable with the scholarly commitments that should characterize every college and university, Catholic or secular?

As developed by Greenburg, Catholic commitment would eclipse the scholarly commitment on the Catholic campus, and would result in the limitation of academic freedom and scholarly autonomy.

The question that should be raised is whether Greenburg's notion of Catholic commitment arises out of a conception of the Catholic college or university that is far too pastoral. Is not the notion that the Catholic college or university participates in the Church's "ministry of evangelization" an inappropriate one?[70] It seems to the present author that this notion indicates a confusion of the Church's preaching mission and its involvement in higher education, and is incongruous with the Catholic university as a university.

Grisez interprets Catholic institutional commitment in a narrowly doctrinal fashion, and in terms of the strict subordination of the university to the *Magisterium*. In his view, the Catholic institution, its theologians, and—ideally—its scholars in all disciplines, must be committed to the Christian faith as it is "expressed by definitive articles" that are proposed and interpreted by the *Magisterium*.[71] Grisez seems to identify Catholic commitment precisely with commitment to the *Magisterium*, saying that "the Catholic character of a college or university is at stake" if the authority of the *Magisterium* is rejected.[72]

It would seem that Grisez's understanding of Catholic commitment is not reconcilable with the basic scholarly commitments of the university. Institutional commitment in and of itself is not incongruous with a necessary academic freedom. It becomes so only when it is interpreted in a narrowly doctrinal manner and, hence, necessitates the imposition—by trustees, administrators, or sponsoring Church officials—of an orthodoxy upon university scholars.

> *What conception of university theology undergirds restrictive models of academic freedom, and is this conception consonant with the nature of the Catholic university as a university?*

Grisez's and Rock's approaches to academic freedom are based upon what might be termed an ecclesiastically centered conception of Catholic theology in the university.[73] This conception of theology has a number of distinguishing characteristics. First, it is characterized by the insistence that a Christian theologian must have a Christian faith commitment.[74] As Grisez argues, "Genuine theology is impossible unless the principles of faith are accepted."[75]

Second, this conception of theology affirms that the faith commitment required of the professor is a commitment to the faith as expressed by the hierarchical *Magisterium*. Rock's thought on this issue is more nuanced than that of Grisez, in that Rock *explicitly* recognizes that the type of assent required of the theologian depends upon the level of engagement of the *Magisterium*.[76] In the works under consideration, Grisez argues that what is normative is "the Church's teaching at a given time."[77]

Third, this ecclesiastically centered conception of theology includes the affirmation that, insofar as the principles of theology are not humanly verifiable, "the theologian must turn for certitude as to his principles to the *Magisterium*."[78] Rock and Grisez utilize this assertion to justify *Magisterial* intervention when orthodoxy is threatened in the university context. Rock's and Grisez's descriptions of the form of such intervention are vague and are offered without principles that might safeguard some measure of institutional autonomy.[79]

Finally, this conception of university theology tends to view the tasks of such theology as *directly* pastoral, as well as academic. This directly pastoral dimension of university theology is apparent in Rock's article:

Pastoral necessity seems to call for gentle but firm correctives from the local magisterial authority when. . . teachings are consistently proposed even in universities, Catholic or not, which are in opposition to the teaching of the magisterium. . . . This seems especially true when those who propose such teachings propose them to undergraduates in Catholic colleges and in Catholic universities which are little more than colleges. Students look to such teachers to teach according to the mind of the Church, especially if these teachers are priests. The local ordinary can hardly be expected to stand helplessly by watching the belief of youngsters undermined by wolves in sheep's clothing.[80]

Is this conception of theology consonant with the nature and purposes of the Catholic university as a university—as a relatively autonomous institution dedicated to the free pursuit and dissemination of knowledge? This question must be answered negatively. First, it would seem that such a conception of Catholic theology is irreconcilable with even the most basic principles of academic freedom and autonomy. The model fails to prevent non-scholarly external interventions into the affairs of the university, and sanctions the imposition of an orthodoxy upon theology professors (and indirectly, upon students) by making faith a prerequisite for sound theological scholarship. In light of the criteria developed earlier in this chapter, such a conception of theology is incongruous with the purposes of *any* American university.

Second, this conception of theology, because of its pastoral presuppositions, dangerously identifies the roles of professor and Church catechist. Moreover, it perpetuates the attitude (1) that "the faithful" are to be shielded from views contrary to Church teaching; (2) that college students are gullible and impressionable children whose spiritual welfare is the responsibility of theology professors; and (3) that most Catholics are neither intelligent enough nor discerning enough to know the difference between Church teaching and the theological speculation of university professors.

The usual riposte of those who defend the restrictive model of academic freedom and its accompanying conception of theology is that the foregoing critique represents the application of criteria that are *foreign* to the nature of Catholic theology. They claim that the distinguishing characteristics outlined above are inherent in the discipline of Catholic theology. Though this may be true, it is not the issue. If Catholic theology deserves a place in the *college* or *university* curriculum, it must respect the basic principles that distinguish the American college or university from other types of educational institutions. It is not the legitimacy of ecclesiastically centered theology that is at issue. Such theology undoubtedly has a place. The question is: Is that place the Catholic college or university? The argument that ecclesiastically centered theology is incongruous with the college or university, raises a further question: Is this the only configuration that theology can legitimately take in the Catholic college or university?

Revised Secular Models of Academic Freedom

Do Revised Secular Models provide an adequate rationale for the freedom necessary for the fulfillment of the Catholic university's purposes as a university?

John E. Walsh justifies academic freedom on the basis of the nature of teaching and the exigencies of the learning process.[81] He writes that

the primary obligation of the teacher is intellectual honesty. . . . He cannot suppress ideas or relevant facts. He cannot be disloyal or dishonest to his own convictions in order to teach what some outside person wishes him to teach. University teaching requires that the teacher and the student together follow the argument wherever it may lead. If the argument leads to conclusions that are unpopular, the professor must be protected.[82]

According to Walsh, the right to teach of one who has become "a knower," and the corresponding right to academic freedom mean the same on the Catholic campus as they do in all other colleges and universities.[83] Although the Catholic university is the locus of scholarly teaching, it is not a locus of the teaching Church. To confuse the teaching mission of the Church with the mission of the Catholic university leads to distortions of both realities. Rather, in Walsh's view, the Catholic university is a manifestation of the Church learning. Genuine learning requires an atmosphere of free and open inquiry.[84]

Walsh's justification of academic freedom on the basis of the nature of teaching is congruent with the approach taken in much of the literature of the AAUP. However, is an adequate rationale provided for its application to the Catholic context?

Walsh claims that the Catholic university is a university in the full sense of the term, distinguished by (among other things) its role as the locus of the Church learning. Walsh's argument that the teaching mission of the Church and the role of the Catholic university must be distinguished is a valid one. However, there are problems with simply identifying the Catholic university with the Church learning. One criticism voiced by Charles E. Curran is that "the teaching function of the church cannot be reduced only to the teaching function of the hierarchical magisterium. In one sense, all the baptized also share in the teaching function of Jesus."[85] Walsh's distinction between the Church teaching and the Church learning does seem to be based upon a narrow conception of the Church's teaching function.[86] However, it can be questioned whether this criticism is fatal to Walsh's central argument. In this particular article Walsh's intention is to distinguish between the official teaching Church and the learning Church. There is nothing in his argument that would prevent him from acknowledging the broader dimensions of the Church's teaching function. In acknowledging these dimensions, however, he would be forced to confront the interesting question of how precisely the teaching Church—conceived in broad communal terms—might be manifest on the Catholic campus.

Walsh's approach to academic freedom can also be criticized for failing to confront some of the problems raised by its application. Walsh argues on behalf of the importance of theology in the university curriculum. Furthermore, he assumes the applicability to theology of his approach to academic freedom. Yet, he offers no specific descriptions of the shape the discipline of theology might take in a Catholic college or university understood as a locus for the Church learning.[87] Moreover, he does not address the question of what role—if any—the official teaching Church should have in the discipline of university theology.

Walsh's approach to academic freedom includes a number of valuable insights, including his argument for distinguishing the official teaching mission of the Church from the purposes of the Catholic university. Although his model supports in theory the extension to the Catholic university of the academic freedom necessary to it as a university, his model is not developed enough nor unambiguous enough to provide an adequate rationale for the extension of such freedom.

Ladislas Orsy constructs a model of academic freedom for university theology based upon the distinction between, and reconciliation of, the charism of bishops and that of theologians. Bishops have the Spirit-assisted task of preserving and proclaiming the Word of God. The theologian, on the other hand, is "to be creative in the understanding of the faith."[88] According to Orsy, the unique charism of fidelity held by the Pope and the body of bishops and the charism of exploration possessed by the theologian complement each other.

Orsy argues that the theologian requires freedom for his or her creative scholarly work.[89] In cases when there is a conflict between theological scholarship and Church doctrine, the Pope or the bishops as a group have the responsibility to point out that a theologian is advancing a position that is irreconcilable with Catholic doctrine. Orsy would apparently reject taking further action against the "offending" theologian.[90] Hence, Church doctrine is protected while the academic freedom of the theology professor is preserved.

Orsy's model of academic freedom—based upon the complementary charisms of bishop and theologian and on the exigencies arising from theology as a discipline—does provide a rationale for the extension to university theology of the academic freedom necessary to all disciplines in a college or university as these are understood in the American context.[91] However, this rationale is tied to a particular conception of theology and of the role of the theologian, the appropriateness of which will be examined below.

Charles E. Curran, Robert E. Hunt, and Frederick W. Gunti utilize similar arguments to justify the extension of academic freedom to university theology professors. They, like Orsy, build their cases for academic freedom not only upon pragmatic grounds, but also upon the claim that such freedom is necessary in light of the nature of theology and the theologian.

Theology's function is to interpret the sources of revelation and the teachings of the *Magisterium* "in the light of the signs of the times."[92] This interpretive function aids the *Magisterium*, yet also involves a certain subordination of theologians to the *Magisterium*, in that theologians "must deal with and give correct weight to" its teachings. However, "part of this theological function of interpretation of the hierarchical teaching involves the possibility of dissent from noninfallible church teaching. Theology must be free to responsibly exercise this interpretive function."[93] All three theorists appear to argue that the need for academic freedom is rooted in the nature of theology and the theologian's role, while Gunti adds that such freedom is also a human right based upon the dignity of the human being.[94]

Problems surrounding the applicability of the principles of academic freedom to theology so conceived are solved by reference to the principle of competence. Gunti argues that a competent Catholic theologian must "theologize within the context of a Catholic faith commitment" and adhere personally to a Catholic faith commitment.[95]

Hunt and Curran appear to take a similar position in a book they coauthored a number of years ago. They affirm that "theologians must always function *within* the context and according to the claims of the Roman Catholic faith commitment."[96] What are the "essentials" of this faith commitment that cannot be transgressed? Curran and Hunt identify these as the dogmas of faith—those "proposed by the Church to be believed as divinely revealed, either in solemn judgment (papal or conciliar definition) or through the ordinary and universal magisterium."[97] Such dogmas of faith are infallible.

In his more recent article on academic freedom, Curran describes theological competence in apparently broader terms, and without reference to the personal faith commitment of the theologian. He writes that "competency requires that one be true to the presuppositions, sources and methods of the discipline" of Catholic theology.[98] However, in Curran's view, these presuppositions are not merely procedural or methodological, but rather include specific content—the dogmas of faith. Catholic theologians cannot advance conclusions clearly in opposition to dogmas of faith and continue to be considered competent Catholic theologians.[99]

Do the conceptions of competence outlined by Gunti, Curran, and Hunt resolve adequately the problem of academic freedom in the Catholic college or university?[100] Does their application engender the freedom necessary to the Catholic institution as a college or university? These authors' conceptions of competence are excellent foundations for a model of the freedom of *the theologian in the Church*. They are not, however, conceptions of competence whose application will lead to a necessary academic freedom for the theologian who is a professor of Catholic theology in the Catholic college or university. Although these conceptions of competence preserve institutional and scholarly autonomy, they do not truly protect scholarly freedom.

First, the criterion represented by Gunti's interpretation of "theologizing within the Catholic faith-commitment" or Curran's definition of being "true to the presuppositions of the discipline" of theology ultimately engenders only a freedom to teach "the truth." This truth is enforced by scholarly peers and, hence, a measure of academic autonomy is salvaged. However, it remains questionable whether the professor to whom this notion of competence is applied is any freer than if the application were at the hands of an authority external to the university.

Second, such a criterion is not, despite claims to the contrary, truly comparable to any standard used to assess competence in secular disciplines.[101] The presuppositions (there are many!) and "principles" of these disciplines are subject to ongoing revision. They do not constitute a static orthodoxy against which all scholarly conclusions are measured (although undoubtedly they are sometimes so regarded). Breakthroughs or "scientific revolutions" remain possible. In addition, the standards by which competence is judged in secular disciplines are formulated by scholars themselves via a long process of development. Finally, the function of the criteria of competence in secular disciplines is quite different from the function of the faith commitment criterion in Gunti's model and the required adherence to dogmatic presuppositions in Curran's model (and presumably in Hunt's).

Secular criteria of competence do not include standards by which scholarly conclusions are judged; rather they insure the soundness of the *methods* used to reach such conclusions. Sidney Hook writes:

We have a right to demand of the inquirer into truth, and of those who aim to teach the truth or aid in its search, that their assertion be warranted. What makes a conclusion warranted is how it is derived from evidential grounds. The scholar and teacher has a right to teach the truth as he sees it in the light of reflective inquiry and in relation to all the evidence available to him. When a man receives his credentials as a scholar and teacher from his peers it is presupposed that he has demonstrated his capacity and inclination to reach conclusions according to the best methods of rational inquiry current in his particular field. It is not necessary that he agree with any specific doctrine. It is the way in which he reaches his conclusions which makes him a member of the community of scholars.[102]

Therefore, in light of the Catholic community's understanding of the nature and role of the hierarchical *Magisterium*, the professor of Catholic theology has the responsibility to portray accurately and fairly official Catholic teaching (as proposed and interpreted by the *Magisterium*) on specific theological issues when presenting positions on, or interpretations of, these issues labeled as Catholic. He or she also has the responsibility to distinguish official Church teaching from the conclusions of theologians. These responsibilities flow from the basic requirements of scholarly honesty and fairness to evidence. Any lack in this area is to be considered a problem of competence to be addressed by scholarly peers. A theologian's own scholarly conclusions should not reflect upon his or her competence unless the scholar's research methods or integrity are found to be lacking. The professor of Catholic theology should be free to reach conclusions and assume theological positions at variance even with dogmas of faith, so long as the official teaching of the Church on the particular question under consideration is made clear. The *Magisterium* must, when necessary, exercise the right to publicly declare that a particular theological position is contrary to the Catholic faith. Such a declaration, however, should not in any way jeopardize the academic position of the theologian that assumes such a position.[103]

Third and finally, the notion of scholarly competence developed by Gunti contains within it conceptions of the role of the professor of Catholic theology and of the nature of Catholic academic theology that are quite foreign to the American academy. Why is a *personal faith commitment* to the dogmas of faith as proposed by the *Magisterium* necessary to the competence of the theology professor? Why is not an understanding of these dogmas, and an intellectual acceptance of their binding status in the Catholic community enough?[104] The Catholic (including the Catholic theologian) *who as an individual professes to be a Catholic-Christian* would be expected to possess such a faith commitment. If such a commitment is lacking, this is a matter to be addressed by the individual in the depths of his/her conscience. If the absence of such commitment is publicly expressed or indicated, it is also a matter for the individual's bishop. The status of one's faith commitment is, however, irrelevant to the performance of one's scholarly duties.

On the other hand, the requirement that the professor of Catholic theology have a personal faith commitment to the dogmatic presuppositions of Catholic theology makes sense if the professor of Catholic theology is conceived as a spokesperson for the *Magisterium*—a Church theologian, or if academic theology on the Catholic college or university campus is conceived as an extension of the pastoral teaching mission of the Church—a higher catechetics if you will. Such a requirement makes little sense if, as is claimed, Catholic theology is a full academic discipline and the university theologian a true scholar.

The presence of a Catholic "faith-commitment" and "adherence to the dogmas of faith" in scholarly work may be criteria applicable to theologians who exercise quasi-official or official roles as Church theologians. Moreover, they may not be unreasonable requirements for theologians in Church-sponsored institutes of theology and those who teach in a seminary sponsored by a diocese or religious order. However, for the Catholic college or university as a college or university, and for the theological school that forms a part of a university, such requirements appear to be inappropriate in that they unnecessarily qualify basic academic freedom.

The revised secular models of academic freedom are founded upon unambiguous arguments in support of the extension of full academic freedom to university theology and, indeed, include cogent justifications for the extension of such freedom. However, the inadequate conceptions of theological competence that accompany Gunti's, Curran's, and Hunt's models prevent them from being totally acceptable as models to guide the contemporary Catholic college or university.

> *Do Revised Secular models of academic freedom contain—either implicitly or explicitly—a rationale for intellectual openness to the full range of human experience, thus avoiding both a narrow empiricism and a dualism that would radically separate the theological and "secular" disciplines?*

Insofar as their aims include the integration of theology into the university as a full (and free) discipline, the revised secular models of academic freedom harmonize well with what might be termed a holistic approach to knowledge. However, the only theorist that addresses this issue directly is John E. Walsh.

Walsh argues that theology must have a place in the university if it is to be a center of universal learning. He underscores, however, the importance of maintaining the autonomy of other disciplines.

Theology could not, even if it should so desire, dictate the content or the direction of learning in other disciplines. Rather, theology learns from the other disciplines, just as they from it. . . . The Catholic university makes it possible for theologians, scientists, and lawyers to learn together, to confront each other with vital and real problems, and hopefully to find both the objective and subjective bases for a unifying view of man and of the universe and the relationship of both to God.[105]

Walsh's is a fine description of the approach to knowledge that should characterize the Catholic university. His emphasis is upon the *integration* of the partial perspective of the *autonomous* disciplines; hence, he eschews any hint of theological imperialism, recognizing that theology can and must learn from other disciplines.

Can the Revised Secular models of academic freedom adequately reconcile the scholarly and religious commitments of the Catholic university?

None of the theorists examined directly addresses the problem of Catholic institutional commitment. It does seem, however, that at least implicitly, the theorists under consideration avoid what has been termed a narrow interpretation of such commitment.

First, Walsh and Curran explicitly reject the identification of the purpose of the Catholic college or university with the teaching or pastoral mission of the hierarchical *Magisterium*.[106] Second, there is no tendency in any of the revised secular models toward theological imperialism. As we have seen, Walsh explicitly rejects such a violation of the autonomy of university disciplines by Catholic theology. Third and finally, the theorists being considered apparently reject an interpretation of Catholic institutional commitment that involves direct subordination of the college or university to the hierarchy, since in the models of Curran, Hunt, Gunti, and Orsy, direct intervention by the hierarchy into the affairs of the university is excluded.

The revised secular models of academic freedom that have been examined are not incongruous with the development of a creative notion of Catholic commitment that is reconcilable with the scholarly commitments of the Catholic university. There are some indications of how Catholic institutional commitment might be positively conceived by the proponents of these models. The closest thing to a positive statement of the shape Catholic institutional commitment should take is found in Walsh's article. Included in this essay is an editor's note that relates pertinent comments made by Walsh at the public presentation of his article. When asked about the characteristics that should distinguish a Catholic university (another way of asking about the practical ramifications of a Catholic commitment), Walsh identified three. First, the Catholic university should devote particular attention to the study of theology. Second, on the Catholic campus, an integration of the insights of theology and those of other areas of learning should be attempted. "Finally, a Catholic university should provide a total context of living: a mutuality of sympathy, a kind of connaturality of aims and goals productive of a distinctive and self-deepening community spirit."[107]

Two of the three distinctive characteristics mentioned by Walsh are directly related to the presence of the academic study of theology on the Catholic campus. Yet, the presence of a Roman Catholic-oriented department of theology on a college campus should not be the chief manifestation of a Catholic commitment.[108] It will be argued in the conclusion below that a truly Catholic institutional commitment—if it is to be vibrant—must imbue all aspects of university life, from the approach to curricular organization, to the ethical quality of the university's relations with students, faculty, the local community, and the universal human community.

What conception of theology undergirds the Revised Secular models of academic freedom, and is this conception consonant with the nature of the Catholic university as a university?

According to Curran, "Theology is a scientific discipline, a human activity which presupposes faith," the function of which is the "interpretation of the sources of revelation and of the teaching of the hierarchical magisterium in light of the signs of the times."[109] Hunt conceives of the task of theologians in terms of the evaluation of "the faith of God's people as actually lived, and their aims, in order to bring them into harmony with the Word of God and the doctrinal heritage faithfully handed down by the Church, and in order to propose resolutions to questions which arise when this faith is compared with actual life, with history and with human inquiry."[110]

The task of the theologian, according to Orsy, involves an intellectual exploration of God's revelation.[111] It is best described, in his view, by Anselm's notion of *fides quaerens intellectum*. "The theologian must be aware that he is fulfilling an important function in the body of Christ, and the members are relying on him and are with him." For indeed, Orsy argues, "in the person of the theologian the people of God are searching for a deeper understanding of the truth."[112] Accordingly, the qualifications of the theologian require that he or she be "a man of the Church, not in the sense of being a speaker for the hierarchy, still less in the sense of seeking favor of the highly placed in the external power structure of the Church, but in the sense of belonging to the whole Christian community . . . and feeling a responsibility for all of them."[113]

Finally, Gunti argues that it is the task of the theologian "to scientifically investigate the meaning of the faith, and to draw from Revelation and the data of the human sciences ever more of the unfathomable riches of the Gospel."[114] The theologian performs a "theological ministry for the Church," and holds a "special position . . . in the teaching church."[115]

Certainly, the foregoing conceptions of the nature of Catholic theology and the function of theologians are representative of the general position of a large number of Catholic theologians.[116] Upon close examination of these conceptions, it becomes apparent that they place great emphasis on theology as an intellectual endeavor performed "*in* and *for* the Church."[117] Similarly, the role of the theologian is conceived in highly ecclesiastical terms. Curran and Hunt stress the theologian's interpretive role in the Church. Orsy speaks of the theologian as one who performs an important function in the Church, a "man of the Church" responsible to all of its members. Gunti conceives of the theologian as performing a "ministry" for the Church.

In these conceptions, comparatively little emphasis is placed upon the theologian as a university professor and scholar, or on Catholic theology as a university discipline. One is sometimes left with the impression that the college or university happens to be the place where the theologian carries out his or her churchly role. Moreover, the arguments in support of academic freedom for theological professors (particularly those of Gunti and Orsy) seem at times to be arguments for the *freedom of the theologian in the Church* which, because of the locus of most theological work in the United States—the college and university, conveniently adopt and utilize the American principles of academic freedom and autonomy.

There appears to be a failure in the revised secular models to distinguish clearly between theology as a church-centered endeavor—a ministry, and theology as a university discipline; between the theologian as churchman/minister, and the theologian as university scholar. The failure to distinguish the churchly and academic functions of theology could be due to the fact that such a distinction is contrary to the nature of theology and, hence, inappropriate. On the other hand, it very well could be that the failure to make such a distinction in the United States is the result of certain historical factors discussed in Chapter 2, for example, the overriding religious/ecclesiastical aim of early Catholic institutions and the clerical dominance over Catholic higher education. Theology courses were traditionally taught by clerics and were usually catechetical rather than academic in tone.[118] Because theology has been a field often interpreted in catechetical terms and dominated by clerical instructors with a preestablished faith commitment and role in the Church, it is

understandable that a clear distinction between the academic and ecclesiastical functions of theology and theologians has not developed.

In light of the Catholic university's purposes as a university, and the
academic nature of college and university theology, it seems inappropriate to consider theologian-professors as primarily "men of the church"
or "ministers." Some individuals may, indeed, be both professors and
churchpersons involved in the ministry of theology. However, it seems
that the virtual fusion of the two roles into one—as reflected in the
conceptions of theology that undergird most Catholic theoretical models
of academic freedom—has postponed the development of a conception
of the professor of Catholic theology that takes account of the exigencies
arising from the Catholic university as an American university, and a
conception of university theology as an academic discipline.

A CRITICAL REFLECTION ON RECENT TEACHINGS
OF THE *MAGISTERIUM*

Apostolic Constitution *Sapientia Christiana* of John Paul II

The norms contained in *Sapientia Christiana* are applicable only to
ecclesiastical universities and faculties, and must be understood in light
of the specialized purposes of such institutions. These purposes—the
promotion, through research, of the various disciplines and of knowledge of the Christian revelation, the training of students, and participation in the church's mission of evangelization—together with the
regulations that flow therefrom, do raise doubts as to whether an ecclesiastical university so conceived can be considered a true university as
this is understood in the United States.

The norms contained in the Apostolic Constitution do not engender
the measure of institutional autonomy and academic freedom necessary
to the Catholic university as a university. First, the model of university
governance implicitly contained in the document stands in stark contrast
to that generally accepted in the United States. For "the governing board
of an institution of higher education in the United States operates, with
few exceptions, as the final institutional authority."[119] However, in the
context of the norms of the Apostolic Constitution, the governing board
of the ecclesiastical university does not technically exercise such final
authority. Rather, ultimate authority over the approval of the statutes
of the university and the appointment of its rector or president is vested
in the Vatican's Sacred Congregation for Catholic Education.[120]

Second, the Constitution qualifies academic freedom in keeping with
the stated principles of an ecclesiastical university. "True freedom in
teaching is necessarily contained within the limits of God's Word, as this

is constantly taught by the Church's Magisterium" and "true freedom in research is necessarily based upon firm adherence to God's Word and deference to the Church's Magisterium, whose duty it is to interpret authentically the Word of God."[121] No specific safeguards for faculty members accompany this revised definition of academic freedom. In an earlier section, it is merely stated that the statutes of a particular university must outline "for what reasons and in which ways a teacher can be suspended, or even deprived of his post, so as to safeguard suitably the rights of the teachers, of the Faculty or University, and, above all, of the students and also of the ecclesial community."[122]

Third, in light of the purposes of the ecclesiastical university or faculty, the notions of scholarly competence and juridical competence are also revised in the Constitution. "All teachers must be marked by an upright life, integrity of doctrine, and devotion to duty," while "those who teach matters touching on faith and morals are to be conscious of their duty to carry out their work in full communion with the authentic Magisterium."[123] These criteria of competence, which extend beyond the immediate realm of the scholarly, are formulated in an ambiguous manner. Moreover, contrary to the most basic principles of scholarly freedom and autonomy, the judgment of scholarly competence is placed indirectly in the hands of individuals external to the scholarly community. Hence, the document states that "those who teach disciplines concerning faith or morals must receive, after making their profession of faith, a canonical mission from the Chancellor or his delegate, for they do not teach on their own authority but by virtue of the mission they have received from the Church." Furthermore, all teachers, before given a permanent post or promoted to the highest professorial level, "must receive a declaration of *nihil obstat* from the Holy See."[124]

In view of the norms of the Apostolic Constitution, the ecclesiastical faculty or university is not merely committed to the hierarchical *Magisterium*, but also controlled by it. The need for such control arises out of the perception of the ecclesiastical faculty or university as a continuation of the teaching mission of the hierarchical *Magisterium*. As Curran has pointed out, such a perception "explains why teachers need the *nihil obstat* from Rome, and teachers in disciplines concerning faith and morals also need a canonical mission."[125]

Certainly the Church has the right to establish institutions of research and teaching that, under its direct control, function to serve its narrowly defined ecclesiastical interests and mission. However, it is at best misleading to call these institutions universities when such a description has, in a particular context, come to represent certain characteristics that these institutions simply do not possess. It would seem that the norms outlined in the Constitution—when literally enforced—transform the

Catholic ecclesiatical university into something other than a university, as this is understood in the American context.

The Code of Canon Law

Depending upon how it will be interpreted and implemented, the new Code of Canon Law could relegate the debate concerning academic freedom in the Catholic university to the purely theoretical realm. If interpreted and implemented strictly, the canons that deal with Catholic colleges and universities will greatly curtail the enjoyment of academic freedom on Catholic campuses.

The new Code does recognize the theological scholar's basic right to freedom in research and expression. Yet this right is qualified by, among other things, the relation of the theologian to the hierarchical *Magisterium*. Canon 218 affirms that scholars in the sacred disciplines do enjoy a just freedom of research and expression "while observing a due respect for the *magisterium* of the Church." The exercise of this right, already inherently qualified, is further restricted by Canon 812.[126]

Those canons that are particularly inimical to the enjoyment of the academic freedom necessary to the Catholic university as a university are Canons 810 and 812. Canon 810§1 states:

It is the responsibility of the authority who is competent in accord with the statutes to provide for the appointment of teachers to Catholic universities who besides their scientific and pedagogical suitability are also outstanding in their integrity of doctrine and probity of life; when those requisite qualities are lacking they are to be removed from their positions in accord with the procedure set forth in the statutes.[127]

The notion of scholarly competence that is implied in Canon 810§1 is not without difficulties. The major problem that this canon poses for a necessary academic freedom is the vague nature of the criteria by which competence is judged. What is "integrity of doctrine" and "probity of life?" Who decides when such are lacking, and on what basis is this decision made? It would seem that these tend to be the type of criteria that could be used to justify just about any challenge to professorial competence.

The AAUP has looked unfavorably upon such criteria as found in the faculty handbooks of many Catholic colleges simply because they are far too vague to convey to the professor exactly what is expected of him or her. As early as the "1915 Declaration of Principles," the AAUP insisted that "in every institution the grounds which will be regarded as justifying the dismissal of members of the faculty should be formulated with reasonable definiteness."[128] (Grounds for dismissal are an indication of what constitutes a competent scholar.)

An additional problem with Canon 810§1 is its inclusion of "probity of life" as a criterion of competence. It would seem both unwise and unrealistic to reject all character considerations when judging fitness in any field. However, the notion of "probity of life" constitutes a far too ambiguous standard. Specific rubrics in this area are nearly impossible to formulate. Indeed, they may even be counterproductive. However, it would appear that, in general, any specific faculty character criteria developed by a particular institution should have a reasonably direct relation to the performance of a professor's scholarly duties.

Although the AAUP has tended to define professional fitness largely in academic terms, character considerations have not been entirely ignored. In the "1940 Statement of Principles," the AAUP recognizes (albeit indirectly) "moral turpitude" as grounds for dismissal.[129] Likewise, a 1953 resolution of the organization states that "the test of the fitness of a college teacher should be his *integrity* and his professional competence, as demonstrated in instruction and research."[130]

Finally, clarifying the notion of "moral turpitude," the 1970 "Interpretive Comments" on the 1940 document state:

> The statement applies to that kind of behavior which goes beyond simply warranting discharge and is so utterly blameworthy as to make it inappropriate to require the offering of a year's teaching or pay. The standard is not that the moral sensibilities of persons in the particular community have been affronted. The standard is behavior that would evoke condemnation by the academic community generally.[131]

The AAUP does not dismiss character considerations in determining fitness to teach. However, despite the foregoing clarification, the problem and a residual ambiguity surrounding the AAUP's treatment of it have not been resolved entirely.

Returning to the examination of Canon 810, it should be noticed that the canon does defer to the statutes of the particular university. The canon states that the removal of a professor lacking one or more of the listed qualities must be in accord with statutory procedures. Unless Catholic universities specify clearly the moral and doctrinal grounds for dismissal, it is difficult to imagine how this canon can be reconciled with accepted principles of tenure protection.

Particularly troublesome is Canon 812. This canon, which has no precedent in the earlier Code, states: "It is necessary that those who teach theological disciplines in any institute of higher studies have a mandate from the competent ecclesiastical authority."[132] Prior to examining the implications of this canon for academic freedom on the Catholic campus, points clarifying this canon will be offered.[133]

First, the requirement of a mandate applies only to Latin Rite Catholics and to those professors appointed after November 27, 1983, the date the new Code became effective.[134] Second, Canon 18 states that "laws which . . . restrict the free exercise of rights . . . are subject to a strict interpretation."[135] Therefore, Canon 812 must be interpreted strictly, for it restricts the exercise of a right—the theologian's right to freedom of research and expression that is affirmed in Canon 218. Third, the duty to have a mandate is imposed upon the individual, not the institution.[136] Canonist Ladislas Orsy comments:

There remains still the question, if out of the context and spirit of the new legislation a legal duty can be affirmed in the case of Catholic universities which are persons in canon law [subjects of rights and duties] to appoint only teachers correctly "mandated." The fact is that no evidence can be found for the affirmation of such a duty.[137]

Fourth, Catholics who teach *theology* in Catholic colleges or universities are bound by the law. Theology includes biblical, historical, systematic, and moral theology, and could possibly include canon law and Church history. It does not include religious studies. Fifth, the mandate "is a commission to teach. It is less weighty than a canonical mission . . . but it is more than a mere permission, because 'mandate' includes an element of acting in the name of someone else."[138] Unless otherwise clarified, the "competent ecclesiastical authority" that grants the mandate would appear to be the local bishop.

Finally, it is possible that the American tradition of academic freedom and autonomy will be judged a custom that takes precedence over the law. Orsy writes:

Anyone familiar with the life of universities, including Catholic universities, knows that there has always been a persistent and strong insistence on academic freedom and autonomy of government. *That* can be custom.

But if it is recognized as custom, it is clearly against the present law. Canon 5 gives direction how to handle such conflict: if the custom is explicitly reprobated, it must cease forthwith; if not, it can be tolerated if it is "centenary and immemorial" and the ordinary judges that in the circumstances it could not be prudently removed. Canon 812 includes no clause condemning contrary customs.[139]

The ramifications of the canon—if enforced—for academic freedom in the Catholic college or university would be quite serious.[140] The canon stands in stark contrast to the basic principles of academic autonomy. For the canon vests the ultimate power to decide who will be hired to teach in departments of theology in the bishop or his representative. Moreover, anything granted can be rescinded. What implication might this have for professors who are accused of having violated their mandate by scholarship, teaching, or behavior considered unacceptable by the bishop? Who is juridically competent to judge such an individual? Scholarly peers? Or would the bishop retain the right to rescind a mandate without giving the faculty member the benefit of the procedures of academic due process?

Implied in Canon 812 is the notion that the Catholic university, and especially the department of theology, are extensions of the Church's mission of evangelization.[141] The mandate is considered necessary in that the theology professor is conceived as teaching on behalf of another—namely the hierarchy. The requirement of a mandate for teachers of theology is destructive both of the autonomy of the university and of the freedom necessary for the theological scholar as a full academic partner in the Catholic college or university.

CONCLUSION

In light of the Catholic university's nature and purposes as an American college or university, current Catholic theoretical models of academic freedom are inadequate. Those models that have been labeled restrictive fail to support in theory, or engender in practice, a necessary freedom of teaching, research, and publication. They tend to be wedded to a narrow conception of institutional commitment, one based upon direct subordination to the Church's *Magisterium* and fidelity to its doctrines. Moreover, the model of theology that undergirds these approaches to academic freedom is ecclesiastically centered and, hence, irreconcilable with basic principles of academic freedom and autonomy.

The revised secular models surveyed support the extension to university theology of the principles of academic freedom as understood in secular academia. However, the particular conception of theology upon which these models are founded also tends to be ecclesiastically centered. The reconciliation of this notion of theology with the principles of academic freedom leads—in most of these models—to the formulations of revised notions of competence. While these notions of competence correctly underscore the preeminent place *Magisterial* teaching occupies in the Catholic faith community, they do so in a manner that ultimately imposes upon the professor of theology a personal faith commitment and/or a standard of orthodoxy, in light of which scholarly peers are to judge his or her conclusions. Although basic principles of autonomy are preserved in these models, a necessary freedom—as understood in the American academy—is not.

The inadequacies of both types of models are, for the most part, rooted in their underlying theological presuppositions. All these models, to varying degrees, betray an ecclesiasticism that defines Catholic university theology as primarily a Church-centered discipline and the theology professor as a quasi-official Church spokesperson or minister. The result has been that the nature of university theology as an academic discipline and the role of the theologian as a university scholar have been largely eclipsed.

In the final chapter of this book, the results of the present critique will be utilized in an effort to outline directions for a balanced interpretation of academic freedom in the Catholic context, one that attempts to be true both to the Catholic university's Catholicity and its nature as a genuine university. Presently, however, attention will be turned to a critical examination of the secular model of academic freedom and to a consideration of its applicability to the Catholic college or university.

NOTES

1. These will be more fully explored below.

2. AAUP, "1915 Declaration of Principles," p. 99.

3. Gleason, "Academic Freedom," p. 71.

4. See Thomas Aquinas, *Summa Theologica* I, q. 16, a. 5, in *Basic Writings of St. Thomas Aquinas*, ed. Anton C. Pegis, 2 vols. (New York: Random House, 1945), 1:174.

5. Gerhart Niemeyer, "The New Need for the Catholic University," *Review of Politics* 37 (1975): 483.

6. David Tracy, *Blessed Rage For Order* (New York: Seabury Press, 1975), p. 98. For a discussion of "limit questions" in science, see Tracy, pp. 97–100.

7. "Land O'Lakes Statement," pp. 154–55.

8. Greenburg, *Sapientia Christiana: Impediments to Implementation*, p. 32.

9. Ibid., p. 25.

10. C. Joseph Nuesse, "Assessing Catholic Purpose in American Catholic Higher Education," *Social Thought* 7 (Summer 1981): 35.

11. Catalogues of The Catholic University of America, 1981–83; Nazareth College, 1982–83, p. 2; and Assumption College, 1982, p. 2.

12. Michael P. Walsh, "Nature and Role Today," in *The Catholic University: A Modern Appraisal*, ed. Neil G. McCluskey (Notre Dame, Ind.: University of Notre Dame Press, 1970), p. 52.

13. Hence, what the AAUP, "1915 Declaration of Principles," called proprietary institutions would not qualify as colleges and universities in the American sense.

14. See the AAUP 1915 and 1940 statements.

15. See AAUP, "1915 Declaration of Principles," pp. 94–99.

16. AAUP, "1940 Statement of Principles," p. 108. We are assuming the necessity of some form of tenure protection.

17. Hofstadter and Metzger, *Development of Academic Freedom*, p. 393.

18. See the "Land O'Lakes Statement," p. 154.

19. See Hofstadter and Metzger, *Development of Academic Freedom*, pp. 344–52, especially p. 351.

20. Julian N. Hartt, *Theology and the Church in the University*, (Philadelphia: Westminster Press, 1969), p. 58.

21. James T. Burtchaell, "Hot Gospel in a Cool College? The Question of Advocacy," in *Religion in the Undergraduate Curriculum*, ed. Claude Welch (Washington, D.C.: Association of American Colleges, 1972), p. 23.

22. "Editor's Introduction," in *Colleges and Commitments*, ed. Lloyd J. Averill and William W. Jellema (Philadelphia: Westminster Press, 1971), p. 107. John Paul II has stated: "Because he is bound by the total truth on man, the Christian will, in his research and in his teaching, reject any partial vision of human reality." In "Truth and Freedom," p. 307.

23. See John O'Grady, *Christian Anthropology* (New York: Paulist Press, 1976), pp. 48–49.

24. See O'Grady, *Christian Anthropology*, pp. 42–59; Richard P. McBrien, *Catholicism*, Study Edition (Minneapolis: Winston Press, 1981), pp. 158–61; and the collection of Karl Rahner's essays in *The Rahner Reader*, ed. Gerald A. McCool (New York: Crossroad Publishing Co., 1975), pp. 173–99.

25. McBrien, *Catholicism*, p. 161.

26. Rahner, "The Order of Creation and the Order of Redemption," in *Rahner Reader*, pp. 193–94. As Rahner explains on p. 194, this understanding does not lead to religious imperialism.

27. Tracy, *Blessed Rage for Order*, p. 96.

28. Ibid., p. 98.

29. Niemeyer, "The New Need for the Catholic University," pp. 486–87. Italics mine.

30. Walsh, "Nature and Role Today," p. 53.

31. Henle, "Catholic University of Today," pp. 57–60.

32. *The Code of Canon Law*, Canons 810 and 812, pp. 574–75.

33. As outlined, for example, in the "Land O'Lakes Statement."

34. 1972 Congress of Delegates of Catholic Universities, "The Catholic University in the Modern World," p. 199.

35. This problem might well be exacerbated by the new Code of Canon Law.

36. Hassenger, "What Makes a College Catholic?" p. 181.

37. Clyde A. Holbrook, *Religion: A Humanistic Field* (Englewood Cliffs, N.J.: Prentice-Hall, 1963), p. 41.

38. Ibid., p. 53. Holbrook defines religion as "the study of those forms of conviction, belief, and behavior and those systems of thought in which men express their concerned responses to whatever they hold to be worthy of lasting and universal commitment" (p. 36). It should be noted that Holbrook considers theology a component part of the field of religion.

39. McBrien, *Catholicism*, p. 129.

40. "Land O'Lakes Statement," p. 155.

41. "The Catholic University in the Modern World," p. 200. See also the National Catholic Education Association, "The Relations of American Catholic Colleges and Universities with the Church," *Catholic Mind* 74 (October 1976): 54.

42. NCCB, "Catholic Higher Education and the Pastoral Mission of the Church," p. 5.

43. Ibid. Italics mine.

44. See Holbrook, *Religion: A Humanistic Field*, p. 50.

45. The term *model* is being used in a general rather than a technical fashion. No claim is being made that the ideas of the authors to be examined represent comprehensive and coherent theories.

46. Greenburg, *Sapientia Christiana: Impediments to Implementation*, p. 25.

47. Ibid., p. 19.

48. Ibid., p. 25.

49. Ibid., p. 26.

50. Ibid., p. 33.

51. In the United States, universities are generally considered by most to be, *by definition*, relatively free institutions. Few would deny religious or most other special interest groups the right to establish institutes of higher education for the perpetuation of particular doctrines. However, should such institutions where the pursuit of truth is bridled be called colleges and universities, when in the American context such titles imply a measure of intellectual freedom?

52. Grisez, "Academic Freedom," p. 19. Italics mine.

53. Ibid., p. 18.

54. Ibid.

55. Ibid.

56. Grisez, "Catholic Higher Education," p. 51.

57. Ibid.

58. Grisez, "Academic Freedom," p. 18.

59. Rock, "The Catholic and Academic Freedom," p. 251.

60. Rock does not specify the type of hierarchical intervention into the university that he would allow.

61. McBrien, *Catholicism*, pp. 126–27. Bernard Lonergan writes: "What Karl Rahner refers to as *Denzinger-theologie*, the late Pierre Charles of Louvain named *Christian positivism*. It conceived the function of the theologian to be that of a propagandist for church doctrines. He did his duty when he repeated, explained, defended just what had been said in church documents." See *Method In Theology*, pp. 330–31.

62. Grisez, "Academic Freedom," p. 18.

63. Grisez, "Catholic Higher Education," p. 52.

64. Grisez in "Summary of Discussion," p. 97.

65. Ibid. Here Grisez does acknowledge the need to distinguish between the levels of teaching of the *Magisterium*. See "Summary of Discussion," pp. 98–99.

66. Grisez readily admits to being a "fundamentalist" who holds "fast to the living *magisterium* of the Church." See "Academic Freedom," p. 20.

67. Grisez, "Catholic Higher Education," p. 51.

68. Greenburg, *Sapientia Christiana: Impediments to Implementation*, p. 26.

69. Ibid., p. 11. See also p. 25.

70. Greenburg incorrectly applies the purposes of ecclesiastical universities and faculties to all Catholic colleges and universities.

71. Grisez, "Academic Freedom," p. 18.

72. Ibid.

73. Greenburg offers no explicit model of theology, but it would seem that his conception is similar to Grisez's. See Greenburg's commentary in *Symposium*

on the Magisterium: A Positive Statement, ed. John J. O'Rourke and S. Thomas Greenburg (Boston: St. Paul Editions, 1978), pp. 15–17.

74. Rock, "The Catholic and Academic Freedom," p. 258.

75. Grisez, "Academic Freedom," p. 18. Grisez does not explicitly define the meaning of "principles of faith" in the work under consideration.

76. See Rock, "The Catholic and Academic Freedom," p. 251.

77. See Grisez, "Academic Freedom," p. 19, and his comments in "Summary of Discussion," p. 97.

78. Rock, "The Catholic and Academic Freedom," p. 252.

79. Ibid., pp. 257, 260; Grisez, "Academic Freedom," p. 19.

80. Rock, "The Catholic and Academic Freedom," p. 259.

81. Walsh specifies that his approach is based upon a limited perspective—that of the philosophy of education.

82. Walsh, "University and the Church," p. 106.

83. Ibid., p. 107.

84. Ibid., p. 109–10.

85. Curran, "Academic Freedom," p. 750.

86. See Walsh, "University and the Church," p. 109.

87. He merely discusses the importance of doing theology in dialogue with other disciplines. Ibid., pp. 112–13.

88. Orsy, "Freedom and the Teaching Church," p. 488.

89. Ibid., p. 486.

90. Ibid., pp. 494–96. Orsy could be interpreted as allowing the theologian to reach conclusions contrary to the faith without his or her academic position being compromised. This is the position that will be assumed by the present author.

91. One drawback of this model is that it does not include a categorical rejection of all direct intervention into the university by the hierarchy, although such a rejection *is implied*.

92. Curran, "Academic Freedom," p. 750.

93. Ibid., p. 751. See also Curran and Hunt, *Dissent*, chaps. 2–5.

94. See Gunti, "Academic Freedom as an Operative Principle," p. 188. See also pp. 183–87.

95. Ibid., pp. 262–63.

96. Curran and Hunt, *Dissent*, p. 107. The discussion on pp. 108–9 would *seem* to indicate that, like Gunti, Hunt and Curran include a personal faith dimension in their notion of competence, although this is not entirely clear.

97. Ibid., p. 109.

98. Curran, "Academic Freedom," p. 752.

99. Curran, interview, 16 June 1984.

100. These positions are also similar to that adopted by AATS in its 1960 statement "Academic Freedom and Tenure in the Theological School." *AATS Bulletin* 24 (1960): 35.

101. See Gunti's argument in "Academic Freedom as an Operative Principle," pp. 261–62.

102. Hook, *Heresy Yes Conspiracy No*, p. 164.

103. Ladislas Orsy *appears* to take a similar approach to the academic freedom of the theologian. See "Freedom and the Teaching Church," p. 496. The present

author would argue that a scholar should be protected even if the position assumed is one that directly or indirectly questions, on the basis of theological and related scholarship, the Catholic community's present understanding of the nature and role of the hierarchical *Magisterium*—so long as (in deference to scholarly honesty and fairness to evidence) that present understanding is made clear.

104. Addressing the issue of whether personal faith is required to do (revelation) theology, Avery Dulles writes that it does not seem that such faith is essential. "The theologian does need the capacity to perceive, at least by empathy, what beliefs are implied in (or compatible or incompatible with) commitment to the tradition of the Church. Tradition, like the body and its organs, is best known in a subsidiary way by dwelling in it, rather than in a focal way, by looking at it. . . . But many other factors beside existential commitment enter into the equipment of the theologian, and thus the absence of this one factor could perhaps be compensated for by other factors." *Models of Revelation* (Garden City, N.Y.: Image Books/Doubleday, 1985), p. 15.

105. Walsh, "University and the Church," pp. 112–13.

106. Ibid., pp. 108–9; and Curran, "Academic Freedom," p. 752. However, there appears to be a conflicting tendency toward "ecclesiasticism" in models of Orsy, Gunti, Curran, and Hunt.

107. Walsh, "University and the Church," note 2, p. 117.

108. It is not being assumed that Walsh believes that it should be.

109. Curran, "Academic Freedom," p. 750.

110. Hunt, "Academic Freedom and the Theologian," p. 264.

111. Orsy, "Freedom and the Teaching Church," p. 488.

112. Ibid., p. 493.

113. Ibid., pp. 493–94.

114. Gunti, "Academic Freedom as an Operative Principle," p. 184.

115. Ibid., pp. 188, 258.

116. See *Sacramentum Mundi: An Encyclopedia of Theology*, 1969 ed., s.v. "Theology," by Karl Rahner, and the discussion of the International Theological Commission's "Theses on the Relationship Between the Ecclesiastical Magisterium and Theology," in Sullivan, *Magisterium*, pp. 174–218.

117. Hunt, "Academic Freedom and the Theologian," p. 264.

118. See William J. Sullivan, "The Catholic University and the Academic Study of Religion," in *Religion in the Undergraduate Curriculum*, ed. Claude Welch (Washington, D.C.: Association of American Colleges, 1972), pp. 39–40; and Burtchaell, "The Question of Advocacy," p. 19.

119. AAUP, "1966 Statement on Government of Colleges and Universities," *AAUP Bulletin* 52 (Winter 1966): 377.

120. *Sapientia Christiana*, Article 7; Article 18.

121. Ibid., Article 39.

122. Ibid., Article 30.

123. Ibid., Article 26.

124. Ibid., Article 27. The "canonical mission" was originally designed to insure some measure of Church control over the appointment of teachers of Catholicism in the state-controlled schools of nineteenth-century Europe. See

John P. Boyle, "The Academy and Church Teaching Authority: Current Issues," *Proceedings of the Catholic Theological Society of America* 40 (1985): 172–80.

125. Curran, "Academic Freedom," p. 753.

126. *Code of Canon Law*, Canon 218, p. 151; Canon 812, p. 575. See also Orsy, "Glosses on Canon 812," p. 481.

127. *Code of Canon Law*, Canon 810, p. 574.

128. AAUP, "1915 Declaration of Principles," p. 111. Examples of unacceptably vague criteria can be found in Hunt et al., *Responsibility of Dissent*, pp. 88–89.

129. "1940 Statement of Principles," p. 109.

130. Quoted in Joughin, *Academic Freedom and Tenure*, Editor's note 8, p. 37.

131. AAUP, "Interpretive Comments," p. 326.

132. *Code of Canon Law*, Canon 812, p. 575.

133. For this section, the author is indebted to Orsy's article "Glosses on Canon 812."

134. *Code of Canon Law*, Canon 1, p. 26; Canon 11, p. 31; and Canon 7, p. 29. See also Orsy, "Glosses on Canon 812," p. 483; and the commentary in *Code of Canon Law*, p. 575.

135. *Code of Canon Law*, Canon 18, p. 36. Orsy, "Glosses on Canon 812," p. 481.

136. Orsy, "Glosses on Canon 812," pp. 481–82.

137. Ibid., p. 483.

138. Ibid., p. 480.

139. Ibid., pp. 485–86.

140. Orsy also points out that the civil law implications of Canon 812 "can be momentous in the United States." Ibid., note 1, p. 476.

141. In his commentary, James Coriden points out that the mandate is not "a *formal* association with the Church's mission or ministry of teaching." *Code of Canon Law*, p. 576. Italics mine. However, if at least an indirect relation between theology and the Church's mission were not assumed, the canon would be unnecessary.

6.

A Critical Examination of the American Secular Model of Academic Freedom

Despite widespread agreement concerning the principles that constitute the American secular model of academic freedom, interpretations of these principles have often varied. Some interpretations of academic freedom have included what might be termed a reductionistic approach to knowledge and a rather naive view of the relation between neutrality and objectivity.[1] Specifically, some early proponents of academic freedom tended to identify genuine knowledge with the products of empirical investigation based upon the scientific method.[2] This view of the nature of knowledge was often coupled with a tendency to make bold claims concerning the possibility of value-free scientific inquiry.

Such interpretations of academic freedom have, in the past, led some to the conclusion that the American secular model is incongruous with the Catholic college and university and particularly inapplicable to the theological disciplines within these institutions. However, the guiding thesis of this chapter is the claim that, in theory, what is inapplicable to the Catholic college or university is not the secular model of academic freedom, but rather some interpretations of that model. In the context of a fuller critique of the secular model, it will be argued that these interpretations are not inherently related to or constitutive of this model and, hence, that the principles of academic freedom that have evolved in the United States—if correctly understood—are indeed applicable to the Catholic context.

EMPLOYING THE CRITIQUE

As in the previous chapter, the critical examination to be carried out below is based upon selected critical questions, although the form of these questions will differ somewhat, owing to obvious differences between the current Catholic models of academic freedom and the secular model presently under consideration. Nevertheless, the substance of the critique will remain the same. The specific critical questions helpful in assessing the secular model and its applicability to the Catholic context can be formulated as follows:

1. Does the secular model of academic freedom provide the freedom necessary for the fulfillment of the Catholic university's purposes as a university?
2. Is this model of academic freedom reconcilable with an openness to the study of the full range of human experience and, hence, applicable to all disciplines, including the theological?
3. Are the scholarly and religious commitments of the Catholic university community reconcilable within the secular model of academic freedom?

Each of these questions will be addressed in turn.

Freedom in the University

Does the secular model of academic freedom provide the freedom necessary for the fulfillment of the Catholic university's purposes as a university?

The basis of the secular model of academic freedom is the claim that the achievement of the aims and the proper performance of the functions of the American college or university (whether conceived in theoretical or practical terms) require an atmosphere of freedom. Professors and students must have the right to *"pursue the truth unhindered."* However, as Edmund L. Pincoffs has observed, this general principle "is nearly as vague and full of difficulties as the general understanding that the *summum bonum* is happiness."[3] As we have seen, specific principles, rubrics, and protections have been developed (largely through the efforts of the AAUP) to expand upon this general principle and to make its application to specific situations possible.

The principles, rubrics, and procedural norms that comprise the secular model of academic freedom are designed to safeguard—to the greatest extent possible—the freedom of the professor to pursue and disseminate the truth as he or she sees it. Moreover, there have been, in recent decades, some attempts to broaden the woefully faculty-centered American notion by developing principles aimed at the protection of student freedom.[4] Nevertheless, despite its relative effectiveness in protecting the free pursuit of truth and the dissemination of knowledge in the past, questions can be raised concerning the adequacy of the secular model in the present and for the future.

The secular model of academic freedom evolved largely in response to threats to scholarly freedom and autonomy arising—directly or indirectly—from sources external to the scholarly community; namely, from religious authorities, state legislatures, and donors.[5] Hence, the principles and norms that comprise the model were designed chiefly to address situations within which trustees or administrators, under pressure from these external authorities, disciplined or dismissed "offending" faculty members. In protecting professors from such externally originated threats, the secular model of academic freedom has been at least partially effective.

As Fritz Machlup observes, permanent tenure has been an extremely important means of protecting academic freedom.[6] Tenure, together with the recognized principles of academic due process, has been effective in protecting from dismissal scholars whose professional or personal opinions and conclusions have been judged offensive by his or her institution's trustees, or by other external groups and authorities—religious, financial, or governmental.

However, one can admit only to the partial effectiveness of the principles of academic freedom in protecting the individual scholar from external threats to his or her freedom and autonomy. While such principles have been generally effective in protecting professors from dismissal, they have not been very effective in protecting them from other types of intimidation. "A scholar who, through his writing, speeches, or lectures, offends the sensibilities of others . . . may thereby jeopardize the realization of several of his claims and prospects."[7] These might include a promotion, the approval of his or her courses, and an increase in salary. Subtle forms of infringement on academic freedom can be quite difficult to respond to and often impossible to prove.

Questions have also been raised concerning the adequacy of the secular model and its accompanying rubrics to protect the scholarly community as a whole from external challenges to its autonomy. Theorist Russell Kirk has recently argued that regulatory intrusions by the federal government into the affairs of the university constitute a serious threat to academic freedom.[8] Most colleges and universities rely heavily upon federal funding—either direct (through institutional and research grants) or indirect (through student loan programs, etc.).[9] The power of the federal purse is quite extensive; hence, many colleges and universities are involved in a complex relationship of dependence with the government. This situation has at least the potential of unnecessarily eroding even further the always precarious freedom and autonomy of the institution of higher learning. It would seem that the complex problems that characterize this situation are not easily addressed in terms of the traditional rubrics of the secular model of academic freedom.

Although the principles and rubrics of the secular model of academic freedom have been at least partially successful in protecting faculty members from threats to freedom arising outside the scholarly community, they have had little success in addressing the often complex *internal* challenges to scholarly freedom characteristic of contemporary times. As Edward LeRoy Long, Jr. points out, the traditional secular model of academic freedom is based upon the assumption that most threats to academic freedom originate outside the community of scholars.[10] However, a faculty member's freedom can be restricted by intolerant peers as well as by trustees, administrators, or external powers. Moreover, in some sectors of higher education a growth in faculty independence and power has called into question the tendency to look to administrators, trustees, and external authorities as the only sources of challenges to academic freedom. For example, the freedom and order of the academic community, particularly in larger universities, have been threatened internally by the advent of independent faculty "entrepreneurs"—faculty members who also function as industrial or governmental consultants, or whose research is underwritten by government or industry in ways that circumvent effective university controls.[11]

The AAUP and other organizations have attempted to address new problems by issuing guidelines aimed at expanding and applying basic principles of academic freedom.[12] However, because of the intricate nature of contemporary challenges to academic freedom, principles and regulations can at best only effect ambiguous resolutions to current problems. The complexity of our contemporary situation may call for conceiving of academic freedom, not in terms of codes or rubrics alone, but in terms of a dynamic ethos.[13] It is to this point that attention will now be directed.

Academic Freedom as a Dynamic Ethos

A distinction may be drawn between academic freedom as a principle (with its attendant norms and structured protections) and academic freedom as a dynamic ethos.[14] Long explains:

Academic freedom should encourage (not merely permit) inquiry, exploration, adventuresome creativity, honest social criticism, and the expression of personal convictions. It is often spoken of as a principle, but becomes real only as an atmosphere or working ethos that removes the fear of disadvantage or reprisal from the lives of those who work in educational institutions.[15]

Guiding principles and procedural norms are quite important. Yet, the development of academic freedom on a particular campus requires an atmosphere that an adherence to rubrics alone cannot create.

Long presents a framework helpful in understanding academic freedom in terms of such an atmosphere or dynamic ethos. This framework is composed of four assertions. First, Long points out that "academic freedom is related to both the rights of, and the possible misuses of power by every group within the academic community."[16] This assertion underscores the fact that the central issue of academic freedom is not how the academic community will be treated by those outside its ranks, but rather how the members of the scholarly community will treat one another. The nurturing of academic freedom within this community requires the responsible exercise of power by all within it. The relations among various groups and individuals on campus must be characterized by candor and by an openness that does not merely tolerate, but rather appreciates differences.

This leads to Long's second assertion: "Academic freedom involves the search for genuine diversity."[17] Academic freedom can thrive only in an atmosphere in which a pluralism of ideas and convictions is appreciated, and the incongruities that arise in a pluralistic community are tolerated. The drive for an inevitably artificial coherence and uniformity can only destroy freedom.

Third, Long affirms that "academic freedom must be compatible with the making of discriminating judgments," for without such judgments tolerance can become tractability and diversity can degenerate into chaos.[18] Many discriminating judgments aid the process of institutional self-definition. Some colleges are founded for the study of liberal arts, while others, for the study of sciences and technology. "An institution chartered to teach engineering and science does not abrogate its academic freedom by not developing a major in performing arts."[19] It might be added, however, that the academic freedom of the students of such an institution might very well be violated if the study of science or engineering is carried out in an isolated fashion without some reference to the larger context of these fields or to their cultural and valuational dimensions. Long does warn that some discriminating judgments do not serve institutional self-definition but rather threaten the learning process. These would include judgments aimed at censorship—the exclusion of certain points of view or their spokespersons.

Finally, Long asserts that "academic freedom must protect the voluntary covenants of advocacy that arise within the covenant of inquiry."[20] Members of the academic community must have the right to join voluntary organizations committed to a moral or political cause (either on the campus or beyond it). This right has been preserved chiefly because colleges and universities, as communities of inquiry, have refrained from requiring that their members assume particular positions of advocacy. Such a requirement can, in Long's view, change the essential purposes of the college or university.

Members of the academic community should be free to commit themselves to "subgroups of advocacy" within that community. "But it is another matter to coerce a community of inquiry to make an institutional stand that commits each and every member of a voluntary society and academic community brought together on one premise to an action role postulated on another commitment."[21] There might be situations in which an academic community might take a stand based upon an *ad hoc* consensus. However, Long cautions that this is only possible if such a stand does not violate "the convictions of any members of the academic community."[22]

Long sketches an approach to academic freedom that transcends principles and rubrics. When academic freedom is conceived of in terms of a dynamic ethos, rather than merely as a set of principles, the flexibility of the notion is made more apparent. Through such an understanding, academic communities are made better equipped both to enhance and protect scholarly freedom in the face of complex and rapidly changing circumstances.

Reapproaching the Critical Question

Does the secular model of academic freedom provide the freedom necessary for the fulfillment of the Catholic university's purposes as a university? In theory, the secular model provides such freedom. The problem is whether the rubrics and principles that constitute the secular model are adequate to protect in practice the freedom necessary to the university in contemporary times. As has been discussed above, existing principles and rubrics alone are not always able to enhance and protect scholarly freedom in the face of complex and subtle challenges to that freedom.

It is important to emphasize that principles and structured protections are necessary—especially to guard against what have been termed external challenges to academic freedom. In the case of the Catholic college or university, such principles take on an added value for two major reasons. First, although most Catholic colleges and universities have accepted in theory the principles of academic freedom as outlined in the AAUP 1940 statement, questions concerning the applicability of these principles to Catholic institutions are still raised by some.

Second, the secular model of academic freedom has evolved chiefly in response to externally originated intrusions into the university and has been relatively successful in guarding against such intrusions. The principles that comprise the model are both adequate for and necessary to the maintenance of the autonomy of the Catholic college or university and the preservation of the freedom of its scholars in all disciplines. Church hierarchical interference—direct or indirect—remains a potential threat in the Catholic context. This threat is not only underscored by some of the Catholic theorists surveyed, but is also evident in recent Church legislation regarding Catholic colleges and universities.

In short, the secular model and its attendant rubrics are necessary to the maintenance of academic freedom on the Catholic college and university campus. However, as suggested above, the secular model is not entirely adequate for any college or university confronting the complex contemporary challenges to academic freedom. As Long has argued, such challenges require a nuanced approach rather than merely the application of simple propositions. This is especially true in the Catholic context within which unique problems arise: problems concerning the definition of religious institutional commitment, the nature of Catholic university theology, and the status of theology professors.

The Applicability of the Secular Model

Is the secular model of academic freedom reconcilable with an openness to the study of the full range of human experience and, hence, applicable to all disciplines, including the theological?

Inherent in the secular model of academic freedom is nothing that would preclude its application to the study of all aspects of human experience, including the religious. However, in order for such application to be possible, reductionistic interpretations of knowledge that have sometimes accompanied the secular model in the past must be avoided, and the religious or theological study to which this model is applied must assume an appropriate academic form.

Avoiding Reductionistic Interpretations of Knowledge

In the early period of its development, the American notion of academic freedom was sometimes closely aligned with a rather narrow conception of the nature of knowledge and with what, in retrospect, appear to be ambiguous conceptions of the meaning of objectivity and its relation to neutrality.[23] Specifically, some early proponents of academic freedom identified true knowledge with the products of empirical investigation based upon the scientific method. Moreover, this view of the nature of knowledge was often coupled with a tendency to make overzealous claims concerning the possibility of value-free scientific inquiry.[24]

These interpretations of the nature of knowledge and of the possibility of value-free scholarship were sometimes joined to the theoretical philosophy of higher education that had undergirded the growing American research universities of the late nineteenth and early twentieth centuries.[25] It was during this period that the philosophy of higher education in general, and the developing concept of academic freedom in particular, were influenced by the Darwinist revolution in science. Prior to discussing more fully the reductionistic interpretations of academic freedom, the influence of this revolution will be examined in the context of a brief overview of the intellectual roots of the secular model of academic freedom.

The contemporary American notion of academic freedom is heir to a number of historical intellectual currents. These have been emphasized to varying degrees by different scholars. Ralph Fuchs identifies three major foundations upon which rests the notion of academic freedom: the philosophy of intellectual freedom extending back to ancient Greece, the idea of scholarly autonomy that arose in the universities of Europe, and the freedoms guaranteed in the American Bill of Rights.[26]

Robert M. MacIver views the principle of academic freedom as a development out of a broad movement that included "the ending of theocratic overlordship, the establishment of the territorial state, . . . the crumbling of the oligarchical class system, the growth of the consciousness of nationality, the accelerating advancement of science, . . . and the whole process of socioeconomic change that is summed up in the expression 'Industrial Revolution.' " Inherent in these developments were new "thought forms that rejected the usurpations of authority based only on birth or predetermined status and proclaimed the right of man as man to cherish his own doctrines, to worship in his own way, and to compete for power or place on equal terms with his fellow men."[27]

Richard Hofstadter discovers the eighteenth- and nineteenth-century roots of academic freedom in "the ideals of toleration and religious liberty and the intellectual liberalism of the Enlightenment."[28] In a similar vein, commentators and scholars—William F. Buckley and Frederick Gunti, for example—have recognized the specific influence of John Stuart Mill's notion of the free marketplace of ideas and the general tenet of liberal creed that "truth will emerge victorious."[29] Walter P. Metzger, dealing with a later historical period in the work he coauthored with Hofstadter, emphasized the revolution in science brought about by Darwin's work and the influence of the German idea of academic freedom upon American higher eduation.[30]

Metzger considers Darwinism particularly influential in the development of the notion of academic freedom insofar as "a 'new' rationale for the concept grew out of the Darwinian debate."[31] First, Darwinism fostered the development of a new conception of truth. Rejecting the dogmatic and monolithic model of truth operative in colleges of the pre-Civil War era, the evolutionist affirms that all beliefs are *tentatively* true or false. Any claim to truth must be able to withstand continuous inquiry and the scientific methods of verification. Thus Darwinism, through its influence upon science, contributed to a new conception of truth that enables one to tolerate error and leave its correction to the scientific processes of inquiry and verification.[32] This process of open verification quickly became identified in the minds of many with the scientific method of empirical verification and, gradually, "knowledge" became synonomous with scientific knowledge.[33]

Second, the process of verification so necessary to the scientific enterprise is a process that follows certain rules—rules and methods known and employed by experts. This fact aided the development of the notion of scientific (scholarly) competence, which places the prerogative of judging the fitness of a scholar within the domain of his or her professional peers.[34]

Finally, Darwinism introduced into science a number of values. These values include tolerance, honesty, testifiability, cooperativeness, as well as universalism and neutrality. Darwinist science strove to free itself from particularistic criteria whether creedal, racial, or national when assessing the merits of a scholar and his or her work. Correspondingly, from the Darwinist perspective, the search for knowledge must be carried out in a relatively *neutral* manner, transcending any particular ideology. Hence, "professors must renounce all commitments that corrupt the passion for truth."[35]

The Darwinist revolution in science, then, accelerated the development of the importance of the scientific method of empirical verification and contributed to the recognition of the value of objective scientific inquiry. While these developments constituted positive contributions to the advancement of scholarship, they were often subject to exaggeration or misinterpretation. Hence, affirmations of the importance of the empirical methods of the natural sciences sometimes degenerated into a discounting of all knowledge beyond the empirical. As a result, disciplines whose principles are not always empirically verifiable—including theology and philosophy—were often looked upon as "second-class citizens in the academe."[36]

The impact of Darwinism in this area can be perceived in the writings of those who came under its influence. For example, mathematician Chauncey Wright "maintained that science should no longer be concerned with matters beyond factual description."[37] In a more radical vein, Frances E. Abbott wrote: "I vindicate the rights of the human intellect as the sole *discoverer* of truth; I maintain the unique and exclusive claim of the scientific method as the sole organon of its discovery."[38] It should be understood that such positions constitute—at least in part—reactions to the religious dominance over learning that had existed until that time.[39]

There are some commentators who claim that a narrow emphasis upon the scientific method of empirical verification continues to dominate higher learning. Such is the position of James T. Burtchaell, former Provost of the University of Notre Dame, who considers the dominance of the scientific method the source of the "single most powerful bias against religious studies in all colleges: state, private, and church-affiliated."[40]

It would seem, however, that a narrowly empiricist approach no longer imbues American higher learning. First, most scholars have come to recognize that this approach to knowledge is difficult to defend in light of developments in philosophy and sociology. For example, scientists have come to accept (at least in theory) the limitations of the inductive method as first discussed by the eighteenth-century philosopher David Hume.[41] It might be recalled that Hume considered the validity of inferences made on the basis of empirical observation or experience probable rather that absolute. Hume writes:

For all inferences from experience suppose, as their foundation, that the future will resemble the past and that similar powers will be conjoined with similar sensible qualities. If there be any suspicion that the course of nature may change, and that the past may be no rule for the future, all experience becomes useless and can give rise to no inference or conclusion. It is impossible therefore, that any arguments from experience can prove this resemblance of the past to the future, since all these arguments are founded on the supposition of the resemblance.[42]

Thus, although inductive inferences are pragmatically valuable to scientists, they remain only of probable validity. Hence, the notion that there exists order in nature remains an assumption rather than an absolute assertion.[43]

A narrowly empirical approach to knowledge has also been challenged by critiques such as that of phenomenologist Edward Husserl. "Husserl praises the basic thrust of empiricism toward an experiential grounding of knowledge but seeks to warn empiricism against what he considers its unwitting metaphysical bias—the restriction of 'experience' to sensory perception and of sensory perception to passive recording of particular data."[44] Knowlege for Husserl is experientially based. However, experience is not merely the "recording of sense data." Rather, it is "all awareness, the totality of our 'taking-in,' our perceiving, grasping, seeing."[45] Hence, the investigation of the "empirical" world of nature (narrowly understood) could not be the "most basic source of certainty and truth."[46]

Insights derived from the sociology of knowledge have also given rise to questions concerning the adequacy of a narrowly empirical approach to knowledge.[47] The central ideas of the sociology of knowledge are based upon the insight that "reality" (that which is judged independent of human volition) and "knowledge" (the perception of reality as real, and as possessing certain characteristics) are socially relative.[48] As Peter L. Berger and Thomas Luckmann have argued, "reality" and "knowledge" are socially constructed and maintained in an ongoing dialectical process by which the products of social activity and human expressivity (the process of externalization) take on the aura of "facts" that are independent of human activity (the process of objectivation) and which are reappropriated by succeeding generations through social learning or socialization (the process of internalization).[49] Hence, the human being creates society and society creates the human being in a complex, ongoing dialectical process.

Scientists obviously do not exist in a pristine state within a social and historical vacuum. Therefore, from the perspective of the sociology of knowledge, empirical observations are always made from a particular social standpoint—a socially relative standpoint. Moreover, scientific methods, theories, etc. are socially constructed and maintained and are subject to the same conditioning influences as all other socially created systems of knowledge and meaning.[50]

The foregoing represents merely a brief sampling of the types of challenges that have been made to the position of the narrow empiricist. It would seem that very few scholars today would be willing to restrict reality to sensory data. Moreover, it has come to be recognized that uninterpreted facts do not exist. The collector, as a social individual, and his or her methods of collection are subject to conditioning influences that have been variously labeled and emphasized by scholars of different disciplines and schools of thought. Scientists themselves have come to recognize the limitations of the scientific method. Even the "hard" sciences are based upon presuppositions and assumptions not verifiable directly by empirical methods.[51]

The place the humanities occupy in American colleges and universities also belies the assertion that American higher education continues to be dominated by a narrow empiricism or by a naive devotion to the scientific method. It is true that in recent decades the attention directed to the sciences has often eclipsed the importance of the humanities, sparking resentment among some humanists.[52] Nonetheless, no American college or university, and few scholars, if any, would seek systematically to exclude the humanities from the curriculum on the grounds that they are unscientific or unscholarly. The perennially important place of the humanities in the college curriculum is affirmed by the sociologist and theorist of academic freedom Robert MacIver. He writes that in the university, "knowledge itself tends to be identified with the fields of scientific discovery. But the need for the 'humanities' is not lessened, instead it is rather increased by the triumphs of the physical sciences and of the technology that accompanies them."[53]

In light of the challenges to a narrow empiricism, and in view of the place the humanities continue to occupy in the college curriculum, it is difficult to demonstrate that there continues to exist a widespread systematic and conscious bias in favor of empiricism or a naive adherence to the scientific method in American higher education.

The issue pertinent to the present discussion is not the extent to which a narrow empiricism survives in American higher education, but whether such an empiricism is entailed by the secular model of academic freedom.

While some early proponents of academic freedom exhibited a narrowly empirical approach to knowledge (and perhaps interpreted academic freedom in light of this approach), there is no evidence that such an approach to knowledge is inherent in the secular model. The principles that comprise this model are certainly flexible enough to be applicable to the various disciplines and their methods and procedures. It would seem that the secular model of academic freedom would be applicable to any discipline or field that is truly scholarly, that is, one that contains within it "a major component of scholarship that can be validated according to publicly verifiable procedures of disciplined study" or, stated differently, "whose materials and methods are accessible to any scholar with the necessary technical and linguistic equipment."[54] It would seem that, like other disciplines and fields within the humanities, theology can meet this criterion.

Noted Protestant scholars such as Clyde A. Holbrook and Jaroslav Jan Pelikan have unambiguously affirmed the place of theology (as well as religion, of which theology is a subfield) among the humanities and, correspondingly, among those fields suitable for university study.[55] As Holbrook has argued, the fact that a theology may be rooted in or based upon conceptions of the supernatural does not necessarily preclude its acceptance as a humanistic scholarly discipline.[56]

According to Pelikan, the criterion that theological research must fulfill to justify its inclusion in the college or university is that it must contain "a major component of scholarship that can be validated according to publicly verifiable procedures of disciplined study."[57] If the methods or data of a field of study are esoteric rather than public, no true scholarship can be carried out. In Pelikan's view, some types of theology do fulfill this criterion—historical theology and most biblical theology, for example. He can even envision certain types of dogmatic and moral theology meeting this criterion. Beyond these general observations, however, Pelikan offers no detailed descriptions of the mode of theologizing appropriate for the college or university.

Holbrook argues that, when judging the appropriateness of theology as a field of university study, one must avoid the assumption that theology is a monolithic entity. Rather, the various conceptions of theology and modes of theologizing must be assessed on an individual basis.[58] It would seem that Holbrook would find inappropriate any approach to theology that necessitates an adherence to a particular religious commitment by a professor or a student, that involves a theological imperialism over other disciplines, or that includes any unyielding dogmatic stance.[59] Theology within the free university must be "subject to the same kinds of rational evaluation and types of evidential criticism as any structure which makes similar types of claims for its authenticity, whether they be in the religious, scientific, political, or aesthetic realms."[60]

Holbrook rejects the notion that because theology deals with data and experiences that are not open to general inspection that it forfeits its place in the university curriculum. "Any discipline," he states, "which purports to deal with ultimate meanings or comprehensive interpretations of human experience similarly involves prerational assumptions, experiences, or 'givens' which provide the starting points of normative interpretations." He further argues that "since theology is concerned with the rational understanding of these experiences rather than directly with the engendering of them, it, no more or less than other fields in which basic insights are presupposed, maintains a type of esoteric privacy which would make it unfit for a place in the university."[61] What can be included among "prerational assumptions" without a particular theology becoming unacceptably esoteric is not made clear. However, Holbrook insists that theology must remain subject to the same rational evaluation and evidential criticism as other fields and disciplines—scientific, political, and aesthetic—that include assumptions about which educated persons in good faith disagree.

Protestant theologian Schubert M. Ogden has examined in greater detail than have the foregoing theorists the specific question of theology's status as a scholarly ("scientific") discipline.[62] Ogden identifies two suppositions that he considers the source of contemporary doubts concerning the legitimacy of theology as a science: first, "that theology by its very nature involves an appeal to special criteria of meaning and truth to establish some or all of its statements," and second, "that the theologian himself must be a believer already committed to the Christian understanding of reality, and thus to the truth of the statements that theological reflection ostensibly seeks to establish."[63] As Ogden points out, these suppositions are by no means the invention of critics, but represent theology's traditional self-understanding.[64] In his view, they are valid bases upon which to question the status of theology as a scholarly discipline. But need theology conform to these suppositions? Ogden thinks not.

Ogden defines theology as "the fully reflective understanding of the Christian witness of faith as decisive for human existence."[65] Theology so defined presupposes a correlation between the *immediate* object of theology—the Christian witness of faith—and human existence for which this witness claims to be decisive.[66] Because of its correlative dimension, theology is "subject to assessment by dual criteria of adequacy," namely appropriateness and understandability.[67]

Theology is appropriate if "it represents the same understanding of faith as is expressed in the 'datum discourse' of the Christian witness."[68] The explicit witness of faith is manifested in the self-defining acts and normative positions that constitute Christian tradition, in particular, the canon of Scripture.[69]

A theology is understandable if "it meets the relevant conditions of meaning and truth universally established with human existence."[70] Christian witness claims a decisiveness for human existence, and accompanying this claim is an implicit claim to the truth of this witness. This truth-claim must meet the conditions of truth "given with existence itself."[71] Hence, insofar as Christian witness constitutes a conception and understanding of reality, it must—in order to be warranted—confirm and be confirmed by the understanding of reality found in philosophy and the sciences.[72] The understanding of reality represented by the Christian witness is not always compatible with other such understandings. Nonetheless, theology's task remains the same: "to achieve an understanding of the Christian witness that, however different it may be from all previous witnesses and their theological interpretations, appropriately grasps their essential meaning; and that, with whatever differences from current philosophical and scientific opinions, is understandable by the same criteria of meaning and truth to which they, too are subject."[73] Criteria of meaning and truth will vary according to historical circumstances. Hence, theology's understandability is best achieved if theology is carried out in the context of a sustained discussion with secular knowledge.[74]

In light of the foregoing, Ogden rejects the supposition that theology must appeal to criteria of meaning and truth different from those employed by cognate disciplines. He likewise rejects the supposition that the theologian must himself or herself be a believer. Ogden asks: If faith is a condition of the possibility of theological work, how can one know when one is in a position to undertake such work?

Since not even I myself can presume to look upon my heart, which God alone is able to judge, either there is no such test available to human judgment, in which case the condition of my personal faith cannot be known to be met; or else it can be known to be met, but only insofar as faith is certified by the profession of certain beliefs. In that case, the question arises how anyone having the least regard for the scriptural understanding of "faith" could suppose either of himself or of another that the profession of even the most orthodox beliefs is any guarantee of the presence of faith.[75]

According to Ogden, what is required of the theologian in order to understand the Christian witness of faith, "is not that the theologian accept the *answer* of the witness of faith, but only that he ask the *question* to which it is addressed."[76]

Ogden, then, argues that there can be no question about theology's right to be considered a scholarly scientific discipline. The suppositions that would preclude the acceptance of theology as legitimate are, in his view, those to which theology has traditionally conformed rather than suppositions to which theology must conform.[77]

The positions presented thus far in this section are those of Protestant theologians. Hence, the question of the applicability of the criterion of public verification to specifically Catholic theology arises. Is Catholic theology a legitimate scholarly discipline to which the principles of academic freedom are, therefore, applicable? Unless the criterion of public accessibility is construed in a very narrow fashion (that is, in a way that precludes any consideration of the supernatural) it would seem that Catholic theology can be accepted as a legitimate scholarly discipline.

David Tracy is a Catholic scholar who has addressed at length the question of the status of Catholic theology as a legitimate (public) discipline.[78] Tracy offers a general description of Christian fundamental theology as "philosophical reflection upon common human experience and upon the Christian fact."[79] More specifically, such theology involves a critical correlation of these two principal sources.[80]

"The principal method of investigation of the source 'common human experience' can be described as a phenomenology of the 'religious dimension' present in everyday and scientific experience."[81] Through such a method, the phenomena of symbols and gestures of everyday life and language can be analyzed with a view toward uncovering their religious dimensions.[82] The investigation of the Christian fact, on the other hand, is best described as a historical and hermeneutical (interpretive) investigation of the classical Christian texts among which Scripture remains fundamental.[83]

The results of the investigations described above "should be correlated to determine their significant similarities and differences and their truth value."[84] It should be noted that, in Tracy's view, correlation does not complete the theologian's task. The question of the *truth-status* of the meanings of the Christian fact remains. This is the crucial issue in any discussion of the status of theology as a scientific discipline.[85] Tracy argues that the truth-status of the Christian fact can be explored through metaphysical reflection—"the philosophical validation of the concepts 'religion' and 'God' as necessarily affirmed or necessarily denied by all our beliefs and understandings."[86]

In short, Tracy argues that fundamental theology can be considered a full scientific discipline in that it fulfills the criterion that "its mode of argumentation, its criteria, its evidence, its warrants, its methods are available for public investigation."[87] Within Tracy's revisionist interpretation of fundamental theology, the sources, methods of analysis and interpretation, and method of assessing truth-claims (metaphysical philosophy) are indeed "public." Moreover, Tracy rejects the notion that the fundamental theologian must be a believer, a notion that would cast doubts upon theology's status as a scientific discipline in that it implies that special claims to personal esoteric experiences are part of the data of theology.[88]

In recent years, Tracy has also argued on behalf of the public character of confessional systematic theology.[89] Such theology, rooted in a particular religious tradition, recognizes the reality of historicity while it seeks "to retrieve, interpret, translate, mediate the resources . . . of the classic [normative] events of understanding of our fundamental religious questions embedded in the classic events, persons, images and texts of the tradition for transforming our present horizon."[90] Briefly put, the task of systematic theology is the reinterpretation of a particular tradition for the present situation.[91]

In Tracy's view, confessional theology can claim to be public on a number of grounds. First, like fundamental theology, systematic theology utilizes the methods and resources of the contemporary intellectual situation.[92] Moreover, despite the fact that such theology begins with the tradition or "inner history" of the Christian community, it allows the views of others outside this community to illuminate its self-understanding, while directing constant attention to the dialectic between formulations of its revelatory tradition and the contemporary experience of the theologian. Finally, insofar as the systematic theologian deals with a major religious tradition (one having classical—normative—texts, events, images and persons), interprets that tradition in a full and critical sense, and directs this work toward the "public of the church," Tracy believes that his or her theology should be considered public rather than private.

Since even their most skeptical critics grant that the Hebrew and Christian traditions include classical texts, the hermeneutical theologians can argue that they perform a public function analogous to the philosophical interpreter of the classics of philosophy or the literary critic of the classics of our culture.

Any text, event, or person that reaches the level of a classic expression of a particular person, community or tradition serves an authentically public character.[93]

Tracy's arguments on behalf of the public character of systematic theology avoid a narrow interpretation of the criterion of public accessibility. They could be utilized to argue for the public status of other modes of doing Catholic theology—even those whose methodologies differ from Tracy's. In order to be accepted as a legitimate scholarly discipline, however, it does seem that a particular approach to Catholic theology must avoid the requirement of personal faith on the part of the theologian, static conceptions of revelation, and theologically positivistic conceptions of the roles of theologians and the *Magisterium*.

Recent theological work (of Catholics such as Tracy as well as that of many Protestant scholars), has sparked a discussion and fueled a process of reinterpretation, both of which *at least indicate* that contemporary Catholic theology need not conform to the suppositions that have bound its traditional manifestations. Unless the criterion of public accessibility is construed in a very narrow way, Catholic theology can be considered a scholarly discipline that deserves a place in the university. Hence, it can and should enjoy the protection of academic freedom.

Commitment and Objectivity

Are the scholarly and religious commitments of the Catholic college or university community reconcilable within the secular model of academic freedom?

This question has two dimensions. The first is the issue of whether the religious commitments of the scholar and his or her scholarly commitment to the pursuit of truth are reconcilable within the secular model. This issue has particular relevance in the context of the Catholic college or university department of theology where one tends to find a large proportion of religiously-committed instructors.

The issue of the reconcilability of an institutional religious commitment with a necessary academic freedom constitutes the second dimension of the critical question at hand. Is a university's sponsorship by, and commitment to, a particular denomination incongruous with the principles of academic freedom as understood in the American context?

In the sections that follow, it will be suggested that the principles of academic freedom do not preclude religious commitment on the part of a scholar so long as the notion of scholarly objectivity is properly understood. Moreover, it will be argued that institutional religious commitment need not be incongruous with academic freedom unless such commitment is interpreted as necessitating the imposition of an orthodoxy upon an academic community as a whole, or upon a particular department within that community.

The Committed Scholar and Academic Freedom

As noted earlier in this chapter, accompanying the rise to prominence of scientific methods of empirical verification in colleges and universities of the late nineteenth and early twentieth centuries was a corresponding emphasis upon the importance of an "objective" approach to inquiry.[94] However, just as some interpretations of the scientific method of empirical verification led frequently to narrow conceptions of knowledge, so too the notion of objectivity was sometimes subject to exaggerated interpretations that considered the abandonment of (especially religious) commitments a prerequisite to sound scholarship. Philosopher Huston Smith points out that for one who would adhere to such interpretations, "the most important ingredient in the intellectual venture is objectivity, the mind's innocence and transparency before the facts. Since convictions, beliefs, and commitments involve emotional attachments, they necessarily interfere with this transparency. So, on the altar of objectivity, they must be sacrificed."[95] It will be argued that this conception of objectivity is not a constituent part of the American secular model of academic freedom and, indeed, most contemporary scholars would consider such an approach to the notion at best naive.

The notion of scholarly objectivity (and the related ideas of value freedom and neutrality) is a troublesome concept in that its proponents have often disagreed about its specific nature. The roots of this concept have been traced variously to the empiricist heritage, the influence of Darwinism on the scientific method and to thinkers such as Max Weber.[96] Because of the ambiguity that often surrounds the notion of objectivity, it is important to examine its various dimensions prior to assessing its place in the American secular model of academic freedom.

Any discussion of the concept of objectivity must begin with the observation that the mind cannot simply mirror facts without disturbing or rearranging them. First, the human mind must interpret and structure sense data. Moreover, thought is selective and specialized since human beings cannot study everything at once. Finally, as philosophers of history, sociologists of knowledge, and psychologists have emphasized, the human's cultural and historical context, as well as his or her emotions, condition thought and, thus, limit objectivity.[97] In short, "since all observation ultimately implies a human observer operating either directly or through his mechanical extensions, all scientific propositions must of necessity reflect the existence of the subjective observer."[98]

In light of the impossibility of achieving a pure objectivity, how might objectivity be defined? And what is its relation to various types of neutrality? Smith has suggested the definition of objectivity required of the scholar: objectivity is simply *fairness to evidence*. "This involves open-mindedness—the willingness, even eagerness, to entertain seriously every item of relevant evidence that has a bearing on the problem at hand. It involves maximum responsiveness to the facts, seeing each, as far as possible, with discrimination and without distortion to the end that it may be assigned its appropriate and becoming weight."[99] What distinguishes this definition is that the identification of objectivity with neutrality is avoided.

Objectivity cannot imply a complete cognitive neutrality—the suspension of judgment concerning the truth or falsity of statements of fact—since such a neutrality is impossible to achieve. As Smith notes, "The complete skeptic is a philosopher's fiction."[100]

A general value neutrality is also not required for objective scholarship. Sociologists Talcott Parsons and Gerald M. Platt point out that for Max Weber, "the standards of cognitive validity and significance are basically independent of . . . noncognitive value considerations. Although noncognitive values influence what people want to know and what knowledge they want to use, the *cognitive* validity or invalidity of the propositional system itself is not determined by these noncognitive values." Weber's insistence that the standards of knowledge be value-neutral or value-free "does not mean that seekers after knowledge are or should be dehumanized creatures whose action is not guided by any values."[101]

In addition to being unnecessary for objective scholarly work, a general value neutrality is impossible to achieve in a pure form. For "value judgments are as inescapable as judgments of fact, so that generalized neutrality here is as impossible and indefensible as in regard to knowledge."[102] Although general value neutrality may be unattainable in practice, attempts to achieve it could disintegrate into an irresponsible indifference.[103]

Specific value neutrality toward the academic virtues is not required for objective scholarship in that such a requirement would be clearly nonsensical in the academic context. However, whether specific value neutrality toward the social order is required for objective scholarship remains a complex issue.[104] There is considerable debate about whether *as an institution*, a university should remain neutral vis-à-vis the social order. It is not necessarily the case that when an institution assumes a position on a particular question of social policy, the objectivity of the scholarship performed within it is thereby *directly* compromised. In addition, much has been written in support of the assumption by the university of such positions.[105] It has been argued that while universities must avoid power politics and direct participation in political processes, the demand that universities remain aloof from broad questions of social policy and social values could have negative consequences. Education could become "isolated from the mainstream of practical life, and in consequence partially trivialized." Moreover, "complete social neutrality may contribute to a condition in which education (as we know it) is impossible."[106] Such was the experience of the European universities during the Nazi period.

It should be noted that some scholars of the "political left," such as Milton Fisk and Robert Paul Wolff, have argued that the American university is not, in practice, neutral toward the social order. They have suggested that most universities exhibit implicit and explicit value commitments to the capitalistic *status quo* through institutional goals and principles, admission policies, academic standards, criteria of scholarly competence, research projects, and relations with government and industry.[107]

The abandonment of the traditional (ostensibly) neutral stance of the American university can also involve negative consequences. The appeal of the university for public support and for public respect of its autonomy is based, in part, on the fact that the university is a nonpartisan institution devoted to the disinterested pursuit of truth. The assumption by universities of positions on questions of social policy could very well lead to a weakening of the autonomous status of these institutions.[108]

Furthermore, unless a complete consensus concerning an institutional position is achieved, there will always be individuals with differing viewpoints within the university community whose convictions will be violated by such an institutional position. These individuals may very well experience pressures to conform to this position—pressures that can limit their academic freedom, and indirectly affect the objectivity of their scholarship. From this perspective it is argued that "the provision of a setting for open dialogue, safe from pressures for reprisal and ensuing respect for the rights of dissent, is possible only if the institution within which this dialogue is to take place is itself, *as an institution*, neutral on the issues being debated."[109]

It cannot be demonstrated that institutional neutrality toward the social order is required to preserve the objectivity of the work of the scholars within the institution. Indeed, such neutrality might be ultimately injurious to objectivity if a question of social policy involved the survival of the university as an institution devoted to the free pursuit and dissemination of knowledge. On the other hand, the dangers to the academic freedom (and indirectly to the objectivity) of scholars posed by the commitment of an institution to a particular political position are readily apparent.

This issue is not one that can be addressed solely on the basis of a particular principle or rubric. Rather, it is one that requires an approach that understands the college or university community and its academic freedom in dynamic rather than in static propositional terms. As Long points out, the important question is not "Should the college take a stand on a particular social question?" but rather "What ways of either taking a stand or not taking a stand are most compatible with our own freedom and authenticity? What are the values preserved and the values destroyed by each of several kinds of action or non-action?"[110] In this way each individual academic community will be able to examine—in light of its particular context—specific options for institutional commitment as they arise and to address them in a manner that maximizes that community's responsible freedom.

Scholarly objectivity does not require neutrality toward the social order on the part of the professor as an individual. The professor retains all the rights accorded to every other citizen. In the United States, these include the right to engage in appropriate political activity. When dealing with controversial political/value questions, the professor is bound by the norm of objectivity to be fair to the evidence—that is, to treat controversial issues as controversial issues. Although free to offer his or her opinions, the professor should make every attempt to place those opinions within the context of a fair representation of opposing viewpoints.

If scholarly objectivity is understood in the general sense outlined above, then it can be safely affirmed that, from the AAUP "1915 Declaration" onward, this concept has been considered in the United States a defining characteristic of the genuine scholar, that is, of one who can justly assert a claim to academic freedom.[111] However, there appears to be nothing inherent in the principles or procedures that constitute the American secular model of academic freedom that requires a religious, political, or general value neutrality on the part of scholars for sound research—even if such a neutrality were possible.

On the question of responsible, objective teaching, the focus within the secular model has been on the avoidance of indoctrination—particularly when teaching immature students.[112] When dealing with controversial matters in the classroom, the professor is obliged to expose students in a fair manner to the competing scholarly opinions on these matters.[113] However, the professor "is under no obligation to hide his own opinion under a mountain of equivocal verbiage. . . ."[114] Hence, the teacher is not required to remain neutral on controversial matters treated in the classroom, if neutrality is understood as refraining from formulating or expressing an opinion on these matters.

In light of the foregoing discussion, it appears that the secular model of academic freedom does not require the absence of religious or value commitments on the part of a scholar (even if such a state of neutrality were possible). What is required is objectivity—fairness to evidence—in research and teaching.

Some scholars, Smith and Holbrook for example, have convincingly argued that religious commitment need not be incongruent with objective research. As Smith observes, openmindedness and objectivity are the principal marks of genuine conviction. When one genuinely believes, one will be confident that all new evidence will reinforce rather than challenge one's belief. Dogmatism, it would seem, is born of the fear that new evidence will contradict established belief.[115]

What should accompany this posture of openness is a recognition of what Smith calls *fallibilism*—the notion that all human ideas are incomplete.[116] While fallibilism requires that human beings be openminded, it does not require that ideas be held without confidence. "Does not fallibilism necessarily curb the depth of conviction? The answer is, No. Is it not a contradiction to give full assent to something which one suspects contains an element of error? The answer is, Yes, but fallibilism does not require that we suspect all our beliefs of error, only of incompleteness."[117]

A notion of fallibilism can be accepted even by the committed Catholic.

As Gunti has stated, there is a "distinction between 'things-as-they-are' and 'things-as-they-are-*known*' by the human mind."[118] This distinction was implicitly recognized by Vatican II. Referring to divine law, the Council Fathers wrote that "man has been made by God to participate in this law, with the result that, under the gentle disposition of divine Providence, he can come to *perceive ever increasingly the unchanging truth*."[119] In the "Pastoral Constitution on the Church in the Modern World," the Fathers affirmed that "the deposit of faith or revealed truths are one thing; the manner in which they are formulated without violence to their meaning and significance is another."[120]

This distinction has, for years, been recognized by many Catholic theologians. "In the 1940s the *nouvelle theologie* of Henri de Lubac, Henri Bouillard, and others pointed out that man's religious knowledge is necessarily embedded in contingent notions that depend upon particular cultural circumstances."[121] There remains the need for the reformulation of religious statements according to sound hermeneutical principles. As Avery Dulles points out, "Even in its infallible definitions, which are few and far between, the Church is subject to human and historical limitations. In the minds of those who formulate and interpret the definitions, the absolutely binding dogmatic teaching is accompanied by interpretations and representational elements that are not so guaranteed."[122]

Because of the limited nature of human apprehension and its historical and cultural "conditionedness," eternal truth can never be fully grasped (or grasped without some measure of provisionality). In each new historical and cultural situation, formulations that convey religious truth must be "reconceptualized" in an effort to more nearly approximate the meaning of such religious truth.[123]

Religious commitment then, need not corrupt the objectivity of research so long as a scholar's commitment does not involve a fear of contradiction, the avoidance of self-criticism, or a blindness to the limitations of all human conceptualization.[124] Nor should such commitment lead to the abandonment of objectivity in the classroom. As the philosopher and mathematician Alexander Wittenberg has observed, "The university has room for, and welcomes, many particular commitments— and this . . . includes the exposition of these commitments in teaching, subject naturally to normal standards of fairness and scholarship."[125]

What religious commitment *should not* and *need not* lead to is the indoctrination of students, which involves "bypassing the critical judgment of the student."[126] Burtchaell correctly points out that "the difference between an ideologue who abuses the academic privilege, and a legitimate teacher, is this: the latter, albeit resolutely committed to certain beliefs, values, policies, initiates his students in the documents and skills wherewith to evaluate the convictions of their teacher, themselves, and others."[127]

Institutional Religious Commitment and Academic Freedom

The second dimension of the critical question under consideration is the issue of the reconcilability of an institutional religious commitment with a necessary academic freedom. Is a university's sponsorship by, and commitment to, a particular denomination irreconcilable with the principles of academic freedom? The answer to this question is largely dependent upon the type of institutional commitment at issue.

The brief discussion of institutional neutrality on political issues presented above indicates that the question of institutional neutrality vs. commitment is a debated one. It is, moreover, a difficult question to address wholly from the vantage point of the secular model of academic freedom. No unambiguous answer can be determined by utilizing the principles that comprise the secular model. This is illustrated by the fact that the AAUP considers the question an open one.

The specific issue of institutional religious commitment is hardly less difficult to address. It is, indeed, a more troublesome question in that what is at issue when dealing with institutional religious commitment is not whether the university ought to take a stand on an isolated political issue, but rather whether the university can be committed in general to an ecclesiastical community and still remain a university or college as these are understood in the American context.

In the United States, religious groups have the right to establish and support colleges and universities, and such institutions have the right to define themselves in terms of their relations with a particular church. Furthermore, from the time of its establishment, the AAUP has recognized the legitimacy of church-related colleges and universities.[128] There appears to be nothing inherent in the secular model of academic freedom as developed in the AAUP literature that would indicate that the state of church-relatedness is, by necessity, incongruous with a full academic freedom.[129]

However, institutional religious commitment can, indeed, be incongruous with a necessary academic freedom if such commitment involves imposing a religious orthodoxy upon members of the academic community or necessitates the abandonment of the academic autonomy of the institution. Hence, in light of the accepted American principles of academic freedom, a Catholic college or university cannot limit—in the name of its institutional commitment—academic discourse in any department, including theology.[130] Nor can it enforce a particular religious commitment upon its members. Philosopher Morton White writes that "every creative scholar does and should begin with certain basic beliefs and commitments, but any attempt to legislate what they should be is bound to imperil our scholarly tradition and educational system." In light of this view, he argues that "we should construe the required commitment of a professor in all parts of a free university—*the divinity school included*—in a way that transcends substantive belief. Such a commitment would imply no more than a serious, intellectually honest, dedicated concern with the problems of whatever subject he studies."[131]

Long avers that academic freedom must be compatible with a college's right to make judgments that serve institutional definition—those that make the institution what it is.[132] Long's point is well taken. Could it not be argued, therefore, that Catholic institutions (or those of other denominations) have the right to insure that all or some members in their theology departments be Catholic? It must be borne in mind that—as Long cautions—self-defining judgments can degenerate into exclusionary judgments aimed at excluding differing points of view. Exclusionary judgments are destructive of the learning process, of academic freedom, and, it might be added, of the nature of the university.

Limiting a theology faculty to members of an institution's sponsoring church (a policy that, to the author's knowledge, is not widely practiced in Catholic institutions) might very well indicate that at least within the theology department, a type of exclusionary policy makes full academic freedom unrealizable. The question that could be raised is whether various points of view would be sufficiently represented in such a department to foster genuine, critical, and creative scholarship. It can be asserted that truly fruitful theological scholarship can be best achieved through the dialogue that results from ecumenical and interdisciplinary encounter.[133]

When conducting searches to fill faculty positions, the departments of most colleges and universities take into consideration factors beyond a candidate's scholarly qualifications—factors such as personal and educational philosophy, character, etc. Could not the Catholic university, therefore, legitimately take into consideration a candidate's religious outlook or affiliation when making some appointments, particularly in its department of theology? It can insofar as this discriminating judgment *need not always* be injurious to an atmosphere of academic freedom. However, appointment decisions made in light of religious affiliation might, indeed, be incongruous with accepted American principles of academic freedom if religious affiliation was given disproportionate weight vis-à-vis scholarly credentials, if such decisions constituted an instance of an overall exclusionary policy, or if the maintenance of a particular religious commitment was made a condition of continued employment. In the Catholic context, this last condition might take the form of an insistence that a "Catholic faith commitment" (however construed) is conterminous with Catholic theological competence.[134]

An institutional religious commitment would also be irreconcilable with the American secular model of academic freedom if such a commitment necessitated the abandonment of the academic autonomy of

the university. "The governing board of an institution of higher education in the United States operates, with few exceptions, as the final
institutional authority," while the university faculty—limited only by the
board's authority—"has primary responsibility for such fundamental areas
as curriculum, subject matter and methods of instruction, research, faculty status, and those aspects of student life which relate to the educational process."[135] Within the American secular model of academic
freedom and in accordance with the American pattern of college and
university governance, interference by church authorities in the internal
affairs of a church-related college or university is totally unacceptable.

The state of church-relatedness is not necessarily incongruous with
the principles and procedures that comprise the secular model of academic freedom. Much depends upon the form that institutional religious
commitment assumes in a particular context. In Chapter 7, a framework
for an interpretation of Catholic institutional commitment broader than
those of the past will be offered.

CONCLUSION

The principles and rubrics that comprise the American secular model
of academic freedom provide an important measure of protection for
the teaching and learning scholar and, hence, must be retained and
respected. However, the complex challenges to academic freedom in
contemporary times call for a flexible and nuanced approach that transcends the simple application of rubrics or propositions. The creation
of an atmosphere of academic freedom on a particular campus requires—on the part of all groups within the academic community—the
responsible exercise of power, a willingness to dialogue (especially about
the meaning of academic freedom itself), an openness to pluralism, and
a toleration of ambiguity.

It would seem that there is nothing inherent in the principles and
procedures of the secular model that would limit their applicability to
the Catholic context. It has been shown that the narrow interpretations
of knowledge and the rather overzealous interpretations of the objectivity required of the scholar that sometimes accompanied the secular
model in the past (or were sometimes held by its proponents) are in no
way necessarily implied in it.

The faculties and students of Catholic colleges and universities, like
those of public and private institutions, can and should enjoy the protection afforded by the principles and procedures contained within the
secular model. Although alone not entirely adequate, these rubrics provide the type of necessary minimum protection that can allow individual
Catholic academic communities to create on their campuses the dynamic
atmosphere of academic freedom so necessary to fruitful scholarship.

NOTES

1. See Curran's brief discussion of this in "Academic Freedom," p. 748.

2. Ibid. See also Hofstadter and Metzger, *Development of Academic Freedom*, pp. 344–52. For one view of the relation of truth to knowledge, see MacIver, *Academic Freedom in Our Time*, pp. 4–6.

3. Pincoffs, "Introduction," p. viii.

4. See the discussion of the AAUP, "1964 Statement on the Academic Freedom of Students," and "1967 Joint Statement on the Rights and Freedoms of Students," in Chapter 4.

5. See the AAUP, "1915 Declaration of Principles," pp. 101–4.

6. Machlup, "Concerning Academic Freedom," p. 760.

7. Ibid.

8. See Russell Kirk, *Decadence and Renewal in the Higher Learning*, chap. 23.

9. In 1979, Federal support for university research exceeded $3 billion. See AAUP, "Corporate Funding," p. 18a.

10. Edward LeRoy Long, Jr., "The Dynamics of Academic Freedom," *Faculty Forum* 49 (May 1969): 1.

11. See Nisbet, *Academic Dogma*, chap. 5; T. R. McConnell, "Faculty Interests in Value Change and Power Conflicts," *AAUP Bulletin* 55 (1969): 342–43; Long, "Dynamics of Academic Freedom," p. 1; and AAUP, "Corporate Funding," pp. 18a–21a.

12. See, for example, AAUP, "Statement on Preventing Conflicts of Interest in Government-Sponsored Research at Universities," in *Academic Freedom and Tenure*, ed. Louis Joughin (Madison, Wis.: University of Wisconsin Press, 1967), pp. 82–86; and AAUP, "Corporate Funding," pp. 18a–21a.

13. Long, "Dynamics of Academic Freedom," pp. 1, 6.

14. This distinction was first brought to my attention by Edward LeRoy Long, Jr. Murray G. Ross has made a similar observation. See *The University: The Anatomy of Academe* (New York: McGraw-Hill, 1976), pp. 217–18.

15. Long, "Dynamics of Academic Freedom," p. 1.

16. Ibid.

17. Ibid., p. 2.

18. Ibid., p. 3.

19. Ibid.

20. Ibid., p. 4.

21. Ibid.

22. Ibid.

23. Curran, "Academic Freedom," p. 748; and Hofstadter and Metzger, *Development of Academic Freedom*, pp. 344–52.

24. Wylie Sypher writes that "during the nineteenth century science became identified with the use of a certain method that was adaptable to the technological imperative, associated as it was with a naive ideal of 'objectivity,' a naive materialism, a naive logic of induction, a naive reliance upon observation, a compulsion to discipline the mind by making it 'accurate.' " *Literature and Technology: The Alien Vision* (New York: Vintage Books, 1971), p. 10, quoted in Norman R. Bernier and Jack E. Williams, *Beyond Beliefs: Ideological Foundations of American Education* (Englewood Cliffs, N.J.: Prentice-Hall, 1973), p. 68.

25. Brubacher, *Philosophy*, p. 14.

26. Fuchs, "Academic Freedom," p. 243.

27. MacIver, *Academic Freedom in Our Time*, p. 253.

28. Hofstadter and Metzger, *Development of Academic Freedom*, p. 238.

29. See Gunti, "Academic Freedom as an Operative Principle," pp. 108–9; and William F. Buckley, Jr., *God and Man at Yale: The Superstitions of "Academic Freedom"* (Chicago: Henry Regnery Co., 1951), p. 144.

30. Hofstadter and Metzger, *Development of Academic Freedom*, pp. 363–66, 383–407.

31. Ibid., p. 363.

32. Ibid., pp. 363–64.

33. MacIver, *Academic Freedom in Our Time*, p. 7.

34. Hofstadter and Metzger, *Development of Academic Freedom*, pp. 364–65.

35. Ibid., p. 366.

36. See Gunti, "Academic Freedom as an Operative Principle," pp. 107–8. See also Holbrook, *Religion: A Humanistic Field*, pp. 62–63.

37. Hofstadter and Metzger, *Development of Academic Freedom*, p. 344.

38. "The Scientific Method in Religion," *The Index* 8 (March 1877): 136, quoted in Hofstadter and Metzger, *Development of Academic Freedom*," p. 349. Harvard president Charles W. Eliot, in his article "On the Education of Ministers," urged the adoption, by religious scholars, of the scientific method of inquiry: "Protestant theologians and ministers must rise to that standard, if they would continue to command the respect of mankind." *Princeton Review* 59 (May 1883): 345–46, quoted in Hofstadter and Metzger, p. 351.

39. See the discussion, in Hofstadter and Metzger, *Development of Academic Freedom*, pp. 344–52.

40. Burtchaell, "Question of Advocacy," p. 23.

41. Bernier and Williams, *Ideological Foundations of American Education*, p. 66.

42. Hume, "Skeptical Doubts Concerning the Operations of the Understanding," in *Meaning and Knowledge: Systematic Readings in Epistemology*, ed. Ernest Nagel and Richard B. Brandt (New York: Harcourt, Brace and World, 1965), p. 329.

43. Bernier and Williams, *Ideological Foundations of American Education*, p. 66. See Andrew Tudor's brief discussion of "Hume's problem" in *Beyond Empiricism: Philosophy of Science in Sociology* (London: Routledge and Kegan Paul, 1982), pp. 122–26.

44. Erazim Kohak, *Idea and Experience: Edmund Husserl's Project of Phenomenology in Ideas I* (Chicago: University of Chicago Press, 1978), p. 155. C. Robert Freeman points out that Husserl recognized that the natural sciences were based upon unexamined foundations. "Phenomenological Sociology," in *Introduction to the Sociologies of Everyday Life*, ed. Jack D. Douglas (Boston: Allyn and Bacon, Inc., 1980), p. 119.

45. Kohak, *Husserl's Project of Phenomenology*, p. 159.

46. Freeman, "Phenomenological Sociology," p.119.

47. The term *sociology of knowledge* was first introduced by philosopher Max Scheler in the 1920s. See Peter L. Berger and Thomas Luckmann, *The Social Construction of Reality* (Garden City, N.Y.: Anchor/Doubleday, 1967), pp. 4–18.

48. Ibid., pp. 1–3.

49. Ibid., Parts 2 and 3. Examples of such products of human expressivity include language and social roles.

50. Berger and Luckmann consider science a "symbolic universe." Human beings seem to have a propensity for order and meaning that necessitates the creation of overall universes of meaning (comprehensive symbolic totalities that legitimate—explain—and integrate all facets of reality), or symbolic universes. While these symbolic universes legitimate and integrate the various facets of socially constructed reality and an individual's place within this reality, they are themselves socially created and maintained. Ibid., pp. 92–104. Prior to the ascendance of the scientific worldview, religion more generally served as *the* symbolic universe, what Berger terms the all encompassing "sacred canopy" that placed (and legitimated) socially constructed reality within a transcendent frame of reference. See Berger, *Sacred Canopy* (Garden City, N.Y.: Anchor/Doubleday, 1969), and *Rumor of Angels* (Garden City, N.Y.: Anchor/Doubleday, 1970).

51. Curran, "Academic Freedom," p. 748. See also Jaroslav Jan Pelikan's, "In Defense of Research in Religious Studies at the Secular University," in *Religion and the University*, York University Invitation Lecture Series (Toronto: University of Toronto Press, 1965), p. 8.

52. See Holbrook, *Religion: A Humanistic Field*, p. 40.

53. MacIver, *Academic Freedom in Our Time*, p. 7. MacIver does betray a bias when he writes on p. 141: "What the scholar investigates is not values but evidences."

54. Pelikan, "Research in Religious Studies," p. 11.

55. Ibid., pp. 9–12; Holbrook, *Religion: A Humanistic Field*, pp. 30, 126, 160–68. On p. 30, Holbrook defines theology as a "discipline involving systematic explication, articulation, and defense of a particular standpoint of faith."

56. Holbrook, *Religion: A Humanistic Field*, p. 30.

57. Pelikan, "Research in Religious Studies," p. 11. Pelikan argues that this criterion should be respected in both the secular and church-related university.

58. Holbrook, *Religion: A Humanistic Field*, p. 165.

59. Ibid., pp. 106, 165.

60. Ibid., p. 165.

61. Ibid., pp. 165–66.

62. Schubert M. Ogden, "What is Theology?" *Journal of Religion* 52 (January 1972): 22–40; Ogden, "Response to Professor Connelly—I," *Proceedings of the Catholic Theological Society of America* 29 (June 1974): 59–66.

63. Ogden, "What is Theology?" p. 38.

64. Ibid. This is especially true of the Roman Catholic tradition. See Rahner's conception of theology in *Sacramentum Mundi*, 1969 ed., s.v. "Theology."

65 Ogden, "What is Theology?" p. 22.

66. Ogden points out that witness and existence "have variable as well as constant aspects" insofar as Christian witness is present in the various kinds and manifestations of that witness, and existence can be "understood only through the whole of human history and all the forms of culture." Ibid., pp. 24–25.

67. Ibid., p. 25.

68. Ibid.

69. Ogden considers human activity and culture influenced by the Christian

religion bearers of the "implicit" witness of faith. Ibid., p. 28. On the difficulty of determining the witness of faith, see Ibid., p. 26.

70. Ibid., p. 25.

71. Ibid., p. 26.

72. Ogden comments: "The requirement that theological statements be understandable, and thus universally meaningful and true, is far from merely the demand of an alien rationalism. It is . . . what the witness of faith itself essentially demands." Ibid.

73. Ibid., pp. 31–32.

74. Ibid., p. 27.

75. Ogden, "What is Theology?" pp. 36–37. Ogden raises a further question: "If, in order to understand the Christian witness, one must first believe it, under what conditions could one ever possibly disbelieve it?" (p. 37)

76. Ibid., p. 37. Addressing the question of what distinguishes theology from the study of religion, and the theologian from the religious scholar if the former does not by definition hold a faith commitment, Ogden writes: "What discipline, other than Christian theology, however closely connected with the Christian witness, is itself constituted by the question as to the meaning and truth of that witness?" Ogden, "Response to Professor Connelly—I," p. 62.

77. For a Catholic (negative) critique of Ogden's positions, see John J. Connelly, "The Task of Theology," *Proceedings of the Catholic Theological Society of America* 29 (June 1974): 1–55. See also Ogden's reply in "Response to Professor Connelly—I," pp. 59–66.

78. See Tracy's, "The Task of Fundamental Theology," *Journal of Religion* 54 (January 1974): 13–34; and *Blessed Rage For Order*.

79. Tracy, "Fundamental Theology," p. 13.

80. Tracy, *Blessed Rage For Order*, p. 32.

81. Tracy, "Fundamental Theology," p. 19.

82. Tracy, *Blessed Rage For Order*, p. 48.

83. Tracy, "Fundamental Theology," p. 22.

84. Ibid., p. 29.

85. David Tracy, "Response to Professor Connelly—II," *Proceedings of the Catholic Theological Society of America* 29 (June 1974): 72.

86. Tracy, "Fundamental Theology," p. 34.

87. Tracy, "Response to Professor Connelly—II," p. 72.

88. Ibid. Tracy writes that "in all the human and philosophical disciplines and thereby in theology, the interpreter in order to understand the texts, symbols, events, and witnesses requiring interpretation must have some pre-understanding of the subject matter expressed in those texts. . . . If that pre-understanding alone is what is needed, then our common human indeed secular experience precisely as human will more than suffice for the properly subjective or experiential element needed to interpret the Christian tradition. This seems to me to follow unless we are to maintain . . . that religious meaning (either as a religious dimension to our common human experience or as explicitly religious experience) is somehow radically separated from our common human experience." Ibid., pp. 70–71.

89. He has also affirmed the public character of practical theology. See Tracy, "The Public Character of Systematic Theology," *Theology Digest* 26 (Winter 1978):

400–11; Tracy and John B. Cobb, Jr., *Talking About God: Doing Theology in the Context of Modern Pluralism* (New York: Seabury Press, 1983), chap. 1.

90. Tracy, "Systematic Theology," p. 407. Tracy defines "classics" as "those texts which form communities of interpretation and are assumed to disclose permanent possibilities of meaning and truth." *Talking About God*, p. 11.

91. Hence, the overriding task of systematic theology is hermeneutical. See Tracy, *Talking About God*, p. 9. Insofar as systematic theology "will ordinarily assume . . . the truth-bearing nature" of the classic religious tradition which it reinterprets for the present, Tracy observes that systematic theologians "will ordinarily assume personal involvement in" the particular religious tradition. *Talking About God*, p. 4. However, it would appear that questions can be raised concerning the necessity of such personal involvement.

92. Tracy, "Systematic Theology," p. 401.

93. Tracy, *Talking About God*, p. 11. See "Systematic Theology," pp. 401–2. Tracy questions the assumption that "only the model for objective, public argument employed in fundamental theologies can serve as exhaustive of that which functions as . . . public discourse." *Talking About God*, p. 9.

94. See Brubacher, *Philosophy*, pp. 12–14.

95. Smith, "Objectivity vs. Commitment," p. 35.

96. Hofstadter and Metzger, *Development of Academic Freedom*, pp. 402–3, 363–66; Max Weber, "Science as a Vocation," in *From Max Weber: Essays in Sociology*, trans. and ed. H. H. Gerth and C. Wright Mills (New York: Oxford University Press Paperback, 1958), pp. 144–52.

97. Smith, "Objectivity vs. Commitment," pp. 35–38; Pelikan, "Research in Religious Studies," p. 8; and Berger and Luckmann, *Social Construction of Reality*, chap. 1.

98. Bernier and Williams, *Ideological Foundations of American Education*, p. 68.

99. Smith, "Objectivity vs. Commitment," p. 45. In a similar vein, Edward LeRoy Long, Jr., has defined objectivity as "the calculated elimination of the defined position of the observer." *Science and Christian Faith* (New York: Association Press, 1950). See also Holbrook, *Religion: A Humanistic Field*, p. 95, for a similar treatment of the notion.

100. Smith, "Objectivity vs. Commitment," p. 39.

101. Parsons and Platt, *The American University* (Cambridge: Harvard University Press, 1973), pp. 88–89.

102. Smith, "Objectivity vs. Commitment," p. 39.

103. Ibid., p. 40.

104. See the discussion of the varying interpretations of this question in Chapter 4.

105. See Arrowsmith, "Idea of a New University."

106. Smith, "Objectivity vs. Commitment," p. 42.

107. Milton Fisk, "Academic Freedom in Class Society," in *The Concept of Academic Freedom*, ed. Edmund L. Pincoffs (Austin: University of Texas Press, 1975), pp. 5–26; and Robert Paul Wolff, *The Ideal of the University* (Boston: Beacon Press Paperbacks, 1970), pp. 69–76.

108. See Long, "Dynamics of Academic Freedom," p. 4.

109. AAUP, "The Question of Institutional Neutrality," *AAUP Bulletin* 55 (December 1969): 488.

110. Long, "Dynamics of Academic Freedom," p. 6.

111. See, for example, the AAUP "1915 Declaration of Principles," pp. 104–5.

112. Ibid., p.105

113. On the difficulty of excluding bias even in such presentations, see Holbrook, *Religion: A Humanistic Field*, pp. 88–89.

114. AAUP, "1915 Declaration of Principles," p. 105.

115. Smith, "Objectivity vs. Commitment," pp. 46–48. This openness should particularly characterize the Catholic whose tradition includes the affirmation that faith and reason can never disagree.

116. Ibid., p.50.

117. Ibid., p. 52

118. Gunti, "Academic Freedom as an Operative Principle," pp. 146–47.

119. Vatican II, "Declaration on Religious Freedom," no. 3, p. 680. Italics mine. See also Vatican II, "Constitution on Divine Revelation," no. 8, p. 116.

120. Vatican II, "Church in the Modern World," no. 62, pp. 268–69.

121. Dulles, *The Survival of Dogma*, p. 117.

122. Ibid., p.197.

123. Ibid., p.198.

124. James T. Burtchaell writes: "Sincere research manages to combine unabashed preferences and advocated positions with self-criticism." "Question of Advocacy," p. 24.

125. Alexander Wittenberg, "The Relationship Between Religion and the Educational Function of the University," in *Religion and the University*, York University Invitation Lecture Series (Toronto: University of Toronto Press, 1964), p. 127.

126. Holbrook, *Religion: A Humanistic Field*, p. 88.

127. Burtchaell, "Question of Advocacy," p. 24. Holbrook writes in a similar vein: "A genuinely effective objectivity would seem to call not for an uncommitted professor without worthwhile convictions of his own to share . . . but one who with as full recognition of his commitments and presuppositions as human nature permits is willing to place them in the public arena and to change them in light of the insights he receives in the battle of ideas which is bound to ensue." *Religion: A Humanistic Field*, p. 95.

128. See the AAUP "1915 Declaration of Principles," pp. 94–95.

129. Not all secular commentators would agree. See Wittenberg, "Religion and the Educational Function of the University," pp. 125–36.

130. See AAUP, "Interpretive Comments," p. 325.

131. Morton White, *Religion, Politics, and the Higher Learning* (Cambridge: Harvard University Press, 1959), p. 109.

132. Long, "Dynamics of Academic Freedom," p. 3.

133. A strictly "sectarian" department is also injurious to the student's academic freedom.

134. Arguing that religiously committed scholars should have an important place in all universities (so long as such commitments are freely held), Wittenberg adds that these scholars should be free to change their commitments. "Religion and the Educational Function of the University," pp. 127–28. For an overview

of the exemptions from Title VII of the Civil Rights Act of 1964 available to church-related colleges, and a legal analysis of religious preference in employment policies, see Gaffney and Moots, *Government and Campus*, chap. 2.

135. AAUP, "Government of Colleges," pp. 377–78.

Criteria for Interpreting Academic Freedom in the Catholic Context

The critical reflection carried out in Chapter 5 indicates that, in their present form, current Catholic models of academic freedom are inadequate to guide the contemporary American Catholic college or university. What we have termed *restrictive models* of academic freedom neither support in theory, nor engender in practice, a sufficient measure of freedom to research, teach, and learn. Indeed, within these models, the definition of academic freedom—as commonly understood—is so extensively qualified as to raise the question of whether the result can honestly be considered a definition of academic freedom at all. Such qualifications are the direct result of conceptions of Catholic institutional commitment and of university theology inherent in these models. Institutional commitment tends to be identified with institutional adherence to orthodoxy, and institutional subordination to Church authority. In a related vein, university theology is conceived of as an ecclesiatically centered undertaking that is related to the official teaching mission of the Church.

Revised secular models of academic freedom, in contradistinction to restrictive models, support the extension of academic freedom (as understood in the American context), to all university disciplines, especially Catholic theology. However, these models fail to engender such freedom in practice because they have not fully resolved the ambiguity surrounding their conceptions of the nature of university theology and the role of the university theologian. University theology and the theology professor tend to be defined principally in light of their relation to the Church, and only secondarily in light of their role and function in the Catholic university as a university.[1]

The secular model of academic freedom, which is composed of the principles and rubrics developed in the literature of the AAUP, does provide a necessary measure of academic freedom for the Catholic college and university. This model is applicable to Catholic institutions insofar as the reductionistic approach to knowledge and the overzealous claims concerning neutrality that have sometimes accompanied the secular model in the past are by no means constituent of it and, hence, can be avoided.

It has been suggested in Chapter 6 that the secular model is not without defect. While the rubrics and structured protections that comprise the secular model are necessary for the protection of academic freedom on the Catholic campus (as well as on the public and private campus), the secular model chiefly addresses challenges to academic freedom that arise outside the scholarly community, largely ignoring internal dangers to such freedom. Moreover, it should be borne in mind that no single rubric or group of rubrics can adequately encompass what is involved in the task of protecting and enhancing academic freedom in the complex contemporary situation. For the creation of an atmosphere of academic freedom requires an ongoing dialogue among all groups within an academic community—a dialogue characterized by genuine openness and mutual respect.[2]

In addressing the problem of interpreting academic freedom in the Catholic context, this concluding chapter will not attempt to develop a detailed code of academic freedom for the Catholic university, but rather will focus upon developing and exploring a set of guiding criteria that may be helpful in interpreting the secular model of academic freedom for the Catholic context, and perhaps be useful to the Catholic college or university in its effort to create a dynamic atmosphere of academic freedom that transcends the mere observance of rubrics.

ACADEMIC FREEDOM AND THE AMERICAN ROMAN CATHOLIC COLLEGE AND UNIVERSITY: CRITERIA OF INTERPRETATION AND APPLICATION

Critical reflection upon the Catholic and secular models of academic freedom has given rise to criteria that aid in determining the direction that an interpretation of academic freedom in the Catholic context might take. These criteria may be formulated as follows:

1. The principles, rubrics, and procedural norms that constitute the American secular model of academic freedom should be interpreted on the Catholic campus in a way that maximizes the freedom to research, teach, and publish enjoyed by scholars in *all* disciplines, and the freedom to learn enjoyed by students in *all* disciplines.
2. Interpretations of academic freedom in the Catholic context should include a recognition of the reconcilability of personal religious commitment and scholarly objectivity.
3. The notion of Catholic institutional commitment should not be interpreted

in a manner that limits a necessary measure of academic freedom and autonomy, but rather should be interpreted in light of the exigencies of the
Catholic university as an American university.

4. Interpretations of academic freedom in the Catholic context should respect
the Catholic university's openness to the study of the many dimensions of
human experience, especially the religious.

5. While recognizing the central place that Catholic theological study should
occupy within the curriculum of Catholic colleges and universities, interpretations of academic freedom in the Catholic context should be based upon
the assumption that such theological study will assume a truly scholarly form
appropriate to the Catholic university as a university.

Maximizing the Freedom to Teach and Learn

*The principles, rubrics, and procedural norms that constitute the American
secular model of academic freedom should be interpreted on the Catholic
campus in a way that maximizes the freedom to research, teach, and publish
enjoyed by scholars in all disciplines, and the freedom to learn enjoyed by
students in all disciplines.*

The Catholic college or university in the United States, as a type of
American college or university, should not interpret academic freedom
on its campus in a way that departs from or limits the accepted American
principles of academic freedom. It may be recalled that the AAUP "1940
Statement of Principles" does contain a clause that implies a toleration
of the limitation of academic freedom in light of the religious aims of
some institutions.[3] However, the AAUP has rejected such a limitation
stating that "most church-related institutions no longer need or desire
the departure from the principle of academic freedom implied in the
1940 Statement, and we do not now endorse such a departure."[4]

The acceptance and implementation of the specific principles and
procedural norms that comprise the secular model of academic freedom
will not automatically effect the enhancement and protection of such
freedom on the Catholic campus. First, as observed by Long, the protection and cultivation of an atmosphere of academic freedom "is a
complex and subtle matter."[5] The creation of such an atmosphere requires that all groups on campus exercise their power in a thoughtful
and responsible manner, that all on campus approach the diversity of
viewpoints found there in a spirit of openness and mutual respect, and
that the academic community continually examine its discriminating
judgments or choices (those that serve institutional self-definition, for
example) to insure that they are not "exclusionary"—that is, aimed at
excluding certain points of view from consideration or unfairly limiting
the scope of academic inquiry.[6]

Second, the acceptance and implementation of the principles and procedural norms of the secular model are not sufficient to insure the enhancement and protection of academic freedom simply because such principles and norms are open to varying interpretations. For example, a department of theology in a Catholic college or university can initiate dismissal proceedings against a theologian on the grounds of incompetence, do so in a manner that respects accepted norms of academic due process (including judgment by scholarly peers), and still possibly violate the academic freedom of that theologian. Whether or not the scholar's freedom is being violated by these dismissal proceedings might depend upon how the department and/or faculty committee is interpreting scholarly theological competence.

It would appear that the question of scholarly theological competence is one that must be addressed by Catholic colleges and universities with great care, lest judgments of competence become the type of excluding judgments that destroy academic freedom. Criteria of scholarly theological competence, such as *faith commitment and adherence to the dogmas of faith as presuppositions of the discipline of Catholic theology*, are difficult—if not impossible—to reconcile with the atmosphere of freedom required by all scholars in every college and university.

The relation of character traits to teaching fitness is also an issue that raises complex questions, not merely for theology departments in Catholic universities, but for all departments in all universities. This is an issue that requires, on the part of academic communities, both discerning judgment and critical self-examination so that assessments of fitness will not be unjust or covertly exclusionary. As discussed in Chapter 6, the AAUP has attempted to clarify and specify the meaning of "moral turpitude," a notion that is alluded to in the "1940 Statement" as grounds for dismissal. They have not completely done so by defining it as "behavior that would evoke condemnation by the academic community generally."[7] Specific universally applicable norms in this area are difficult—if not impossible—to formulate. In general, it would seem that colleges and universities should strive toward insuring that criteria of fitness concerning faculty character are as specifically formulated as possible and have a reasonably direct relation to a professor's scholarly duties.

The foregoing discussion serves to underscore the fact that, although the principles and norms that comprise the secular model of academic freedom must be adhered to on the Catholic campus, the complex task of enhancing and protecting academic freedom is not thereby completed. The interpretation of specific norms as well as the creation of a total environment of intellectual freedom requires dedicated effort on the part of all groups that comprise the academic community.

Justifications of Academic Freedom in the Catholic Context

For purposes of analysis, we have subsumed various justifications of academic freedom under one of two categories: theoretical or practical.

In justifying the extension of academic freedom to the Catholic educational context, it appears that *both* theoretical and practical arguments can be utilized.

Recent Roman Catholic discussions of human freedom in general and religious freedom in particular have focused upon the dignity of the human being as the foundation of such freedom.[8] These discussions point the way toward a theoretical justification of academic freedom that is especially suited to the Catholic context.

In the "Pastoral Constitution on the Church in the Modern World" of the Second Vatican Council, the Council Fathers affirm that "man's dignity demands that he act according to a knowing and free choice."[9] This dignity is said to flow from the divine image within the human being and the human being's call to communion with God.[10] Addressing the specific issue of religious freedom, the "Declaration on Religious Freedom," states that such freedom "has its foundation in the very dignity of the human person."[11] It further states that truth "is to be sought after in a manner proper to" this dignity.[12] Most importantly, inquiry must be free.

Catholic scholars such as Karl Rahner have also underscored the close relation between freedom and human dignity. Rahner writes that the essential dignity of the human being consists in the fact that the human being "can and ought to open himself (in the direction of immediate personal communion with the infinite God) to the love of Jesus Christ which communicates God himself."[13] For Rahner, freedom is most basically (yet most profoundly) freedom before God—the capacity for self-realization in the context of a total personal option for God or against God.[14] Although not every individual exercise of freedom involves the same degree of self-disposal, each assumes (at least potentially) a profound significance and a certain inviolability.[15] Summarizing Rahner's thought, Gerald A. McCool writes that "unjustified a priori restriction of human freedom constitutes a grave injury to the dignity of the person."[16]

Philosopher Albert Dondeyne has argued that "among the many occupations which allow man to manifest and realize himself in this world, the unprejudiced search for truth is highest and most specifically human."[17] The free search for truth, then, is self-legitimating in that it is a manifestation of the human drive toward self-realization. It is an eminently human activity, one that distinguishes the human being precisely as human. For the human being "appears in the world as a being capable of *raising questions and reflecting*."[18] To frustrate this activity, then, is to violate the very dignity of the human being.

Like freedom in general and religious freedom in particular, intellectual freedom—the freedom to pursue the truth—is based upon the dignity of the human being. Freedom to pursue the truth, freedom of thought and expression, remain rights held by all human beings. What, then, is the relation of intellectual freedom to academic freedom? The right to academic freedom is not enjoyed by all human beings, nor can it be, since academic freedom is a specific right, the exercise of which is restricted to a select few—teaching and research scholars (and their students) within the college or university. While all should enjoy the right to intellectual freedom, a particular configuration of the right to intellectual freedom—academic freedom—applies only to college or university scholars.[19] Academic freedom, then, is intellectual freedom as developed and applied in the academy and, as such, is at least indirectly rooted in human dignity.

Although a justification of intellectual freedom on the basis of human dignity is defensible, how can a particular configuration of the right to intellectual freedom for the college or university be defended? It is at this juncture that practical arguments must be introduced.

The development of a specific model of intellectual freedom for the academy can be justified on the basis of the nature of the respective roles of the scholar and the university, and the ramifications of the exercise of these roles for society.[20] In the AAUP "1915 Declaration of Principles," it is argued that "the importance of academic freedom is most clearly perceived in the light of the purposes for which universities exist."[21] Those purposes are described as the promotion of inquiry and the advancement of human knowledge in the natural sciences, the social sciences, and the humanities, the instruction of students, and the training of experts for service to society. The effective performance of these purposes requires responsible freedom and institutional autonomy. The university exists for the common good—or better stated, for the good of the universal human community—and, hence, the proper functioning of the college and university is of great importance to the well-being of that community. Insofar as academic freedom is vital to the proper functioning of the university, it indirectly serves the interests of the universal human community.[22]

In a related vein, the right to academic freedom is also justified in light of the nature of the scholar's calling. The professor performs an extremely important social function, the proper discharge of which is necessary for the well-being of the human community. As the authors of the "1915 Declaration of Principles" observe, the proper exercise of this function requires security in position (e.g., through an appropriate system of tenure) and the freedom necessary to fulfill the scholar's tasks.[23]

In the Catholic context, the scholar's right to academic freedom can be justified on two principal bases. As a form of intellectual freedom, academic freedom is rooted in the dignity of the human being theologically conceived. As a specific right to freedom exercised by competent professors within the college or university, academic freedom is justified by the function of the university and the role of the scholar, in that the proper exercise of these is vital to the interests of the human community.

The justification of student academic freedom in part parallels its professorial counterpart. Like their teachers, college students enjoy a right to intellectual freedom rooted in their dignity. This right, when developed in light of the needs of students and the goals of the university, becomes the right to academic freedom.

The student's right to freedom is also a morally based right. There exists an implicit agreement between the student and the university that the student's participation in, and contribution to, the academic community entitles him or her to the resources of the university necessary to the student's intellectual development.[24] These resources include free and unbiased instructors. Moreover, the intellectual development of the student can progress only if the student himself or herself is allowed the freedom necessary to explore, question, criticize, and synthesize the knowledge to which he or she is exposed in the context of research and instruction.

In the foregoing discussion of the justification of academic freedom in the Catholic context, no separate justification for the extension of academic freedom to the Catholic theological disciplines has been offered. For the extension of academic freedom to theology (properly conceived as an academic discipline) does not require justification over and above that offered for the extension of such freedom to all other disciplines.

As a human endowed with human dignity, the theologian and the student of theology have the right to seek the truth while enjoying immunity from external coercion. And, like all scholars, the theologian's basic right to intellectual freedom takes on the specific form of the right to academic freedom in light of the nature of the respective roles of the scholar and the university, and in light of the importance of the proper exercise of these roles for the human community.

Additional arguments can be developed to support the extension of academic freedom to students and professors of Catholic theology, arguments aimed at demonstrating that academic freedom is good for the Church as well as for theology as a discipline.[25] First, the Church needs the aid of the Catholic university—as a center of critical inquiry—in carrying out its "duty of scrutinizing the signs of the times and of interpreting them in light of the gospel."[26] The university can provide the Church with the intellectual resources and scholarship necessary for an understanding of the contemporary human situation. The Catholic college or university must be characterized by a genuine freedom of inquiry if it is to perform this service effectively.

Second, "The Land O'Lakes Statement" conceives of the Catholic university as the critical reflective intelligence of the Church. Hence, it argues that "the university should carry on a continual examination of all aspects and all activities of the Church and should objectively evaluate them. The Church would thus have the benefit of continual counsel from Catholic universities."[27] Needless to say, objective critical examination of the Church can only be carried out if the Catholic university retains its autonomy and freedom.

Third, the Church needs the theological scholarship generated within the Catholic college or university for the ongoing development of its teaching. The fruitful utilization of the historical, hermeneutical, linguistic, philosophical, and social scientific tools that form the basis of sound theological scholarship necessarily requires an atmosphere of freedom. Such scholarship is vital to an ever-deepening understanding of the Christian message as well as to the development of more effective ways of communicating that message.

The impact upon the Church of the adoption of a full, unrevised notion of academic freedom by Catholic colleges and universities would not be negative. It should be clear from the foregoing discussion that the Church has much to gain from free and autonomous Catholic colleges and universities. To qualify or revise the accepted American principles of academic freedom in a single department—theology—can be injurious to the total atmosphere of freedom that should characterize the Catholic institution, an atmosphere necessary to its proper functioning.

If a broad conception of academic freedom were to be accepted within theology departments of Catholic universities, a healthy pluralism would result. Pluralism and dissent, as Catholic theologian Leonard Swidler observes, need not be considered evils that are at best tolerated. Because all statements are conditioned by historical, cultural, linguistic, and class factors, "the more statements we have about a matter, the richer can be our joint grasp of it—the richer and truer, will be any level of consensus attained on it. Thus, rather than be discouraged, or even merely tolerated, a pluralism of statements about important matters should be expected and encouraged."[28]

The pluralism of scholarly opinions tolerated within a department of theology must include opinions that—from the perspective of the *Magisterium*—are in error. The presence of what is considered error in the department of theology can be a source of positive developments. The academic dialogue that results from the confrontation of opposing viewpoints can effect the sharpening and improvement of one or both of the positions. Through confrontation with theological positions that are considered erroneous, those positions considered truthful representations of Catholic faith can be brought to a more sophisticated level of conceptualization or expression.

The argument is sometimes heard that the free theological speculation that takes place in the university can confuse "the faithful" or cause them scandal. Ladislas M. Orsy, who, as we have seen, appears to accept the right of a theologian in error to remain in his or her academic position, recognizes that "the faithful" might be disturbed by theological speculation. He argues that confusion among members of the faithful is, in part, the result of the "misleading training" they have received. "Therefore the answer to the problem of confusion is not in suppressing theological research but in giving the faithful better information about its nature."[29] It is to be hoped that most adult Catholics who might be exposed to the work of theologians would be discerning enough to realize that the positions and conclusions of theologians are not official positions of the Church's *Magisterium*. In any event, the bishops can and should exercise their right to clarify matters of faith when necessary.

One need not reject a full academic freedom for the Catholic university (particularly for its department of theology) on the grounds that the impact of such freedom upon the Church would be negative. As has been discussed, a full academic freedom in the Catholic university— justified on the basis of the dignity of the scholar and on the exigencies arising out of the respective roles of the scholar and the university—can be the source of positive contributions to the Church's life.

The specific focus of our discussion has been upon the issue of academic freedom in the American Catholic college or university. However, the argument in support of the extension of academic freedom to the Catholic university that has been advanced within these pages is entirely applicable to any school of theology or seminary program that forms a part of a Catholic college or university.

It should be noted that the somewhat ambiguous phrase *seminary program* is used purposefully. Although the Protestant pattern of clerical education has been mixed—including both separate seminaries and university-related seminaries—Catholic seminaries in the United States have usually been independent of other institutions of higher learning.[30] In recent years, however, there have developed in some of the larger Catholic universities, academic programs leading to the Master of Divinity degree that allow a candidate for the priesthood to complete the academic component of his studies in a university setting.[31]

Insofar as schools of theology or seminary programs that form a part of a larger college or university share in the overall purposes of such institutions, they should enjoy full academic freedom—as this is understood in the American context.[32] As in the case of the department of theology in a Catholic university, this freedom does not preclude the making of some self-defining judgments on the part of these schools or programs. Thus, for example, the consideration of church membership in the hiring of faculty members for *some* positions need not be injurious to academic freedom if religious affiliation is not given disproportionate emphasis vis-à-vis scholarly credentials, if such judgments are not instances of an overall exclusionary pattern, and if a particular religious commitment is not made a condition of continued employment.

Separate seminaries under ecclesiastical control present a somewhat different problem. Bishops and religious orders have the right to establish educational institutions designed to serve ecclesiastical interests through the training of priests. They have the right to exercise a measure of control over these seminaries that would be considered inappropriate at best were these institutions colleges or universities.[33] Recognizing this, Augustine Rock argues that the professor in a diocesan seminary does not have "a clear title to academic freedom" since such an institution "is established by the ordinary for a purpose, and the purpose is obviously not the pursuit of learning."[34]

No doubt a good many seminary rectors and professors would raise questions concerning Rock's assessment of the purposes of their institutions. The pertinent issue, however, is not what the present purposes of seminaries are, but rather what they should be. Should not the pursuit of learning in general, and theological learning in particular, be the goal of any institution devoted to the education of priests? And in light of this purpose and out of respect for the human dignity of professors and students should not academic freedom be enjoyed by the seminary community?

It should be emphasized that even when the purpose of the seminary is identified as the pursuit of learning, this pursuit is often viewed within the context of a broader ecclesiastically defined goal: the training of clerics for service to the Church. It is this overriding ecclesiastical goal that is sometimes perceived as necessitating the limitation of academic freedom in the seminary. Hence, the 1960 statement on academic freedom issued by the American Association of Theological Schools recognizes the need for academic freedom within all educational institutions and even recognizes the various theological justifications of that freedom. However, the document states clearly that remaining within the constitutional and confessional boundaries of a particular theological school is a condition for the licit exercise of the right to academic freedom. The 1976 revision of the statement, although appearing to lessen the qualification of academic freedom in theological schools, continues to affirm that schools with a confessional or doctrinal standard may expect faculty members to subscribe to that standard.[35] Such an approach to academic freedom is, in a sense, defensible in the *seminary context* in that it represents a noble attempt to reconcile the freedom necessary for any educational institution and the protection of the interests of the church that the seminary directly serves.

However, the qualification of academic freedom on the basis of a seminary's ecclesiastical purpose arises in part out of an assumption—

one that is not *clearly supportable*. This is the belief that better clerics will be produced by and, hence, the church will be better served by seminaries within which an orthodoxy sets the limits of inquiry than by seminaries within which the limits of inquiry are set by adherence to sound scholarly methods, to the canons of scholarly integrity, and to a properly understood objectivity.

Reconciling Religious Commitment and Objectivity

Interpretations of academic freedom in the Catholic context should include a recognition of the reconcilability of personal religious commitment and scholarly objectivity.

In Chapter 6, it was argued that the American secular model of academic freedom does not require a religious or value neutrality on the part of scholars. What is required by the American model is objectivity— understood as fairness to evidence—in research and teaching. To be objective, a scholar need not assume a neutral stance on religious or value questions even if a pure neutrality were possible.[36]

Religious commitment, like other types of commitment, need not corrupt objectivity. For true religious commitment is held with a confidence that allows the individual to be open to all new evidence with the expectation that his or her convictions will be supported. As Catholic scholar William J. Richardson observes, "It is precisely because the Christian believes the revealed Word to be the synthesis of God and man (of truth as revealed to man and truth as discovered by him) that he reexamines his acceptance of the revealed Word without fear—confident that these two ways of experiencing truth can never really conflict."[37] Dogmatism, which is destructive of objective, sound scholarship, is born of the fear of contradiction—*not* of confident conviction. Genuine religious commitment, then, is not synonomous with dogmatism.

Objectivity, understood as fairness to evidence, can be as easily approximated by the religiously committed scholar as by all others. Indeed, it can be argued that objectivity can be more easily approximated by the religiously committed scholar in that such an individual is *consciously* and *explicitly* committed and, therefore, better able to reflect critically upon his or her commitments and upon their influence on his or her scholarly work.

Reconciling Institutional Commitment and Academic Freedom

The notion of Catholic institutional commitment should not be interpreted in a manner that limits a necessary measure of academic freedom and autonomy, but rather should be interpreted in light of the exigencies of the Catholic university as an American university.

During the nineteenth and early twentieth centuries, the Catholic identity of Catholic institutions of higher education was exhibited clearly in a number of ways: through a pattern of direct ecclesiastical or clerical control, in the importance attached to religious institutional goals, and in various curricular emphases, including a depreciation of research in favor of a classical course of studies within which moral and religious training occupied an important place. In the recent past (and for some institutions up to the present), Catholic institutional commitment has been interpreted chiefly in terms of the university's adherence to orthodoxy and subordination to the *Magisterium* of the Church. Translated into the language of college catalogues, this notion of commitment is usually expressed as "a commitment to the Christian message as it comes to us through the Church."

Is the interpretation of institutional commitment as adherence to orthodoxy and subordination to the *Magisterium* an appropriate one for the contemporary Catholic college or university? It would appear that it is not. First, to establish limits that scholarly conclusions cannot transgress, or to impose an orthodoxy upon an entire university or particular department, is to contradict basic principles of academic freedom and to frustrate the exercise of the university's function. Second, if church officials external to the university are given authority over administrative or academic affairs, or are given the right to intervene in these affairs, then the university is deprived of a necessary measure of autonomy. Finally, to interpret Catholic commitment in terms of the university's adherence to orthodoxy and subordination to the Church's *Magisterium* implies that the Catholic college or university is an organ of the Church's mission of evangelization. To view the college or university in this way is to eclipse its function as a *scholarly* institution.

Although religious institutional commitment has been interpreted in ways inimical to academic freedom and the nature of the university, it need not always be so. This view has been affirmed by the Federation of Regional Accrediting Commissions, which has stated that "freedom does not require neutrality on the part of the individual nor the educational institution—certainly not towards the task of inquiry and learning, nor toward the value systems which may guide them as persons or as schools." Therefore, "institutions may hold to a particular . . . religious philosophy as may individual faculty members or students. But to be true to what they profess academically, individuals and institutions must remain intellectually free and allow others the same freedom to pursue truth and to distinguish the pursuit of it from a commitment to it."[38]

At least in theory, there need not be a conflict between institutional commitment and academic freedom. An institution's religious and/or value commitments need not and should not inhibit the free research into and publication of—through teaching and writing—any idea. These assertions require further elaboration.

A Reinterpretation of Institutional Commitment

To be truly responsive to its particular societal context and the needs of its clientele, each Catholic college or university must work out the shape of its commitment in a relatively unique way.[39] This requires ongoing reflection—"scrutinizing the signs of the times and interpreting them in the light of the gospel."[40] Just as there are no ready-made answers for the individual Christian struggling to live in the light of Christian faith, so too there are none available to the Catholic university. However, the general shape that Catholic commitment might take in the American educational context can be sketched. Hence, three ways in which Catholic commitment can be exhibited will be explored. Such a commitment can be manifested through a distinctive approach to the scholarly-educational endeavor, through the presence in the curriculum of Catholic theological and religious studies, and through the university's relations with its faculty, it students, and with the wider human community.

The Catholic college's or university's approach to the scholarly-educational endeavor will be conditioned by its institutional acceptance of the Catholic Christian worldview and of the Christian conception of the human being as created in the image of God and called to a life of grace in Jesus Christ. First, this vision affirms the meaningfulness of the quest for truth. As Edward Schillebeeckx writes, God is for believers "the supreme guarantor of the nonabsurdity of our quest for truth."[41] The Catholic college or university has a specific motivation for its collective pursuit of truth and a foundation for its approach to knowledge, namely the Catholic belief in the intelligibility and meaningfulness of existence grounded in God.

Second, from the Catholic faith perspective, the human being is viewed as a multidimensional unity. "In Scripture, man has bodily aspects (*basar, sarkx*), psychological aspects (*nephesch, psyche*), and spiritual aspects (*ruah, pneuma*). Man is one center with many spokes. There is no immortal soul, but only a personality destined for God for all eternity. Man lives and dies and rises as one."[42] In light of the unified view of the human being reflected in Christian anthropology, the approach of the Catholic university to education should be holistic. As William W. Jellema writes, "The concept of the wholeness of man . . . implies that what is taught ought to recall his wholeness and not further fragment him."[43]

A holistic approach to knowledge should be based upon the affirmation that higher learning is truly reflective of human experience only if it encompasses all dimensions of human existence, philosophical and religious, as well as material and scientific. A Catholic university or college that adopts such an approach to learning should design curricula that give to students in all divisions ample opportunities to explore, in a systematic way, the humanistic fields and disciplines (especially the theological) as well as the social-scientific, scientific, and technological disciplines.

The focus of a holistic approach to learning should be upon the interrelatedness of all knowledge (and, it might be added, upon the relation of learning to life).[44] It would appear that an interdisciplinary approach to study would foster the recognition—among students—of the interrelation of all knowledge more readily than an approach based upon strict departmentalization.[45] Moreover, a college or university within which the interrelation of knowledge is emphasized should attempt to coordinate the work of its various schools and divisions to the greatest extent possible.[46]

The holistic approach to higher education born of the Christian vision of the wholeness of the human being should also include a recognition of the personal/spiritual as well as the academic needs of the student. Such needs should be addressed through the establishment of a campus ministry program and through the availability of on-campus counselling professionals—pastoral and psychological, as well as academic.[47]

Finally, a holistic approach to higher education should also be manifested in the particular attention given to the realm of values. Attempts should be made in every field to isolate and study the ethical dimensions of knowledge and its application. Furthermore, students should not only be given the opportunity to address the major ethical issues confronting society but should also be encouraged to clarify their own values in an academic setting.

Catholic commitment will also be exhibited through the presence in the Catholic university curriculum of both religious studies and Catholic theological studies. The former field, which can be defined as "the study of those forms of conviction, belief, and behavior and those systems of thought in which men express their concerned responses to whatever they hold to be worthy of lasting and universal commitment," constitutes a necessary part of humanistic study in general.[48] However, insofar as the Catholic university or college is a Catholic institution, special academic attention will be focused upon specifically Catholic theology in its interrelation with other fields of study and with non-Catholic theology, particularly that of other Christian traditions. As the American bishops write, "The distinguishing mark of every Catholic college or university is that, in an appropriate academic fashion, it offers its students an introduction to the Catholic theological heritage."[49] The shape that theology assumes on the Catholic college or university campus must respect the nature of the institution as a college or university.

Finally, Catholic institutional commitment will be exhibited through the university's relations with the institutional Church, its faculty and students, and the universal human community in general.

Within the broader conception of commitment as described above, there is a sense in which the Catholic university and its various disciplines remain committed to the institutional Church itself. Although the commitment of the university to the Church has traditionally been conceived largely in terms of subordination of the former to the latter and in terms of the university's strict faithfulness to the hierarchical *Magisterium,* a new type of relation between Church and university is possible, a partnership based upon mutual commitment. Through its sponsorship of colleges and universities, the Church can demonstrate its commitment to higher education in general and to Catholic colleges and universities as independent centers of Christian intellectual reflection. Correspondingly, the college or university remains committed to the Church not only as the source and communal embodiment of the institution's religious vision, but also in terms of the college's responsibility to contribute intellectually to the Church's life. For the university is the Church's "closest resource for social criticism" and self-criticism, and "its primary locus for carrying on research and analysis that relates the advances of learning to the Christian faith."[50]

A Catholic institutional commitment will also be manifested in the quality of the college's or university's relations with its students and faculty. First, the Catholic institution has the responsibility to strive toward being what it claims to be: a college or university. It cannot perceive itself as an agency of evangelization and be true to its faculty and students. Second, as a college or university, the Catholic institution will strive toward excellence. As the American bishops admit, "The Catholic identity of a college or university is effectively manifested only in a context of academic excellence."[51]

Third, Catholic institutional commitment will be manifested in the university's relations with its faculty and students through ongoing institutional self-examination in light of Christian values. Does a Christian spirit of love and community inspire the Catholic academy? Are basic principles of justice as outlined in Christian social teaching imbuing the relations of the university to its faculty and staff? Are the university's hiring practices, salary scales, and student admissions policies consonant with its professed convictions and values? "It is important that Catholic institutions of higher education continually review their policies and personnel practices in order to insure that social justice is a reality on campus."[52]

Catholic institutional commitment will also be exhibited in the Catholic university's relations with the universal human community. The Catholic institution has the ability to rise above the parochialism and narrow nationalism that often characterize American higher education in that its sponsoring body transcends "all classes, nations, continents, and races."[53] So long as Catholic commitment is not allowed to degenerate into a parochial and ecclesiatically self-serving reality—what Protestant theologian H. Richard Niebuhr would term a religious henotheism—it can function as a *catholic* commitment, that is, as a commitment to the universal human community.[54] Such a commitment should lead the university to devote particular attention to the study of universal human problems: war and peace, hunger, economic justice, human rights, and environmental well-being.[55] In light of the Christian vision that undergirds its existence, the Catholic university will focus upon the value dimensions as well as the technical dimensions of these problems.

Circumstances may arise that demand that the university assume an institutional position on specific social or political issues. The legitimacy of a university publicly taking such a stand on a specific issue should not be rejected *a priori*. In some situations, not taking a stand may very well constitute a political act or an act that is ultimately injurious to others or to the university. The university community should reflect upon each individual situation it confronts in light of the question, "What ways of either taking a stand or not taking a stand are most compatible with our own freedom and authenticity?"[56]

An academic community must be careful that in assuming a position on an issue, the convictions of some members of that community are not violated. Moreover, a university community's stands on particular issues must not restrict the free and ongoing scholarly investigation of them. Finally, to protect its autonomy and the integrity of its scholarly work, the university must remain above involvement in power politics or official political processes, opting instead to offer to the body politic (irrespective of the university's position) alternative solutions to social problems and possible scenarios describing their respective impact on society as a whole.

Finally, the Catholic university's commitment to the universal community will also be reflected in its own institutional policies. Thus, it will be "sensitive to its social responsibilities in such areas as . . . purchasing and granting contracts, investments, and honorary degrees."[57]

As a *public* corporation, the Catholic college and university should serve and does serve a diverse student clientele. Moreover, many Catholic institutions have on their faculties individuals of varying religious perspectives. Can such pluralism "within its walls" be reconciled with a Catholic institution's commitment? From its inception, American Catholic higher education has—in general—been open to non-Catholic students, and few would argue for the imposition of restrictions in this area now.[58] Insofar as a Catholic institutional commitment need not impose a dogmatism upon the university as a whole, or upon any particular department, a sympathetic understanding of that commitment would seem to be the only thing required of non-Catholic students and faculty members.[59]

It is important to note that a Catholic Christian commitment as understood above is not a static reality but rather an ongoing process. It is a process that is constituted—in large part—by the many self-defining judgments made by a particular college or university, judgments concerning curricular approach and emphasis, hiring policies, and student admissions policies. The Catholic university community must continually reexamine critically the shape its commitment assumes so as to better apply the Christian faith perspective to the ever changing academic context, and to insure that the community's self-defining judgments are not exclusionary judgments destructive of academic freedom and of the academic enterprise itself.

Reconciling Academic Freedom and the Scope of Study in the Catholic University

Interpretations of academic freedom in the Catholic context should respect the Catholic university's openness to the study of the many dimensions of human experience, especially the religious

The Catholic university should be a place "where the process of learning and teaching is open to the whole of being, including the divine ground of being"; a place where the scientific, artistic, humanistic, and religious dimensions of human experience are considered equally worthy of study and reflection; a place where the value dimensions and philosophical presuppositions of all disciplines can be explored.[60]

Within the Catholic institution, special attention should be focused upon Catholic theology and its interrelation with other religious traditions and all areas of learning. This holistic approach, however, will not take the form of a theological imperialism, but rather will constitute a sustained dialogue among fellow searchers. As John E. Walsh has argued, theology and other disciplines can and must learn from one another.[61]

Interpretations of the accepted American principles of academic freedom developed for the Catholic context must respect the Catholic university's openness to the "whole of being," recognizing the legitimacy of theology as a field of scholarly study. By the same token, however, university theology must assume a form appropriate to the college and university setting. It is to this issue that attention will now be directed.

Reconciling Theological Study and Academic Freedom

While recognizing the central place that Catholic theological study should occupy within the curriculum of Catholic colleges and universities, interpretations of academic freedom in the Catholic context should be based upon the assumption that such theological study will assume a truly scholarly form appropriate to the Catholic university as a university.

Catholic theology in the college or university must be regarded as principally an *academic endeavor*, the aims of which revolve around introducing undergraduates to the Catholic theological heritage and to the methods of the discipline; developing in graduate students advanced competence in theological methodologies and in theological research, as well as an interpretive acumen; and providing a locus for creative and critical Catholic theological scholarship. The goals of Catholic theology in the university will not be *directly* pastoral. Such theology is not catechetics at a higher level, or an extension of the Church's official teaching mission; nor will it be primarily church-directed. Rather, it will contribute to the life of the Church in an indirect rather than a direct or quasi-official manner.

Drawing from the work of Protestant theologian Schubert M. Ogden, theology can be defined generally as "the fully reflective understanding of the Christian witness of faith as decisive for human existence."[62] Insofar as the object of Catholic theology is the Catholic faith expressed in language and symbols, such theology remains "an ecclesiastical science."[63] Put simply, the faith that is the object of theology is the faith of the Church. However, to admit this necessary ecclesiastical dimension of all theology is not to admit the legitimacy of an ecclesiastically centered university theology.

An ecclesiatically centered conception of theology tends to view such theology—implicitly or explicitly—as being at the direct service of the Church. Such theology is conceived as having direct pastoral and/or catechetical dimensions. Moreover, the professor of theology—the university theologian—is thought of as exercising a "ministry" in and for the Church. University theology has pastoral implications as well as pastoral applications. However, it should not be defined principally in terms of these. Nor should the pastoral implications of university theology—its impact on "the faithful"—be utilized as a basis upon which to restrict theological discussions on the college or university campus. As Professor Curran has correctly observed, "Too often we worry about protecting the weak and the scandal that might be given to them. What about the scandal of the strong? Many intelligent lay Catholics would be scandalized if Catholic theologians were not searching for better understandings and proposing new theories." Curran adds that "too often authority in the church acts as if all the people of God were dumb sheep or illiterate masses who must be directed from without in all they do."[64]

It is also important to distinguish university theology from catechetics.[65] The original purpose of Catholic theology courses, in keeping with the overriding religious aims of the institutions where they were offered, "was to maintain the young Catholic in his faith, to arm him against various attacks upon his religious belief."[66] Moreover, such courses were usually taught by clerics— "persons particularly interested in and responsible for the religious life of the students."[67] Hence, a distinction between theology and catechetics was slow to develop.[68] Needless to say, such a distinction must be made if theology is to occupy a deserved place in the college or university curriculum.[69]

Correspondingly, university theology courses should not be conceived as extensions of the Church's official teaching mission, nor should the theology professor be defined as a "minister" of the Church (or as its official spokesperson). Such conceptions call into question the status of Catholic theology as a college or university discipline and invite the imposition of strict church regulation of scholarly work. Needless to say, if theology is to deserve a rightful place among university disciplines, the department of theology—like all others in the university must be immune from interventions by Church authorities into its internal academic affairs.

Respecting the God-given role of the *Magisterium*, the Catholic university will recognize the right of an episcopal conference and the Pope (or his delegate) to declare publicly that the positions of a particular professor of theology are contrary to the Catholic faith. Moreover, Church authorities retain the right to discipline a theology professor as an *individual* Catholic. This should not compromise his or her position in the university unless a clear violation of professional ethics or professional competence is demonstrated.

Criteria of scholarly theological competence and personal fitness to teach should have a reasonably direct relation to the performance of a professor's scholarly duties so to avoid unnecessarily restricting academic freedom. Therefore, while personal faith commitment on the part of theological scholars should be accepted as consonant with objectivity and sound scholarship (and be considered desirable) in the Catholic university, the presence of or adherence to such a faith commitment should not be deemed a criterion on which to judge theological competence.

Most contemporary Catholic theologians affirm that theology presupposes faith on the part of the theologian.[70] John J. Connelly writes that "theology cannot be theology if the theologian speaks of revelation from some uncommitted viewpoint."[71] Rahner affirms that theology is concerned with the Christian "faith as act and content . . . and presupposes it in the Church and in the student of theology."[72] However, the assumption that theology presupposes faith on the part of the theologian is not an undisputed one. Moreover, the question that arises is whether the criterion labeled "faith commitment" is in any way a meaningful criterion in the college or university context. As both Ogden and Tracy point out, judging the presence of a faith commitment is a difficult, if not impossible, task.[73] No one can judge the quality of an individual's adherence to God in trust. Hence, what must be subject to judgment is not personal faith in its fullness, but only that which is usually termed belief. Yet, as Ogden correctly notes, the profession of orthodox beliefs is no guarantee of the presence of faith.[74]

What the requirement of a faith commitment seems to demand is extrinsic adherence to a predetermined orthodoxy. In the Catholic academic context, the judgment of faith commitment can only be made indirectly through an examination of beliefs as reflected in the personal professions and the scholarly work of a university theologian. These could only be judged in light of some type of standard—a standard that represents the minimum beliefs that comprise Catholic faith (presumably based upon dogmas of faith). Thus, what one has when dealing with the criterion of faith commitment is not truly a criterion based on faith but rather a criterion based on orthodoxy.

In light of the Catholic Church's understanding of the nature and role of the hierarchical *Magisterium,* the professor of Catholic theology has the responsibility to portray accurately and fairly official Catholic teachings (as proposed and interpreted by the *Magisterium*) on particular theological issues when presenting positions on or interpretations of these issues labeled as Catholic. He or she must also distinguish official Church teaching from the conclusions of theologians. These responsibilities flow from the nature of scholarly objectivity, and any lack in this area is to be considered a problem of competence to be addressed by scholarly peers. A theologian's own scholarly conclusions should not reflect upon his or her competence unless the scholar's research methods or integrity are found to be lacking. The professor of Catholic theology should be free to reach conclusions and assume theological positions at variance even with dogmas of faith, so long as the teaching of the Church on the particular question under consideration is made clear.

CONCLUSION

The overview of the historical and social context of Catholic higher education presented in Chapter 2 serves as an extensive illustration of the observation that "academic freedom is a new idea to Catholic educators because they have only recently arrived at the point where it has a vital bearing on the activity of their colleges."[75] The educational goals of Catholic institutions, the characteristics of their institutional structure, and the social context in which they arose and operated neither necessitated nor were conducive to the development of academic freedom.

By the middle of the twentieth century, changes were well under way. Catholic colleges and universities more closely resembled their non-Catholic counterparts in the areas of educational goals and academic programs. As the assimilation of American Catholics progressed, the once defensive posture of Catholic institutions began to soften. The expansion of Catholic colleges and universities following the Second World War meant larger numbers of lay faculty members and the transformation of traditional patterns of governance. Finally, the Second Vatican Council—with its renewed vision of the Church, its emphasis on the role of the laity, its teaching on freedom, and its openness to culture—resulted in a profound transformation of all facets of the Church's life, including its universities. As a consequence of all these changes, academic freedom *now has a vital bearing on the activity of Catholic institutions.*

As Catholic colleges and universities face the uncertainties of the future, questions arise: What shape ought academic freedom take on the Catholic campus? Can academic freedom exist in an institution that is both Catholic and a university? Are current models of academic freedom adequate to guide the Catholic college or university as it confronts the dawn of the twenty-first century? It is to this final question in particular that this book has been addressed. It has been argued that Catholic models that have been labeled "restrictive" are generally inadequate. Drawing from a narrow interpretation of Catholic commitment and extremely church-directed conceptions of university theology, these models tend to restrict the academic freedom and autonomy that are necessary to any institution that could honestly be called a college or university. The strict implementation of such models would once again raise the question of whether the phrase "Catholic university" is a contradiction in terms.

What have been termed *revised secular models* of academic freedom, although sound in principle, are likewise inadequate. While they correctly argue for the extension of academic freedom to scholars in all disciplines, the conceptions of the nature of university theology and the role of theologian upon which they are based lead to the adoption of a conception of theological competence that remains incongruous with the nature of a Catholic university as a university.

The secular model of academic freedom, composed of the principles and procedural rules outlined in the literature of the AAUP, does provide a necessary measure of academic freedom for the Catholic college or university. In theory, the secular model is not inherently reductionistic in its view of knowledge, nor does it imply a value neutrality, although empirically, these characteristics have—at times in the past—been closely aligned with this model. If properly understood and interpreted, the secular model of academic freedom is applicable to the Catholic context.

The secular model is not, however, without defect. While it is quite effective in addressing challenges to academic freedom that have traditionally arisen outside the scholarly community, questions can be raised concerning its adequacy in addressing complex contemporary threats to scholarly freedom—many of which are internal in origin. Nonetheless, the principles and rubrics that constitute the American secular model remain necessary to the protection of basic academic freedom on every campus and can serve as a platform upon which to construct rubrics designed to address changing circumstances and new problems.

The creation, enhancement, and protection of academic freedom is, as Long points out, a complex affair that transcends the mere observance of principles and rules. The creation of an atmosphere of academic freedom requires, on the part of all members of an academic community, responsibility in the exercise of power, an attitude of openness to the pluralism of ideas on campus, and an attitude of mutual respect in academic dialogue and in the resolution of conflict.

Critical reflection on the various models of academic freedom has yielded the conclusion that current Catholic models are inadequate to guide the Catholic university as an American university, while the secular model—despite defects—is applicable to the Catholic university and necessary to its proper functioning. Critical reflection has also given rise to criteria that may not only aid in the interpretation of the secular model for the Catholic context, but may also constitute partial guidelines for the development of a necessary atmosphere of academic freedom on particular campuses.

The recently promulgated *Code of Canon Law* includes canons that, if enforced, will make the free and autonomous Catholic university an impossibility. This would be a loss both for the Church and for the world. As it continues its task of interpreting the signs of the times in light of the Gospel, the Church needs an independent, creative, and critical center of reflection. This is what the Catholic university has the potential of becoming.

Furthermore, the human community now faces global problems that call into question its very survival. These problems cannot be addressed by scientists or technologists alone. Nor can they be addressed properly from a parochial or narrowly nationalistic perspective. What they require is a universal vision and a willingness to address scientific and technological alternatives in light of human needs and values. The Catholic university can function as a *catholic* center of reflection—as a locus of, and center for, sound scholarship that is universally directed both in its approach to, and application of, knowledge, and in the community it serves.[76]

The foregoing study is, at best, limited. The problem of academic freedom in the Catholic college or university is a complex one that defies attempts to resolve it through simple or unnuanced solutions. This book does not claim to resolve completely every ambiguity or to answer neatly every question. It is hoped that it will, nonetheless, be received as a small contribution to an ongoing discussion—a discussion that will persist so long as some American colleges and universities continue to indentify themselves as "Catholic."

NOTES

1. Even when theology is understood principally in academic terms, it continues to have at least indirect pastoral implications as well as pastoral applications.

2. Long, "Dynamics of Academic Freedom," pp. 1–6.

3. AAUP, "1940 Statement of Principles," p. 108.

4. AAUP, "Interpretive Comments," p. 325.

5. Long, "Dynamics of Academic Freedom," p. 1. See also Theodore M. Hesburgh, "The Catholic University and Freedom," in *The Hesburgh Papers: Higher Values in Higher Education* (Kansas City: Andrews and McMeel, Inc., 1979), p. 65.

6. Long, "Dynamics of Academic Freedom," pp. 1–4.

7. AAUP, "Interpretive Comments," p. 326.

8. See Rahner, *The Rahner Reader*, pp. 262–70; Vatican II, "Church in the Modern World," no. 17, p. 214; and Gunti, "Academic Freedom as an Operative Principle," pp. 26, 233–35, and 255–58.

9. Vatican II, "Church in the Modern World," no. 17, p. 214.

10. Ibid., no. 12, p. 210–11; no. 19, p. 215.

11. Vatican II, "Declaration on Religious Freedom," no. 2, p. 679.

12. Ibid., no. 3, p. 680.

13. Rahner, *Rahner Reader*, p. 264.

14. Ibid., pp. 255–70.

15. On limitations of the scope for freedom, see Ibid., pp. 268–70.

16. Gerald A. McCool, "Introductory Comments," in *Rahner Reader*, p. 262.

17. Dondeyne, "Truth and Freedom," p. 34.

18. Ibid.

19. MacIver, *Academic Freedom in Our Time*, p. 205.

20. AAUP, "1915 Declaration of Principles," pp. 97–101. See also MacIver, *Academic Freedom in Our Time*, p. 11; and Hook, *Heresy Yes Conspiracy No*, pp. 154–57.

21. AAUP, "1915 Declaration of Principles," p. 99.

22. See AAUP, "1940 Statement of Principles," pp. 107–8; and MacIver, *Academic Freedom in Our Time*, p. 11.

23. AAUP, "1915 Declaration of Principles," p. 97.

24. The university has no responsibility for the progress of such development.

25. In the opinion of the present author, such arguments should not occupy a central place in a discussion of the justification of academic freedom in the Catholic context.

26. Vatican II, "Church in the Modern World," no. 4, p. 202.

27. "Land O'Lakes Statement," p. 155.

28. Leonard Swidler, "*Demo-kratia*: The Rule of the People of God or *Consensus Fidelium*," in *Authority in the Church and the Schillebeeckx Case*, ed. Leonard Swidler and Piet F. Fransen (New York: Crossroad Publishing Co., 1983), p. 237.

29. Orsy, "Freedom and the Teaching Church," p. 493.

30. See Jenck and Riesman, *Academic Revolution*, p. 211. For a discussion of the "isolated" Catholic seminary that reflects the questioning of traditional patterns that followed Vatican II, see Robert J. McNamara, "The Priest-Scholar," in *The Shape of Catholic Higher Education*, ed. Robert Hassenger (Chicago: University of Chicago Press, 1967), pp. 203–12.

31. For an outline of the various types of seminary arrangements, see the National Conference of Catholic Bishops, *The Program of Priestly Formation* (Washington, D.C.: United States Catholic Conference, 1976), chap. 5, art. 2.

32. Generally speaking, it would seem that academic freedom should also characterize the independent school of theology or seminary that is free of ecclesiastical or denominational control.

33. In the NCCB, *Program of Priestly Formation*, chap. 5, art. 3, no. 230, it is stated that the academic freedom of the seminary faculty "must be understood in the context of seminary purposes."

34. Rock, "The Catholic and Academic Freedom," p. 257.

35. AATS, "Academic Freedom and Tenure in the Theological School," p. 35; revised ed., *Theological Education* 12 (Winter 1976): 89.

36. See Burtchaell, "Question of Advocacy," p. 24.

37. William J. Richardson, "Pay Any Price? Break Any Mold?" in *The Catholic University: A Modern Appraisal*, ed. Neil G. McCluskey (Notre Dame, Ind.: University of Notre Dame Press, 1970), p. 288.

38. "Institutional Integrity," Policy Paper 66.4 (October 1966), quoted in Cosmas Rubencamp, "Religion as a Humanistic Study: The Holbrook Thesis," in *Theology in Revolution*, ed. George Devine (New York: Alba House, 1970), p. 195.

39. What follows is merely an outline of one form institutional commitment might take in the Catholic university. For a book-length treatment of various types of church-relatedness, see Robert Rue Parsonage, ed., *Church Related Higher Education: Perceptions and Perspectives* (Valley Forge, Pa.: Judson Press, 1978).

40. Vatican II, "Church in the Modern World," no. 4, pp. 201–2.

41. Schillebeeckx, "Problems and Promise," in *The Catholic University: A Modern Appraisal*, ed. Neil G. McCluskey (Notre Dame, Ind.: University of Notre Dame Press, 1970) p. 72.

42. O'Grady, *Christian Anthropology*, p. 125. See Jellema, "The Identity of the Christian College," in *Colleges and Commitments*, ed. Lloyd J. Averill and William J. Jellema (Philadelphia: Westminster Press, 1971), p. 94.

43. Jellema, "Identity of the Christian College," p. 96.

44. Ibid.

45. See Brubacher's discussion of curricular organization in *Philosophy*, pp. 93–98.

46. This coordination might be achieved through dual sponsorship of selected courses, joint colloquia, etc.

47. Harry E. Smith, "Church-Related Higher Education: Distinguishing Characteristics," in *Church and College*. Vol 2: *Mission—A Shared Vision of Educational Purposes* (Sherman, Tex.: National Congress on Church-Related Colleges and Universities, 1980), p. 33.

48. Holbrook, *Religion: A Humanistic Field*, p. 36.

49. NCCB, *Catholic Higher Education and the Pastoral Mission of the Church*, p. 5.

50. Jellema, "Identity of the Christian College," p. 98. See also David Burrell, "Higher Education and Church: Interdependence and Enrichment," in *Church and College*. Vol. 2: *Mission—A Shared Vision of Educational Purpose* (Sherman, Tex.: National Congress on Church-Related Colleges and Universities, 1980), p. 24.

51. NCCB, *Catholic Higher Education and the Pastoral Mission of the Church*, p. 4.

52. Ibid., p. 9.

53. Langdon Gilkey, *Catholicism Confronts Modernity: A Protestant View* (New York: Crossroad Publishing Co., 1975), p. 16.

54. H. Richard Niebuhr, *Radical Monotheism and Western Culture* (New York: Harper Torchbooks, 1970), pp. 24–28.

55. See Congress of Delegates, "Catholic University in the Modern World," pp. 124–25.

56. Long, "Dynamics of Academic Freedom," p. 6. David O'Brien correctly argues that "when circumstances arise which demand a decision to act as an institution in the public arena, . . . that action should be based on wide consultation and serious deliberation." "Church-Related Higher Education and Social Issues," *Church and College*. Vol 2: *Mission—A Shared Vision of Educational Purpose* (Sherman, Texas: National Congress on Church-Related Colleges and Universities, 1980), p. 100.

57. O'Brien, "Social Issues," p. 100.

58. See Power, *History of Catholic Higher Education*, p. 114.

59. See Edgar M. Carlson's discussion of this issue in "Church-Related Colleges and Universities: Identity and Integrity," in *Church and College*. Vol 2: *Mission—A Shared Vision of Educational Purpose* (Sherman, Tex.: National Congress on Church-Related Colleges and Universities, 1980), pp. 45–47.

60. Niemeyer, "New Need for the Catholic University," p. 481.

61. Walsh, "University and the Church," p. 113. See also Hesburgh, *The Hesburgh Papers*, pp. 43–44.

62. Ogden, "What is Theology?" p. 22.

63. Kark Rahner writes: "Faith, the hearing of the revelation directed to the people of God, is the faith of the Church and faith within the Church; theology is necessarily ecclesiastical. Otherwise it ceases to be itself and becomes the prey of the wayward spirituality of the individual." See *Sacramentum Mundi: An Encyclopedia of Theology*, s.v. "Theology."

64. Charles E. Curran, *Moral Theology: A Continuing Journey*, (Notre Dame, Ind.: University of Notre Dame Press, 1982), p. 7.

65. To distinguish between catechetics and theology in this manner is not to imply that catechetics is merely a form of indoctrination that is incongruent with freedom of thought.

66. Sullivan, "The Catholic University and the Academic Study of Religion," p. 38. This is not to imply that contemporary catechetics has this defensive function!

67. Ibid., p. 40.

68. Ibid., pp. 39–40.

69. See the discussion in Rubencamp, "Theology," p. 190.

70. See Rahner's argument in *Sacramentum Mundi*, s.v. "Theology."

71. Connelly, "The Task of Theology," p. 21.

72. Rahner, in *Sacramentum Mundi*, s.v. "Theology."

73. Ogden, "What is Theology?" pp. 36–37; and Tracy, "Response," p. 73.

74. Ogden, "What is Theology?" pp. 36–37.

75. Gleason, "Crisis," p. 52.

76. John E. Walsh, "The International Dimension," in *The Catholic University: A Modern Appraisal*, ed. Neil G. McCluskey (Notre Dame Ind.: University of Notre Dame Press, 1970), p. 143.

Selected Bibliography

ORGANIZATIONAL STATEMENTS ON ACADEMIC FREEDOM

American Association of Theological Schools. "Academic Freedom and Tenure in the Theological School." *American Association of Theological Schools Bulletin* 24 (June 1960): 34–39; rev. ed., *Theological Education* 12 (Winter 1976): 85–105.

American Association of University Professors. "Academic Freedom and Tenure: 1940 Statement of Principles and Interpretive Comments." *AAUP Bulletin* 56 (Fall 1970): 323–26

———. "Committee A Report: Corporate Funding of Academic Research." *Academe* 69 (November-December 1983): 18a–21a.

———. "Committee A Statement on Extramural Utterances." *AAUP Bulletin* 51 (Spring 1965): 29.

———. "1915 Declaration of Principles." *AAUP Bulletin* 40 (Spring 1954): 90–112.

———. "1958 Statement on Procedural Standards in Faculty Dismissal Proceedings." In *Academic Freedom and Tenure*, pp. 40–45. Edited by Louis Joughin. Madison, Wis.: University of Wisconsin Press, 1967.

———. "1940 Statement of Principles." *AAUP Bulletin* 45 (Spring 1959): 107–10.

———. "1964 Statement on the Academic Freedom of Students." In *Academic Freedom and Tenure*, pp. 66–72. Edited by Louis Joughin. Madison, Wis.: The University of Wisconsin Press, 1967.

———. "1967 Joint Statement on Rights and Freedoms of Students." *AAUP Bulletin* 54 (Summer 1968): 258–61.

———. "1966 Statement on Government of Colleges and Universities." *AAUP Bulletin* 52 (Winter 1966): 375–79.

———. "1966 Statement on Professional Ethics." In *Academic Freedom and Tenure*, pp. 87–89. Edited by Louis Joughin. Madison, Wis.: University of Wisconsin Press, 1967.

————. "Statement on Academic Freedom In Church-Related Colleges and Universities." AAUP Bulletin (Winter 1967): 370–71.

International Federation of Catholic Universities. "1968 Kinshasa Statement: The Catholic University in the Modern World." In The Catholic University: A Modern Appraisal, pp. 342–45. Edited by Neil G. McCluskey. Notre Dame, Ind.: University of Notre Dame Press, 1970.

International Federation of Catholic Universities, North American Region. "Freedom, Autonomy, and the University." IDOC International 39 (January 1972): 79–88.

National Catholic Education Association. "The Relations of American Catholic Colleges and Universities with the Church." Catholic Mind 74 (October 1976): 51–64.

1969 Congress of Delegates of Catholic Universities. "The Catholic University and the Aggiornmento." In The Catholic University: A Modern Appraisal, pp. 346–65. Edited by Neil G. McCluskey. Notre Dame, Ind.: University of Notre Dame Press, 1970.

1972 Congress of Delegates of Catholic Universities. "The Catholic University in the Modern World." Notre Dame Journal of Education 4 (Fall 1973): 197–216.

1967 Land O'Lakes Conference. "The Catholic University of Today." America 117 (August 12, 1967): 154–56.

"Report of the Special Committee on Academic Freedom in Church-Related Colleges and Universities." By W. J. Kilgore, Chairman. AAUP Bulletin 53 (Winter 1967): 369–70.

ROMAN CATHOLIC CHURCH DOCUMENTS AND STATEMENTS OF THE HIERARCHY

The Code of Canon Law: A Text and Commentary. Edited by James A. Coriden, Thomas J. Green, and Donald E. Heintschel. New York: Paulist Press, 1985.

John Paul II. The Apostolic Constitution Sapientia Christiana on Ecclesiastical Universities and Faculties. Washington, D.C.: United States Catholic Conference, 1979.

————. "Excellence, Truth and Freedom in Catholic Universities." Origins 9 (November 1979): 306–8.

————. "Ideal Ascent Towards Truth." L'Osservatore Romano (English), 19 November 1979, pp. 11–12.

National Conference of Catholic Bishops. Catholic Higher Education and the Pastoral Mission of the Church. Washington, D.C.: United States Catholic Conference, 1980.

————. To Teach as Jesus Did. Washington D.C.: United States Catholic Conference, 1972.

Paul VI. "New Tasks for Catholic Universities." The Pope Speaks 17 (1972): 355–57.

————. "To the Delegates of Catholic Universities." L'Osservatore Romano (English), 8 May 1969, p. 4.

———. "The Mission of a Catholic University." *The Pope Speaks* 17 (1972): 131–40.

———. "Vitality of the Mission of Catholic Universities." *L'Osservatore Romano* (English), 20 May 1971, p. 10.

Sacred Congregation for Catholic Education. "Proposed Schema for a Pontifical Document on Catholic Universities." *Origins* 15 (April 1986): 706–11.

Second Vatican Council. "Declaration on Christian Education." In *The Documents of Vatican II*, pp. 637–51. Edited by Walter M. Abbott. Translated by Joseph Gallagher. New York: The America Press, 1966.

———. "Declaration on Religious Freedom." In *The Documents of Vatican II*, pp. 675–96. Edited by Walter M. Abbott. Translated by Joseph Gallagher. New York: The America Press, 1966.

———. "Dogmatic Constitution on the Church." In *The Documents of Vatican II*, pp. 14–96. Edited by Walter M. Abbott. Translated by Joseph Gallagher. New York: The America Press, 1966.

———. "Dogmatic Constitution on Divine Revelation." In *The Documents of Vatican II*, pp. 111–28. Edited by Walter M. Abbott. Translated by Joseph Gallagher. New York: The America Press, 1966.

———. "Pastoral Constitution on the Church in the Modern World." In *The Documents of Vatican II*, pp. 199–308. Edited by Walter M. Abbott. Translated by Joseph Gallagher. New York: The America Press, 1966.

BOOKS

Averill, Lloyd J., and William W. Jellema, ed. *Colleges and Commitments*. Philadelphia: Westminster Press, 1971.

Brubacher, John S. *The Courts and Higher Education*. San Francisco: Jossey-Bass Publishers, 1971.

———. *On the Philosophy of Higher Education*. San Francisco: Jossey-Bass Publishers, 1977.

Brubacher, John S., and Willis Rudy. *Higher Education in Transition: A History of American Colleges and Universities: 1636–1968*. New York: Harper and Row, 1968.

Christ, Frank L., and Gerard E. Sherry, ed. *American Catholicism and the Intellectual Ideal*. New York: Appleton-Century-Crofts, 1961.

Coulson, John, ed. *Theology and the University*. Baltimore: Helicon Press, 1964.

Curran, Charles E., and Robert E. Hunt. *Dissent In and For the Church: Theologians and Humanae Vitae*. New York: Sheed and Ward, 1969.

Donovan, John D. *The Academic Man in the Catholic College*. New York: Sheed and Ward, 1964.

Dutile, Fernand N., and Edward McGlynn Gaffney, Jr. *State and Campus: State Regulation of Religiously Affiliated Higher Education*. Notre Dame, Ind.: University of Notre Dame Press, 1984.

Ellis, John Tracy. *American Catholicism*. Chicago: University of Chicago Press, 1956.

———. *American Catholics and the Intellectual Life*. Chicago: Heritage Foundation, 1956.

Flexner, Abraham. *Universities: English, German, and American.* New York: Oxford University Press, 1930.

Gaffney, Edward McGlynn, Jr., and Philip R. Moots. *Government and Campus: Federal Regulation of Religiously Affiliated Higher Education.* Notre Dame, Ind.: University of Notre Dame Press, 1982.

Greeley, Andrew M. *The American Catholic: A Social Portrait.* New York: Basic Books, 1977.

————. *The Changing Catholic College.* Chicago: Aldine Publishing Co., 1967.

————. *From Backwater to Mainstream: A Profile of Catholic Higher Education.* Carnegie Commission Studies. New York: McGraw-Hill, 1969.

Greenburg, S. Thomas. *Sapientia Christiana: Impediments to Implementation From the Catholic Universities.* Foreword by John Cardinal Krol. San Antonio: The Institute of Catholic Higher Education, 1979.

Gunti, Frederick W. "Academic Freedom as an Operative Principle for the Catholic Theologian." S.T.D. dissertation, The Catholic University of America, 1969.

Hartt, Julian N. *Theology and the Church in the University.* Philadelphia: Westminster Press, 1969.

Hesburgh, Thedore M. *The Hesburgh Papers: Higher Values in Higher Education.* Kansas City: Andrews and McMeel, Inc., 1979.

Hofstadter, Richard, and Walter P. Metzger. *The Development of Academic Freedom in the United States.* New York: Columbia University Press, 1955.

Holbrook, Clyde A. *Religion: A Humanistic Field.* Englewood Cliffs, N.J.: Prentice-Hall, 1963.

Hook, Sidney. *Academic Freedom and Academic Anarchy.* New York: Cowles Book Co., 1970.

————. *Heresy Yes Conspiracy No.* New York: John Day Co., 1953.

Hunt, John F., and Terrence R. Connelly. *The Responsibility of Dissent: The Church and Academic Freedom.* New York: Sheed and Ward, 1969.

Jencks, Christopher, and David Riesman. *The Academic Revolution.* Garden City, N.Y.: Doubleday, 1968.

Kerr, Clark. *New Challenges to the College and University.* Berkeley: Carnegie Commission on Higher Education, 1969.

————. *The Uses of the University.* Cambridge: Harvard University Press, 1963.

Kirk, Russell. *Academic Freedom: An Essay in Definition.* Chicago: Henry Regnery Co., 1955.

————. *Decadence and Renewal in the Higher Learning.* South Bend, Ind.: Gateway Editions, 1978.

McCluskey, Neil G., ed. *The Catholic University: A Modern Appraisal.* Notre Dame, Ind.: University of Notre Dame Press, 1970.

McCormick, Richard A. *Notes on Moral Theology: 1965 Through 1980.* Washington, D.C.: University Press of America, 1981.

McCoy, Charles S. *The Responsible Campus: Toward a New Identity for the Church-Related College.* Division of Higher Education, United Methodist Church, 1972.

MacIver, Robert M. *Academic Freedom in Our Time.* New York: Columbia University Press, 1955.

Maguire, Daniel. *Moral Absolutes and the Magisterium*. Washington, D.C.: Corpus Papers, 1970.

Miller, Alexander. *Faith and Learning*. New York: Association Press, 1960; repr. ed., Westport, Conn.: Greenwood Press, 1977.

Minogue, Kenneth R. *The Concept of a University*. Berkeley: University of California Press, 1973.

Murray, John Courtney. *The Problem of Religious Freedom*. Westminster, Md.: Newman Press, 1965.

Newman, John Henry. *The Idea of a University*. London: Longmans, Green, and Co., 1902.

Nisbet, Robert. *The Degradation of the Academic Dogma*. New York: Basic Books, 1971.

O'Rourke, John J., and S. Thomas Greenburg, ed. *Symposium on the Magisterium: A Positive Statement*. Boston: St. Paul Editions, 1978.

Parsonage, Robert Rue, ed. *Church Related Higher Education: Perceptions and Perspectives*. Valley Forge, Pa.: Judson Press, 1978.

Pattillo, Manning, and Donald MacKenzie. *Church-Sponsored Higher Education*. Washington, D.C.: American Council on Education, 1966.

Power, Edward J. *Catholic Higher Education in America: A History*. New York: Appleton-Century-Crofts, 1972.

————. *A History of Catholic Higher Education in the United States*. Milwaukee: Bruce Publishing Co., 1958.

Rahner, Karl. *A Rahner Reader*. Edited by Gerald A. McCool. New York: Seabury Press, 1975.

Rahner, Karl and Herbert Vorgrimler. *Dictionary of Theology*. New York: Crossroad Publishing Co., 1981. s.v. "Magisterium."

Sacramentum Mundi: An Encyclopedia of Theology, 1969 ed. s.v. "Magisterium," by Karl Rahner.

Sacramentum Mundi: An Encyclopedia of Theology, 1969 ed. s.v. "Theology," by Karl Rahner.

Steinberg, Stephen. *The Academic Melting Pot: Catholics and Jews in American Higher Education*. Carnegie Commission Studies. New York: McGraw-Hill, 1974.

Sullivan, Francis A. *Magisterium: Teaching Authority in the Catholic Church*. New York: Paulist Press, 1983.

Tracy, David. *Blessed Rage For Order*. New York: Seabury Press, 1975.

Tracy, David, and John B. Cobb. *Talking About God: Doing Theology in the Context of Modern Pluralism*. New York: Seabury Press, 1983.

Trent, James W. *Catholics In College*. Chicago: University of Chicago Press, 1967.

Wolff, Robert Paul. *The Ideal of the University*. Boston: Beacon Press Paperbacks, 1970.

ARTICLES IN BOOKS AND PERIODICALS

Alberigo, Giuseppe. "The Authority of the Church in the Documents of Vatican I and Vatican II." In *Authority in the Church and the Schillebeeckx Case*, pp. 119–45. Edited by Leonard Swidler and Piet F. Fransen. New York: Crossroad Publishing Co., 1982.

Alfaro, Juan. "Theology's Role Regarding the Magisterium." *Theology Digest* 25 (Fall 1977): 212–16.

Arrowsmith, William. "Idea of a New University." *Center Magazine* 3 (1970): 47–60.

Averill, Lloyd J. "The Sectarian Nature of Liberal Education." In *Colleges and Commitments*, pp. 74–84. Edited by Lloyd J. Averill and William W. Jellema. Philadelphia: Westminster Press, 1971.

Boyle, John P. "The Academy and Church Teaching Authority: Current Issues." *Proceedings of the Catholic Theological Society of America* 40 (1985) 172–80.

Burrell, David. "Higher Education and Church: Interdependence and Enrichment." In *Church and College*. Vol. 2: *Mission: A Shared Vision of Educational Purpose*, pp. 21–27. Sherman, Tex.: National Congress on Church-Related Colleges and Universities, 1980.

———. "The Ideal of a Catholic University." *The Furrow* 31 (1980): 555–60.

Burtchaell, James T. "Hot Gospel in a Cool College? The Question of Advocacy." In *Religion in the Undergraduate Curriculum*, pp. 19–25. Edited by Claude Welch. Washington, D.C.: Association of American Colleges, 1972.

Carlson, Edgar M. "Church-Related Colleges and Universities: Identity and Integrity." In *Church and College*, Vol. 2: *Mission: A Shared Vision of Educational Purpose*, pp. 37–48. Sherman, Tex.: National Congress on Church-Related Colleges and Universities, 1980.

Cogley, John. "The Future of an Illusion." In *The Catholic University: A Modern Appraisal*, pp. 291–306. Edited by Neil G. McCluskey. Notre Dame, Ind.: University of Notre Dame Press, 1970.

Congar, Yves. "The Magisterium and Theologians: A Short History." *Theology Digest* 25 (Spring 1977): 15–20.

Connelly, John J. "The Task of Theology." *Proceedings of the Catholic Theological Society of America* 29 (June 1974): 1–58.

Curran, Charles E. "Academic Freedom: The Catholic University and Catholic Theology." *The Furrow* 30 (December 1979): 739–54.

———. "Authority and Dissent in the Church." *Origins* 16 (November 6, 1986): 375–76.

Donahue, Charles. "Freedom and Education III: Catholicism and Academic Freedom." *Thought* 29 (1955): 555–75.

Dondeyne, Albert. "Truth and Freedom: A Philosophical Study." In *Truth and Freedom*, pp. 27–48. Translated by Henry J. Koren. New York: Ad Press Ltd. for Duquesne University, 1954.

Ellis, John Tracy. "A Tradition of Autonomy?" In *The Catholic University: A Modern Appraisal*, pp. 206–70. Edited by Neil G. McCluskey. Notre Dame, Ind.: University of Notre Dame Press, 1970.

Fisk, Milton. "Academic Freedom in Class Society." In *The Concept of Academic Freedom* pp. 5–26. Edited by Edmund L. Pincoffs. Austin: University of Texas Press, 1975.

Fuchs, Ralph F. "Academic Freedom—Its Basic Philosophy, Function, and History." In *Academic Freedom and Tenure*, pp. 242–63. Edited by Louis Joughin. Madison, Wis.: University of Wisconsin Press, 1967.

Gleason, Philip. "Academic Freedom: Survey, Retrospect and Prospects." *National Catholic Education Association Bulletin* 64 (August 1967): 67–74.

————. "American Catholic Higher Education: A Historical Perspective." In *The Shape of Catholic Higher Education*, pp. 15–53. Edited by Robert Hassenger. Chicago: University of Chicago Press, 1967.

————. "The Crisis in Catholic Universities: An Historical Perspective." *Catholic Mind* 65 (September 1966): 43–55.

————. "Freedom and the Catholic University." *National Catholic Education Association Bulletin* 65 (November 1968): 21–29.

————. "Immigration and American Catholic Intellectual Life." *Review of Politics* 26 (1964): 147–73.

Greenburg, S. Thomas. "The Problem of Identity in Catholic Higher Education: The Statement of the Question." In *Why Should the Catholic University Survive?*, pp. 13–27. Edited by George A. Kelly. New York: St. John's University Press, 1973.

Grisez, Germain. "Academic Freedom and Catholic Faith." *National Catholic Education Association Bulletin* 64 (November 1967): 15–20.

————. "American Catholic Higher Education: The Experience Evaluated." In *Why Should the Catholic University Survive?*, pp. 41–55. Edited by George A. Kelly. New York: St. John's University Press, 1973.

Gryson, Roger. "The Authority of the Teacher in the Ancient and Medieval Church." In *Authority in the Church and the Schillebeeckx Case*, pp. 176–87. Edited by Leonard Swidler and Piet F. Fransen. New York: Crossroad Publishing Co., 1982.

Hassenger, Robert. "What Makes a College Catholic?" *Commonweal* 99 (November 1973): 181–82.

Hebblethwaite, Peter. "Human Rights in the Church." In *Authority in the Church and the Schillebeeckx Case*, pp. 190–201. Edited by Leonard Swidler and Piet F. Fransen. New York: Crossroad Publishing Co., 1982.

Henle, Robert J. "The Pluralism of North America and the Catholic University of Today." In *The Catholic University: Instrument of Cultural Pluralism to the Service of Church and Society*, pp. 22–79. Paris: International Federation of Catholic Universities, 1979.

Hesburgh, Theodore M. "The Catholic University in the Modern Context." *Catholic Mind* 78 (October 1980): 18–25.

Hunt, Robert E. "Academic Freedom and the Theologian." *Proceedings of the Catholic Theological Society of America* 23 (1968): 261–67.

Jellema, William W. "The Identity of the Christian College." In *Colleges and Commitments*, pp. 86–99. Edited by Lloyd J. Averill and William W. Jellema. Philadelphia: Westminster Press, 1971.

Jones, Hardy E. "Academic Freedom as a Moral Right." In *The Concept of Academic Freedom*, pp. 37–51. Edited by Edmund L. Pincoffs. Austin: University of Texas Press, 1975.

Jones, Howard Mumford. "The American Concept of Academic Freedom." *The American Scholar* 29 (1960): 94–103.

Kelly, George A. "The Relationship Between Catholic Higher Education and the Hierarchy." In *Why Should the Catholic University Survive?*, pp. 87–91. Edited by George A. Kelly. New York: St. John's University Press, 1973.

Kreyche, Gerard F. "American Catholic Higher Education and Academic Freedom." *National Catholic Education Association Bulletin* 62 (August 1965): 211–22.

Leo, John. "Some Problem Areas in Catholic Higher Education: The Faculty." In *The Shape of Catholic Higher Education*, pp. 193–201. Edited by Robert Hassenger. Chicago: University of Chicago Press, 1970.

Long, Edward LeRoy, Jr. "The Dynamics of Academic Freedom." *Faculty Forum* 49 (May 1969): 1–6.

Luyten, Norbert A. "Why a Catholic University?" In *The Catholic University: A Modern Appraisal*, pp. 29–48. Edited by Neil G. McCluskey. Notre Dame, Ind.: University of Notre Dame Press, 1970.

Lyons, Peter A. "Academic Freedom at Catholic Universities." *The Ecumenist* 10 (May-June 1972): 60–64.

McCluskey, Neil G. "Rome Replies (Act II)." *America* 122 (March 28, 1970): 330–34.

Machlup, Fritz. "In Defense of Academic Tenure." *AAUP Bulletin* 50 (1964): 112–24.

———. "On Some Misconceptions Concerning Academic Freedom." *AAUP Bulletin* 41 (1955): 751–84.

McKenzie, John L. "The Freedom of the Priest-Scholar." In *Academic Freedom and the Catholic University*, pp. 164–77. Edited by Edward Manier and John W. Houck. Notre Dame, Ind.: Fides Publishers, Inc., 1967.

May, William E. "The Magisterium and Moral Theology." In *Symposium on the Magisterium: A Positive Statement*, pp. 71–94. Edited by John J. O'Rourke and S. Thomas Greenburg. Boston: St. Paul Editions, 1978.

Niemeyer, Gerhart. "The New Need for the Catholic University." *Review of Politics* 37 (1975): 479–89.

Nuesse, C. Joseph. "Assessing Catholic Purpose in American Catholic Higher Education." *Social Thought* 7 (Summer 1981): 35–51.

O'Brien, David. "Church-Related Higher Eduction and Social Issues." In *Church and College*. Vol. 2: *Mission: A Shared Vision of Educational Purpose*, pp. 95–102. Sherman, Tex.: National Congress on Church-Related Colleges and Universities, 1980.

Ogden, Schubert M. "Reply to Professor Connelly—I." *Proceedings of the Catholic Theological Society of America* 29 (June 1974): 59–66.

———. "What Is Theology?" *Journal of Religion* 52 (January 1972): 22–40.

Orsy, Ladislas M. "Academic Freedom and the Teaching Church." *Thought* 43 (Winter 1968): 485–98.

———. "The Mandate to Teach Theological Disciplines: Glosses on Canon 812 of the New Code." *Theological Studies* 44 (1983): 476–88.

Pelikan, Jaroslav Jan. "In Defense of Research in Religious Studies at the Secular University." In *Religion and the University*. York University Invitation Lecture Series, pp. 1–19. Toronto: University of Toronto Press, 1964.

Place, Michael D. "From Solicitude to Magisterium: Theologians and Magisterium from the Council of Trent to the First Vatican Council." *Chicago Studies* 17 (Summer 1978): 225–41.

Rewak, William. "Commentary on Bishops' Pastoral Letter on Catholic Higher Education," *Current Issues in Catholic Higher Education* 2 (Summer 1981): 3–6.

Ritchie, Alexander. "Tenure and Academic Freedom." In *The Concept of Academic Freedom*, pp. 159–69. Edited by Edmund L. Pincoffs. Austin: University of Texas Press, 1975.

Rock, Augustine. "The Catholic University and Academic Freedom." *Proceedings of the Catholic Theological Society of America* 23 (1968): 245–60.

Rorty, Amelie Oksenberg. "Dilemmas of Academic and Intellectual Freedom." In *The Concept of Academic Freedom*, pp. 97–110. Edited by Edmund L. Pincoffs. Austin: University of Texas Press, 1975.

Roy, Lorenzo. "The Difference." In *The Catholic University: A Modern Appraisal*, pp. 74–83. Edited by Neil G. McCluskey. Notre Dame, Ind.: University of Notre Dame Press, 1970.

Sanks, T. Howland. "Co-operation, Co-optation, Condemnation: Theologians and the Magisterium 1870–1978." *Chicago Studies* 17 (Summer 1978): 242–63.

Sartorius, Rolf. "Tenure and Academic Freedom." In *The Concept of Academic Freedom*, pp. 133–58. Edited by Edmund L. Pincoffs. Austin: University of Texas, 1975.

Schillebeeckx, Edward. "The Magisterium and Ideology." In *Authority in the Church and the Schillebeeckx Case*, pp. 5–17. Edited by Leonard Swidler and Piet F. Fransen. New York: Crossroad Publishing Co., 1982.

———. "Problems and Promise." In *The Catholic University: A Modern Appraisal*, pp. 58–73. Edited by Neil G. McCluskey. Notre Dame, Ind.: University of Notre Dame Press, 1970.

Schoonenberg, Piet. "The Theologian's Calling, Freedom, and Constraint." In *Authority in the Church and the Schillebeeckx Case*, pp. 92–118. Edited by Leonard Swidler and Piet F. Fransen. New York: Crossroad Publishing Co., 1982

Searle, John R. "Two Concepts of Academic Freedom." In *The Concept of Academic Freedom*, pp. 86–96. Edited by Edmund L. Pincoffs. Austin: University of Texas Press, 1975.

Smith, Harry E. "Church-Related Higher Education: Distinguishing Characteristics." In *Church and College*. Vol. 2: *Mission: A Shared Vision of Educational Purpose*, pp. 29–35. Sherman, Tex.: National Congress on Church-Related Colleges and Universities, 1980.

Smith, Huston. "Objectivity vs. Commitment." In *Colleges and Commitments*, pp. 34–59. Edited by Lloyd J. Averill and William W. Jellema. Philadelphia: Westminster Press, 1971.

Sullivan, William J. "The Catholic University and the Academic Study of Religion." In *Religion in the Undergraduate Curriculum*, pp. 37–45. Edited by Claude Welch. Washington, D.C.: Association of American Colleges, 1972.

Swidler, Leonard. "*Demo-kratia*, The Rule of the People of God or *Consensus Fidelium*." In *Authority of the Church and the Schillebeeckx Case*, pp. 226–43. Edited by Leonard Swidler and Piet F. Fransen. New York: Crossroad Publishing Co., 1982.

Tracy, David. "The Public Character of Systematic Theology." *Theology Digest* 26 (Winter 1978): 400–11.

———. "Response to Professor Connelly—II." *Proceedings of the Catholic Theological Society of America* 29 (June 1974): 67–75.

Van Alstyne, William. "The Specific Theory of Academic Freedom and the General Issue of Civil Liberty." In *The Concept of Academic Freedom*, pp. 59–85. Edited by Edmund L. Pincoffs. Austin: University of Texas Press, 1975.

Walsh, John E. "The University and the Church." In *Academic Freedom and the Catholic University*, pp. 103–18. Edited by Edward Manier and John W. Houck. Notre Dame, Ind.: Fides Publishers, 1967.

Walsh, Michael P. "Nature and Role Today." In *The Catholic University: A Modern Appraisal*, pp. 49–57. Edited by Neil G. McCluskey. Notre Dame, Ind.: University of Notre Dame Press, 1970.

Weigel, Gustave. "American Catholic Intellectualism: A Theologian's Reflections." In *Catholic Education: A Book of Readings*, pp. 65–89. Edited by Walter B. Kolesnik and Edward J. Power. New York: McGraw-Hill Book Co., 1965.

Wittenberg, Alexander. "The Relationship Between Religion and the Educational Function of the University." In *Religion and the University*. York University Invitation Lecture Series, pp. 111–28. Toronto: University of Toronto Press, 1964.

Index

AAUP (American Association of University Professors), 97–98, 100, 105, 153–54, 164, 166, 185, 198; on church-related institutions, 102–3, 105. *Documents*: "Academic Freedom and Tenure: 1940 Statement of Principles and Interpretive Comments," 103, 117, 154, 197; "Committee A Statement on Extramural Utterances," 101; "1915 Declaration of Principles," 4, 98–102, 104, 115, 153–54, 183, 200; "1958 Statement on Procedural Standards in Faculty Dismissal Proceedings," 103; "1940 Statement of Principles," 100–103, 114, 128, 137, 154, 198, and Catholic colleges and universities, 41, 74, 102–3, 168, 197; "1964 Statement on the Academic Freedom of Students," 105–6; "1967 Joint Statement on Rights and Freedoms of Students," 105–6; "Statement on Academic Freedom in Church-Related Colleges and Universities," 102–3

Abbott, Frances E., 171

Academic freedom: and civil rights, 112, 116–18; definition of, xix, 4, 98, 100, 107, 116–18, 166, 200; as a dynamic ethos, 166–69, 182, 187, 196–97, 216; German roots of, 2–3, 103–5, 170; philosophical foundations of, 70, 72–73, 108–16, 199–201; threats to, 164–68

Academic freedom, American Secular Model, xix, 2–6, 97–102, 163–66, 168–70, 173–74, 179–80, 183, 185, 195–98; and Catholic colleges and universities, 163–64, 168–69, 179, 187, 195–98, 205–7, 211–12, 215–16; early interpretations of, 169–70, 187; historical and intellectual roots of, 2–3, 103–5, 169–70

Academic freedom, Catholic models of, xx, 57–88, 135–57; in *Code of Canon Law*, 67–68, 132, 153–56; of John Paul II, 63–68; of Paul VI, 61–63; restrictive, 70–77, 90–91 n.86, 135–42, 195, 215; revised secular, 70, 77–82, 142–51, 195, 215; in *Sapientia Christiana*, 65–67, 151–53; of Second Vatican Council, 57–61; in teachings of the *Magisterium*, 57–70, 151–56; of U.S. Catholic Bishops, 68–70

Academic freedom, justifications of, 97–100, 107; Catholic, 79–80, 82, 85, 115–16, 142–44, 198–204;

About the Author

JAMES JOHN ANNARELLI, Ph.D., is an Assistant Professor of Theology at St. John's University, New York.